ALFRED A. KNOPF

100 YEARS 1915–2015

Woody Allen: A Life in Film (2004)

Elia Kazan: A Biography (2005)

*The Essential Chaplin: Perspectives on the Life and Art
of the Great Comedian* (editor) (2006)

Film on Paper: The Inner Life of Movies (2008)

Conversations with Scorsese (2011)

Steven Spielberg: A Retrospective (2012)

KEEPERS

KEEPERS

The Greatest Films
—and Personal Favorites—
of a Moviegoing Lifetime

RICHARD SCHICKEL

 ALFRED A. KNOPF | NEW YORK | 2015

THIS IS A BORZOI BOOK
PUBLISHED BY ALFRED A. KNOPF

Published in the United States by Alfred A. Knopf,
a division of Random House LLC, New York, and in Canada
by Random House of Canada Limited, Toronto,
Penguin Random House companies.

www.aaknopf.com

Knopf, Borzoi Books, and the colophon are registered trademarks
of Random House LLC.

Library of Congress Cataloging-in-Publication Data
Schickel, Richard.
Keepers : the greatest films-and personal favorites-of a moviegoing lifetime /
Richard Schickel. — First edition.
pages cm
Includes bibliographical references and index.
ISBN 978-0-375-42459-5 (hardcover) — ISBN 978-1-101-87471-4 (ebook)
1. Motion pictures.   2. Motion pictures—Evaluation.   I. Title.
PN1993.5.U6S35 2015
791.430973—dc23
2014034997

Jacket design by Chip Kidd

Manufactured in the United States of America
First Edition

Contents

KEEPERS

1

Notes Toward the Definition
of an Obsession

Some months ago, when I started to think about actually writing this book, as opposed to hemming and hawing as one generally does when a book is in the offing, I wondered how many movies I had actually seen in the course of the seventy-seven years since I saw my first film, *Snow White and the Seven Dwarfs,* in 1938.

This was something more than an idle inquiry. I wanted to establish some kind of authority. As a result of my preferences in entertainment and, ultimately, my choice of profession, I had seen in the course of a lifetime a great many more films than all but a handful of people—mostly professional reviewers—had seen. But how many did that amount to? That was a question I had never addressed. "A whole bunch," I am wont to say when people ask, which they quite often do; it is a slightly exotic way of making a living, and people seem idly curious about it.

It's obvious that I've seen more than most people, for besides being a movie addict—a fairly common condition, usually more or less cheerfully abandoned when family and work interrupt the addiction—I became, more or less accidentally, a professional moviegoer. I began reviewing films in 1965. (I have done so, with only one significant hiatus, ever since.) By that time I had written a couple of books on them (and have written many more), and around 1968 I started making documentaries about them, an activity I pursued until quite recently. Throughout these years, I have continued my habit of slipping into movie theaters or screening rooms without having any professional rationale for so doing; I just like to be there in the dark watching something—almost anything, if the truth be known. In this habit—I don't know if it is amiable or a mild, chronic illness—I have been indulged by wives, girlfriends, just plain friends and children. Of course, a lot of the time I'm alone, unashamedly killing an evening, no questions asked.

Here I have to enter a caveat: I am an *American* critic. I have dutifully, mostly happily, seen thousands of films of foreign origin. They are among the most rewarding moviegoing experiences of my life. But this twig was bent early. I know more about American films, historically and aesthetically, than I do about those from other lands. I've sought to remedy that defect, of course, and I've done reasonably well with it. But, yes, I am more comfortable, more authoritative, with American movies. In reading critics from those other countries, in turn, I notice some discomfort when they deal with our films.

Funny thing. When I started reviewing in the 1960s, the movies were a young art. We were less than forty years into the age of the "talkies" and perhaps sixty years into the age of the feature film. It occurred to me—preposterously, I admit—that you could, if you worked demonically, become a scholar of world cinema, knowing something about movies from everywhere. In fact, I am still playing catch-up with the cinema of many countries. It's like being a perpetual grad student, swotting up what you need to know to write a respectable piece when the occasion becomes pressing, which very often becomes fascinating and instructive work.

Because I turned pro in the mid-sixties, most of my omissions can be partially justified by the demands of wearing too many hats. You cannot write a book or make a television show about the movies without seeing films anew—no matter how often you've seen the ones you are taking up in these projects. Movies, obviously, do not change substantively, although nowadays, with the rise of directors' cuts and specialists pawing through the archives finding new material that had been eliminated before the answer print—the "official" one—was struck, movies can change more than we thought they could a decade or two ago. I was involved in such a transformative project a few years ago, restoring some forty minutes of Sam Fuller's *The Big Red One*—whole scenes of which were rescued from a Warner warehouse in Kansas City. I think this version of the film is way better than what was circulating before—it has now the weight of a heartfelt epic; it is not just another war picture. And it honors the intentions of its very honorable director. Anyway, we won some prizes for our work and the good opinion of moviegoing mankind. But I noticed this: People who had been content with the short version were not as enthusiastic about our cut. It was nice and all that, but the bastard version was perfectly okay with them. Finished films, even when everyone knows they could be better, exert a powerful inertial force on the object at hand.

I have found that what I guess could be called my gross judgment of a movie does not often change with the passing years. If I liked it once, I'll probably still like it now—but with an asterisk. You will notice things that make it rise or fall in your estimation, based on your experience and the passing years. And, naturally, you see other films (and read books and articles) that impinge on your feelings for the ones you are reconsidering. So you owe to your readers or viewers—not to mention yourself—a report on the state of your current feelings as you encounter and re-encounter movies in the course of your lifelong engagement with them.

Rarely, as I've said, do you flip from love to hate or vice versa. But changes do occur. It's logical. You loved *My Friend Flicka* when you saw it at age ten. If you see it at age sixty-five, you may respect it, but you won't think it's a masterpiece (which does not mean you should deprive your grandchildren of the pleasure of seeing this picture when they are the perfect age for it).

Remarkably, Pauline Kael thought this was not so. She might have seen a film when she was ten years old, and she might be writing about it as a sixty-five-year-old, but that made no difference to her. It was what it was, world without end. She was sometimes wont to say it was like an old fuck—forever frozen in memory's amber. I don't think the argument applies to fucking, and I don't think it applies to movies, either. Memory has a way of playing tricks on us—even Pauline's, whose recall for films was capacious.

That discussion is for later. Now it's time to start counting. That is pretty easy in the early years. There was *The Wizard of Oz,* naturally, and what I still think is my first viewed masterpiece, *Pinocchio,* and a whole slew of other Disney titles *(Dumbo, Bambi* and, God help us, *Saludos Amigos).* There were other treats as well—birthday party items (my own and others') and some special events, like *The Great Dictator* (which my parents thought I should see, although I understood very little of it at the time), and *Harmon of Michigan,* about the famous football player (Tom, father of the television actor Mark), which I insisted on seeing on a school night, no less. There was no regularity in this—no rhyme or reason, either. But by the time I was nine or ten I was probably going to the movies once every week or two.

Shortly after that, the movies became a more serious habit. There were two sub-run theaters—as opposed to first-run—

within walking distance of my house, and two regular companions who lived on my block and liked the movies as much
as I did. Friday nights or Sunday afternoons, Danny Seifert or
Kenny Siegesmund and I, or all three of us, trotted off to the
movies almost without fail, not much caring what was playing
and pretty much liking everything we saw, no genres excluded.

I don't suppose those two friends kept up this habit later in
life, but I did. Let's say that from the time I became a teenager
until the day before yesterday, I have seen at least two movies
a week. When I was a kid, my mother, who liked to shop in
downtown Milwaukee, would of a summer's afternoon park me
in one of the several first-run downtown theaters, armed with
candy and popcorn, while she pursued her bliss. It was—you'll
have to take my word on this—completely safe. Ushers were
everywhere. Later, we would meet at my father's office and go
out for hamburgers. I'm not sure I was ever happier than at
the movies those days. If you multiply two movies a week by
sixty-nine years, you come out at around 7,000 movies in all,
as a baseline—a not inconsiderable sum, especially when we are
told that the average American of my age nowadays sees only
four movies a year in a theater.

When I went to the University of Wisconsin, I basically
doubled my moviegoing. Yes, four of them a week. It was easy.
There were four or five movie theaters on State Street and Capi-
tol Square in Madison, and one repaired there regularly for the
current releases. The university, which now has a rather distinguished film department, at that time offered no courses in film,
practical or theoretical. But a small theater in the student union
functioned as an art house on the weekends, playing mostly the
latest releases from abroad. (There was not much in the way of
American independent films in those days.) I missed very few
of those pictures. On Thursday afternoons this theater played
classic titles of the past, and it was at these screenings that I saw
for the first time *Intolerance* and *Metropolis* and Buster Keaton
and the Russian and French classics of the twenties and thirties.

I was making up my own mind about all the films, unguided by the academic scholarship of the era. What we had for authority was Paul Rotha's latest edition of *The Film Till Now*, which was considerably better than nothing, though kind of so-so on American cinema. What *I* had was something like 100 more movies per annum and, in my last year, a founding membership in a film club, which for our enrichment played Leni Riefenstahl's *Olympia* and for our profitability played *Ecstasy*. Imagine that! Hedy Lamarr, a minor, but an authentic MGM star, jaybird naked in the dappled forests of Czechoslovakia! Movies occasionally are wondrous things.

And the gift that keeps on giving. After I graduated, I moved to New York, where I went to work for a few years as a staff writer on magazines. I didn't know many people. I didn't have a television set. But I lived in Greenwich Village, which was Madison on steroids. That is to say, it had plenty of movie theaters—the Sheridan for second-runs of current releases, the Art (for art), the Waverly (for repertory), the Greenwich for odds and ends. I fed my habit as I had in Madison—a couple hundred movies a year. Five years of college plus five years of— I guess you'd call it bohemia—adds up to another 1,000 movies. So by the time I married, at age twenty-seven—to a woman who shared my moviegoing passion—I was already on track for a lifetime total of 8,000 films, give or take.

And I was not yet a professional moviegoer. That occurred in 1965, when, at first casually, then not so casually, I began reviewing for *Life* magazine. I persisted there until it folded, in 1972, then I moved over to *Time,* where I lasted until 2009. I took some time off and then landed an agreeable job at a website called Truthdig.com. So in my fifty or so years of reviewing, I've added 10,000 movies to my total, which works out to 18,000 titles in sum.

But we are not finished. From 1965 to date, I've written thirty-seven books and made the same number of television documentaries, mostly about the movies. I'd guess each of those enterprises has entailed seeing (or re-seeing) around thirty-five films—2,590 of them in all. In addition, I've done all sorts of shorter films and articles for a variety of occasions, and it's probably safe to say I saw another thousand movies in the course of those activities. And then there were speeches and TV appearances for which I took in even more movies, and there were film festivals, of course—I don't like them; too many bad movies in a short span of time—which quickly added substantially to the total, probably another thousand or so.

For a grand total of, shall we say, 22,590 movies, or about 294 of them a year. Which means that two out of every three days, for a long time now, I have been at the movies.

I suppose you could say that I have overdone it, but I have nearly always had a good time doing what I do. I'm not great at quoting immortal lines from famous films (most critics aren't; that's a specialty of amateur enthusiasts) or referring to great scenes at apposite moments. But I think I've been able to see movies unblinkered—and in the end, that's what this book's about. It contains reflections on a large number of movies that are, by any standard, masterpieces. It is silent about a large number of movies that are significant milestones in the history of the art that I have no interest in seeing ever again, because, quite frankly, they are ponderous, or running on reputations that have not been reexamined in decades, or prisoners of styles that are no longer relevant—to me at least.

I want to make this point about moviegoing: It includes for me a lot of things that are not, strictly speaking, about going to the movies. The truth, very simply, is that most movies are lousy or, at best, routine. We go to see them, much of the time, in search of something else—the comforting darkness of the theater, the play of light and shadow on the screen, the consolations they offer for some temporary trouble. A lot of the time we don't give a hoot what's playing. We are at a public event for private reasons, which we don't always recognize until later, if at all. It is the occasion, the atmosphere, that we crave. The art of the film has to break through our preoccupations and distractions if it is to somehow seize us. Come to think of it, the amazing thing about movies is how often that happens, not how rarely.

So back to counting—22,250 movies. Not many of them were pleasurable at any level, but you learn as much about film from the bad ones as you do from the good ones. Thankfully, there are enough of the latter to make this book a feasible undertaking. W. H. Auden, in one of his superb critical essays, wrote that masterpieces are for the "High Holidays of the Spirit," suggesting that the intensity of the responses they engender is not something that we can freely indulge. It would be too much for us, put too much pressure on us. We need the routine, the merely all right, if only as a benchmark against which to measure the extraordinary when it happens along.

The main thing I want to stress is the pleasure principle. Movies being movies, they exist, first and foremost, to entertain—especially those made in America. A critic from another country, setting out on a task similar to mine, would probably find very little overlap with my list of favorites. Which is all right with me. We are not drawing up a "best" list. All of the movies I've chosen as my keepers are expertly made, of course. There are movies among them that are awkward and clumsy yet are still, in their way, fun—and sometimes instructive—to see. At the very least, I want to reward expertise herein. Especially with American films, I want to praise the sheer professionalism of their making. It is such a dominant industry—I sometimes think its chief glory lies in the fact that so much energy and passion and, yes, cleverness are expended on material that is largely tosh. But very often the sheer slickness of the effort leads us to think—at least temporarily—that the movie is better than it actually is, which may (or may not) sort itself out as the years wear on.

There are other values, of course, in the contemplation of movies, and I intend to attend to them. But if this book is not a pleasure to read and does not trigger some reflection on your part, then it will have failed in its purpose. You are supposed to argue with me—*Why this? Why not that?* We should agree to disagree, but I hope in a civilized way. Where once we did not take movies seriously enough, we now, I think, oftentimes take them too seriously, arguing our cases too loudly.

As I have worked on this book, to be honest, its purpose has changed. I didn't quite realize it at first, but it has become a history—a personalized history, to be sure, but a history none-theless. Through the lens of my favorite films, I have written the story of the movies as I have perceived them over the years. There are lots of omissions—I couldn't see *everything,* and there are plenty of things I don't want to comment on—and it is deliberately positive in overall tone. I've mostly enjoyed my life at the movies, and I've only occasionally felt the need to chas-tise them herein. Life is too short to dwell heavily on their many sins. That's for another book that I won't be writing.

"It's only a movie, Ingrid," Alfred Hitchcock famously said (or perhaps wished he had said) to Ingrid Bergman when she pressed him about how she should play a scene or read a line or some such. Well, yes, of course, that's necessary perspective. But I came to know Hitch in his later years, and I am here to testify that no man ever took movies more seriously than he did. That is true of almost everyone who has spent his life, cynically or idealistically, in their service. To put it simply: Movies are, in some sense, nothing—a pastime, an evening's entertainment. And yet they are, for quite a few of us, everything; well, almost everything. On that irony this book is poised.

2

Speaking of Silence

Silent film is, let's face it, something of an inconvenience to movie history. Mary Pickford once said that it would have been more logical if movies had evolved toward silence instead of the other way around. It's a rather arresting statement, but I guess she meant that silence implied a removal from reality, one of the limitations on which art normally depends. Opera, dance, even the stage are not "real"; all are highly stylized representations of reality, effective to the degree that their conventions separate these works from raw, unmediated reality. To state the case most radically, silents are, with exceptions, more romantic, more abstract, than talking pictures. I sometimes think they are not movies as we understand the term.

They obviously partake of some of their values. But notably in their acting styles, and in their preferred genres, they are different from sound movies. For proof of that, you need only look to Chaplin or, indeed, Pickford herself. They are major artists, of course, but I think neither would have had the impact they had if sound had preceded them to the screen.

Not that, at the time, anyone was complaining. There were, of course, a minority who thought that the movies were silly and stupid and perhaps even immoral, but we can safely say there was, in general, a very high consumer satisfaction with the silents. Throughout the 1910s and into the 1920s, quite a few people were content with that state. There were a number of theoreticians who thought that, far from being a defect, the lack of spoken dialogue was the very thing that set this medium gloriously apart from all the others. By the later twenties, it has been argued by George Lucas, among others, that film had attained a visual sophistication that has not been matched perhaps to our very day. A film like *The Crowd* (of which more later), with its sophisticated expressionism, argues that point brilliantly—and it was one among many.

There was, however, a general sense—not really a complaint, more of an unease—that this medium was not yet complete, that sooner or later it would have to talk and sing and wisecrack. And from the time feature-length films became the industry standard, much effort and treasure was expended on marrying sound to film, until that was achieved, first with a series of Warner Bros. shorts and then, of course, with the 1927 feature *The Jazz Singer,* which was, in truth, only a part talkie and, as a film, about as bad as they come. Panic and greed competed briefly but, all things considered, sorted themselves out rather quickly. A few voices mourned the passing of the old order; D. W. Griffith, for instance, thought that a universal language was being lost. It was a lot easier to translate a few intertitles for the foreign markets and rely on richly modulated pantomime to tell a story than it was to dub pictures with voices not belonging to the players on the screen, or sometimes to make whole new versions of the film in alien tongues. But Griffith himself was pretty much a back number by then.

There were, however, some minor but palpable losses. It's probably true that the silent era was the most prosperous period the movies ever enjoyed. Woody Allen has argued that this was largely a matter of costs. Sound effectively doubled the expense of production and the complexity of filmmaking. The free and easy way of knocking off epics on a relative shoestring mostly disappeared for much of sound's first decade; the predominant genres became relatively low-cost comedies and crime pictures, not that many in the audience paid much attention, such was the continuing appeal of the moving image.

There's no question that movies lost some of their spaciousness when actors started speaking in them, that the taste in acting styles became rougher, more urban and less exotic, that definitions of both male and female attractiveness became more naturalistic. (One cannot imagine James Cagney or Edward G. Robinson becoming silent picture stars.) Similarly, writing also grew wittier as men and women who'd had a hit play or novel in New York were shipped west, seemingly by the trainload, to enter into the well-paid studio servitude, complaining all the way to the bank. The myth—well, all right, the half myth—of servitude to an idiot system took stubborn hold. No one seemed to notice that this was a true golden age of the movies, lasting pretty much until the advent of television.

3

Exceptions

My loyalty, historically and emotionally speaking, is to the first two decades or so of the talkies. That's not because I was seeing many movies in the first part of that era. It's because, coming late to them, I somehow found it romantic and glamorous and enormous fun. Back when I was first beginning to appreciate movies at some slightly sophisticated level, we were much closer to the silent era—perhaps twenty-five or thirty years from it. (My late father-in-law told me of seeing riders in Ku Klux Klan outfits, thundering down Broadway, promoting *The Birth of a Nation,* and that didn't seem far distant to me.) It was what we had for history; we were too close to the snappy thirties and forties—a less grandiose period in any case—to truly appreciate it. It would need to simmer for a while in memory.

I'm going to omit from lengthy consideration here the Marx

Brothers. They seem to me to have slipped down history's page in recent decades. Chico is never really funny with his lame Italian accent. Harpo works his mime pretty well, but his innocence wears less well. Groucho is, of course, the wiseguy supreme, and he is the only brother who had a career outside the family troupe—a prosperous one. They managed some sublime bits, but somehow our (maybe I should say "my") affection for them is now muted. The three of them do not add up to one great comedian, try as they might, and God knows they tried.

So I want instead to focus our attention on Charles Chaplin and Buster Keaton, who stand outside the broad stream of silent film history, proudly sui generis. Chaplin was the greatest star of his era, perhaps of any era, and he was, like Keaton, a grotesque. That's an important point to make about silent picture stars. The beautiful ones, male and female, tended to be preternaturally so; the comical ones more weirdly strange. When he was off camera, Chaplin was a moderately handsome fellow, but paste on his mustache, dress him in his curious costume, and he became something else. You might say that the singularity of his appearance had the odd effect of universalizing him. That is to say, we had to broaden our definition of humanity to include him. If we did not, we would be forced to exile him. The action in most of his films was meant to make this odd little duck an acceptable member of the human race.

Which says nothing about his uncanny skills as a mime. This universality was enhanced by the great specificity of his intricate gags. There was rarely any doubt about his intentions; what was most amazing about his work was the way he would extend it beyond all our expectations. It was dazzling to watch him, for instance, play a drunk trying simply to get up the stairs and into bed. In retrospect, the sequence seems perfectly logical, even inevitable, in the way one gag leads to another, but no one ever approached his sheer skill in milking such a relatively simple act.

If Chaplin had a physical weakness, it was his voice. It was thin and rather prissy. It was a factor, I think (though not the only one), in his long refusal to speak from the screen. And when he started to speak (and, sometimes, speak and speak, as if he wanted to test the limits of his appeal in pictures like *The Great Dictator* and *Monsieur Verdoux*), it represented another kind of weakness, a taste for sentiment, which had a distancing effect.

At the time, this quality was accepted by audiences. It was part of what made Chaplin Chaplin. Later, he was condemned for it, and his stock sank while Buster Keaton's rose in the not yet finished (though marginalized) debate over the two great silent comedians. Woody Allen is very good on this topic. "When anyone tries to be sentimental or moving, and they fail at it, you know you want to strangle them . . . you have such an adverse reaction to it." But as Allen points out, "a portion of the time he didn't fail at it."

He cites in this regard the sublime ending of *City Lights,* where the blind girl belatedly discovers who her secret admirer is. In that moment he went "for seriousness and pathos and brought it off." I would certainly add the conclusion of *The Kid,* where Chaplin must rescue Jackie Coogan's waif from the officialdom intent on bearing the lad away to the orphanage. It is as masterful an orchestration of comedy, action and pathos as anyone has ever achieved.

This is an important thing to say about Chaplin. Yes, his sentimentality is sometimes over the top, but it provides a necessary balance to the purity of his comedy, which sometimes runs the risk of becoming totally mechanical, invention piled on invention. It allows us, from time to time, to relax, to take stock of "the Little Fellow."

There are, perhaps, more relevant criticisms of him. There is solipsism in Chaplin's work, immense self-regard, a sense that he thinks he is the only thing the camera really needs to care about. And there is the manic need he had to do everything on the picture. He was always the Man. He had his foils, and they were often very good. But they were interchangeable and disposable.

We sometimes wish he would relax a little. But in fact, if he was stuck he would simply shut the picture down, keeping the company idle (but paid) until genius struck, which it generally did. It is startling how few (if any) shoddy, half-thought-out sequences survive in the finished films. Some are better than others, naturally, but none of the fully comic ones can be judged full-scale failures. At the height of his fame, people routinely attached the word "genius" to his activities—and I think correctly so, if by that word we mean doing something sublime that he, as much as anyone, could not fully explain.

So what is my favorite Chaplin film? (And remember, we're talking favorite, not best.) It would be easy to say *City Lights*. It's a very fine film, no doubt about that, somewhat burdened, oddly, by the fact that we tend to remember its love story more than its divine comic sequences. (A boxing match is particularly well done, and Charlie as a white wing, clearing the streets of horse manure, leads to one of the biggest laughs in Chaplin history.) But I'm going to opt for what is probably the least well regarded of his features, *The Circus* (1928).

It was made in the most difficult circumstances. A fire at Chaplin's studio delayed production for months, and he was undergoing one of his periodic bouts of romantic stress. When he came to write his autobiography, decades later, he spared but one mention for the film and provided no anecdotes about its production whatsoever. Yet it is a marvel of pure comedy—with only a hint of romance (between a bareback rider and a lion tamer). There's the circus owner (and father of the rider) for not very menacing menace. Mostly there's three extensive set-piece comedy routines (and a lot of incidental bits, all of which are perfectly executed). The climax features Chaplin doing a high-wire act while beset by a troop of monkeys.

Doesn't sound like much, does it? But it's breathtaking in its intricacy, and its thrills. Of all Chaplin's extensively developed comic routines, it is, I think, his greatest—especially when you consider that monkeys are fundamentally undirectable. The sequence leaves you breathless, both with laughter and fear. And the film's only poignancy comes at the very end, when the circus leaves town and Chaplin can only sit in the shadow left on the ground by its ring. Alone again—his preferred situation, obviously—he rises, dusts himself off and waddles jauntily into his unknowable future. Those final shots are, I think, far more hopeful than gloomy, and very lightly done. Chaplin would not be Chaplin without resorting to sentiment, earned or not, dubious or not. We all recognize that. But for him to make this unpretentious film at the height of his fame and then basically forget it almost entirely when he came to write his final summing up, that is something else. "Old men forget," Shakespeare said. But this is close to a monumental case of memory loss.

The Circus brings me back to the Chaplin–Keaton debate, in part because it is most like Keaton's work in its lack of pretense—and because the monkey sequence is as fine as anything Keaton did in blending thrills and comedy. Buster had no philosophical ambitions. He wanted only to make funny films, and as a constructor of gag sequences he was every bit Chaplin's equal. In recent times, as I said, critical opinion has shifted to Keaton as the greater artist—I believe this is because we now have a far larger taste for the austere than we formerly had. There is also the contrast between their off-screen fates. Chaplin had his troubles, of course, most of them political, but none of them threatened his prosperity or his high regard in critical circles. Keaton, however, was felled by drink and by his careless embrace of sound. (He did not play on his exceptionalism as Chaplin did.) Somehow people eventually could relate to his problems more readily than they could to Chaplin's, which finally eased his path back to grace.

I think this dispute is feckless; they are both great and immortal artists of entirely different stripes. I'll concede that Keaton is the more likable human being. But still, of all the stars of the silent screen, they require the least explanation. If you see a film by either one of them with an audience, he owns the room completely. Our laughter is complete and direct; you forget, as you rarely do with other actors of that era, that *they are not talking*. And in their silence they achieve that "universality" that Griffith believed was the silent cinema's supreme virtue.

If, though, Chaplin and Keaton are doomed to be twinned through the ages, we must be careful to preserve their obvious contrasts. Chaplin was, supremely, an actor. He was, putting it simply, working, working, working all the time—decorating the main line of his gag sequences with throwaway bits by the dozen. You might not even notice all of them until you return to the film for further study. Keaton, by contrast, was a study in stillness. That does not mean, obviously, that he was inactive. Far from it. He was as lively as a cricket or a water bug, devising his escapes from a world that was, in its way, innocently—but constantly—malevolent. The point, however, was that Keaton could never show a facial reaction to his troubles—the great poker face and all that. That was the whole joke, the only joke.

Imagine a career of this magnitude built on variants on a single gag. It is one of the things that commends him to us today. He seems to be doing more with less than Chaplin ever dreamed of, and we respond to that, particularly since he so expertly avoids the merely mechanical in his work. Something of the Victorian always clings to Chaplin. Something of onrushing modernism, not yet fully defined, drives Keaton. There's an irony in that. Chaplin had obvious pretenses to intellectualism; Keaton had none. But yet he was an intellectual of sorts, in that he was the one working the big theme—modernism and its discontents—while Chaplin (*Modern Times* aside) did not have a great deal to say on that topic.

Keaton is, to reference Woody Allen again, by far the "cooler" artist. And there is a quiet brilliance about his work as a filmmaker, a reluctance to sell it out for a quick gag (or a stroke of genius), that Chaplin does not quite match. He was, moreover, working with a handicap unknown to Chaplin: that perpetually frozen face, never allowed to lapse into alarm at the predicaments he stumbled into. It is simply astonishing how the laughter keeps building and building despite the minimalism engendered by this endlessly recurring affectlessness. (Of course, he manifested other, more physical responses to peril—running away from it, for example, though, even then, he maintained a certain dignity as he fled the jurisdiction of chaos.)

There is one other factor that adds to the degree of difficulty in his work. This utterly brilliant athlete had always to appear awkward while doing his stunts—as if he were everyman, confronting unimaginable peril yet soldiering on through it. It is at the heart of the identification he forges with his audience. He must, as we surely would not, stumble through to his ultimate triumphs. He cannot, for a second, look like he knows what he is doing. Or is about to do. And yet, of course, the planning that went into his manically extended thrill sequences is mind-bending.

Oddly enough, I find it difficult to choose a single Keaton film for inclusion in this book. There are wonderful things in almost all of his films—the rescue of his girlfriend from the raging torrent in *Our Hospitality;* the mad near-miss chase between him and his girlfriend on the deserted ship in *The Navigator;* the entire concept of *Sherlock, Jr.* Then there is the epic adventurousness of *The General* (1926), which seems to me less a comedy (though, of course, it has plenty of wonderful comic bits) than an attempt to broaden his canvas. (He spent hugely on the film, for example risking over $40,000 on a shot of a train engine plunging from a bridge into a gorge, which elicits no more than a blank response from a watching officer, truly a spectacular nonevent in the plot.) But the movie, said to be Keaton's favorite of all his works, was a flop at the time, and it does seem to me, at times, a somewhat halting and patchy film.

Pressed, I'm going to give the palm to *The Navigator*. It is an economical film—perhaps an hour long—and it is nonstop and unpretentiously funny, maybe the most inspired and beautifully integrated and sustained of all his comedic efforts. All movies with any aspirations to lingering regard aspire to perfection, and even the best of them usually fail to find it (there are a few exceptions). This movie, because of the modesty of its goals, achieves something like that state. It is just lovely fun. I wouldn't change a frame of it.

4

Ironies

Two of the three greatest stars of the American silent screen were Mary Pickford and Douglas Fairbanks the elder. She was pert, tiny and appealing; he was bold, dashing and appealing in quite a different manner. Together with Chaplin (Fairbanks's best friend) they were the beneficiaries and victims of the modern celebrity system, which they essentially invented with their rather slapdash ways. Yet today they are virtually forgotten—unfairly.

Pickford is condemned (mostly by people who haven't seen many, or any, of her films) as sentimental and too perky by half. Fairbanks, of course, became the muscular, always laughing exponent of costumed athletic spectacle, a genre he virtually owned, and one that did not fare well after sound pictures arrived. These descriptions do not tell the half of their stories. There was more steel in her screen character than she openly admits, and a picture like *Sparrows* (in which she rescues children from a baby farm deep in southern swamp country) is an exciting adventure, bravely enacted by a resourceful actress. His spectacles (notably *The Thief of Bagdad* and *Robin Hood*) were wonderfully overproduced and sensationally rich in "gags," as their many glorious action sequences proved.

But it was not just a shift in taste that reduced these performers to footnotes. In effect, age did them in. They both became too old to sustain their essential youthful character, and neither could reinvent themselves in a new movie era. That was especially true of Fairbanks. He was forty-six in 1929, muscle-bound and uninterested in pursuing his previous course. His later years were devoted, without conviction, to vanity productions. Pickford was the same age and could not transcend her established character, either. She soldiered on a little more successfully than he did, winning an Oscar in 1929. But her relationship with fame was much more ambiguous than his. Their divorce was messy, a comedy of errors, really, and in her later years there was a drinking problem and a taste for seclusion.

They possibly do not demand inclusion here, but I include them anyway—for *Sparrows* and for *Thief of Bagdad*. Pickford and Fairbanks remain potent exemplars of the spirit of their time, and when it comes to movies, you don't have to apologize for liking them. I suspect the American movie would not have developed as it did, with its ineluctable sense of melodrama and spectacle, if these two performers had not so delightfully—and so profitably—existed. Try them some night. You will be more than surprised at how their images transcend their current reputations.

King Vidor, a director about whom we will shortly have more to say, was musing, in the 1970s, about the beginning of his career, some fifty years earlier. He said, in effect, that if he had known about the attention that would be focused on the films of his early days, "he would have made them better." That's perhaps false modesty, but he was also saying that from

1920 to 1925 the more aspirational filmmaking was taking place largely in Europe, not in the United States, which nevertheless began its permanent world box office domination in this era. He cited, for example, the influence of German Expressionism and the rise of the Russian historical spectacles on the relatively few American directors who wanted their films to play for more than a few weeks in general release and not disappear, seemingly forever, from the world's screens. He was speaking at a time when a cinephile audience had arisen, determined to trace the not entirely undistinguished roots of American film history to its beginnings and to honor its pioneers.

It was during the period to which Vidor was referring that Rudolph Valentino crammed most of his career—discovery, huge stardom, a switch to (mostly masculine) contempt and premature death. At the end of that time, Garbo was discovered and soon became the dominant star of her era (though, oddly, not the greatest box office attraction), and Ernst Lubitsch came to America and made what he always considered his best film, *The Marriage Circle* (1924). D. W. Griffith struggled financially and artistically, trying to support a studio of his own and his habit of making historical spectacles that were awkward and seemed old-fashioned to a public that wanted something jazzier.

There was another side to Griffith, which he chose not to exploit, yoked as he was to spectacle and "importance." He was rarely entirely comfortable with the broad canvases of works like *Way Down East* or *Orphans of the Storm,* though he occasionally had some success with them. He was best at films like *True Heart Susie* and *A Romance of Happy Valley,* smaller pictures that referenced his early Biograph days and his own boyhood days in rural Kentucky. They have an ease and charm (and Lillian Gish, not trying too hard) that is sweet and funny and ages better than his more expensive and portentous efforts.

Griffith made, and released in 1924, what I think is one of his best pictures, *Isn't Life Wonderful,* a story of a German family plagued by famine and inflation. It summoned not overblown history, but the austere pleasures of what was his best vein: simple people struggling with simple, yet deadly, issues of survival. As a Griffith biographer, knowing much too much about him, I stand in a more ambiguous relationship to his life and career than most. He was a bit of a humbug and something of a poseur, and—never forget—the author of the noisome *The Birth of a Nation*. He has a lot to answer for. But in his early days he had a taste for simple stories about ordinary people that were gently sentimental, faintly comical and very appealing. *Isn't Life Wonderful* represents a reversion to that vein, and the truest indicator of his feelings.

It is perhaps the least well-known of his feature films—not that any of them are well known anymore—and it did nothing to halt his slide first into irrelevancy and then into silence. Yet it is a beautifully felt and realized work, and though he made many other films with much larger impacts on the public and on film history, I believe *Isn't Life Wonderful* deserves a place in this book.

If you study movie history at all, you learn this, if nothing else: It is all irony. Griffith, for instance, flopped back to bombast and empty spectacle immediately after *Isn't Life Wonderful* and never recovered his former pace or significance. And that says nothing of the largest irony of all: the fact that silent movies reached their highest level of sophistication and achievement (certainly in America) just as they were rendered irrelevant by the coming of sound.

Consider the legendary *Greed* (1925). Basically Erich von Stroheim wanted to make a shot-by-shot version of Frank Norris's novel *McTeague,* with a running time of perhaps seven hours. This he proceeded to do at MGM, with the producer Irving Thalberg, both a friend and an enemy of the director, wisecracking that Stroheim had "a footage fetish." It wouldn't do, of course; the studio cut it to a little over two hours and released it to considerable dubiety, tinged with admiration for Stroheim's undoubted visionary qualities. *Greed* is not, in any sense, a likable movie; and it's not one that I ever want to see again. Yet it is also something that must be reckoned with, if only because this story of murder, theft and blighted romance testifies to the vaulting ambition of Hollywood at the time. Thalberg told Vidor that Hollywood must occasionally indulge itself in follies like *Greed*. It could afford them and it could sometimes make money on them. Implicit in this comment was the notion that film could not truly be a respected art form if it did not do so. Thus *Greed* was, and was not, a signpost on the halting way forward. It has to be seen by anyone who claims a serious interest in film. Even in the cut version, it has passages of great power. Decades later, Hollywood would have known what to do with it—release it at its full length, and enjoy deserved praise for its courage or madness or whatever. But the time was not ripe. Something more disciplined, more in control, less brutish, more self-consciously beautiful was in order.

Something like *Sunrise* (1927). It was a product of F. W. Murnau, a master of German Expressionism who was only thirty-eight when the film was released, and died three years later in an automobile accident. Yet by that comparatively tender age he had made *Nosferatu* (1922), to this day the greatest of the Dracula movies, because of the way it married the grotesque with the poetic in a dreamlike (but not dreamy) way. He had also made *The Last Laugh,* about a hotel doorman demoted to washroom attendant, with Emil Jannings improbably achieving a studio-imposed happy ending that, despite our resistance, touches us.

Now Murnau was in Hollywood, working at Fox, on *Sunrise*. It was the set everyone in Hollywood wanted to visit when the film was in production. (*The Jazz Singer* was shooting, unheralded, at Warner Bros. at the same time. History has a way of sneaking up on Hollywood.) The film tells a very simple, almost abstract story. George O'Brien and Janet Gaynor are a not entirely happy farm couple. He lusts for the bright lights of the big city, just a boat ride away across a lake, and for Margaret Livingston, a temptress from the big town. He thinks about murdering his wife on a visit to the city. Instead, they have innocent fun there—a lovely meal, dancing, having their picture taken—and rekindle their romance. On the boat ride home across the lake, a storm comes up, and she is lost overboard and thought to be dead. The next morning she is found, and all ends happily.

It doesn't sound like much, and maybe it isn't. But the beauty of its making, which triumphs over the banality (and abstraction) of its narrative, forms a wonderful contrast to the frenzied scenes of city life, delirious in their expressionism. The director is perfectly in control of this contrast, and there is a remarkable paucity of intertitles—not always the case in "serious" silent films. Lack of dialogue rendered unto the director unquestioned control over his film. Intertitles were often an afterthought (and often ludicrously out of key with a film's intent), and indeed, Murnau had made *The Last Laugh* without resort to any intertitles at all. Dialogue and a carefully detailed script were requisites for sound production and this, in effect, set up a second power center for films. Unless a director participated in the writing, his authorship of a movie was necessarily diminished.

This was clearly not the case with *Sunrise*. It was so obviously Murnau's vision, elegantly abetted by the moving cameras of Charles Rosher and Karl Struss. The film was not a commercial success. It was only in later years that it achieved its high and deserved reputation, which, even so, is diminished by its having been released at the very end of the silent era. *Sunrise* is unlike any other film ever made—in story, theme and quality of presentation. It has taken decades for people to recognize that it is largely without precedent or successors in film history, and its admirers are a relative few. *Sunrise* has never been entirely lost. But it has never been entirely found, either.

5

The System

By 1925 the studio system was fully empowered. Pictures continued to be made independently, but they were not able, by and large, to make their way unaided by studio backing. In this year, King Vidor, who had been making films outside the major studios, moved to Metro-Goldwyn-Mayer and into the welcoming orbit of Irving Thalberg. Vidor was thirty-one at the time, Thalberg twenty-six, and they took a shine to one another that might have been partially generational but was clearly based on ambition as well—not just for their own interests, I think, but for the medium to which they were devoted. They were among the first men who came to the movies without any special loyalty to other fields, such as the theater. They thought, at least part of the time, that the movies could be, among other things, an art form. Thalberg, as I said, felt that a prospering studio like MGM could from time to time afford to trade profits for the prestige of making thoughtful, occasionally stodgy movies that appealed to the small but influential audience for what we may call the "finer things." Sometimes you didn't even have to sacrifice profits to attain that goal.

A case in point was Vidor's sixth film for the studio, *The Big Parade* (1925). It was time for Hollywood to come seriously to grips with World War I. (A year later, Raoul Walsh would make the equally good *What Price Glory.*) It is an antiheroic movie. An ordinary doughboy (John Gilbert) goes to war, endures some action in France, is wounded, comes home and then restlessly returns to Europe and, still limping from his wound, embraces Renée Adorée, the French girl whom he belatedly recognizes as his true love.

The film achieves its power simply, and is the better for it. There is, for example, a fine sequence in which American troops advance, under fire, through dense woods. Implacability is suggested by having them move to the beat of a large bass drum, one step every time it sounds. (The audience could not hear its booming beat, because it was a silent film.) The important thing about the movie was not its style, but rather Vidor's stress on the ordinariness of his hero (or antihero). For now, and for several years in the future, he wanted his principals to be anonymous, mere faces in the crowd, almost accidentally picked out by his camera. Lots of movies, perhaps the majority of them, aspire to this condition, but most of them eventually succumb to the temptation of exceptionalism—eventually the hero indulges himself in the atypical heroic act or romantic gesture. In this period, Vidor's people did not. And the audience picked up on that. *The Big Parade* was a very successful film, and it encouraged Thalberg to ask for more.

Vidor made other pictures, of course, notably *La Bohème,* during the filming of which he actually thought Lillian Gish had died, so still did she become in one of her swoons. But his masterpiece of this era and perhaps of all his films came in 1928, in response to a casual query from Thalberg about what he was thinking about doing next. He didn't know, but, according to his autobiography, a thought popped into his head: a film about how an ordinary man and woman might wander through life, observing and experiencing the usual ups and downs of its passage, triumphs and tragedies on a fairly modest yet compelling scale. They thought at first to call it "One of the Mob" but eventually settled on *The Crowd*. Vidor shot the film in a highly expressionistic style, using as the couple he follows his own wife, Eleanor Boardman, and an extra, James Murray, whom he had spotted in a crowd leaving the studio one afternoon. One of the film's salient qualities was its ease with expressionism. There were lots of raked and otherwise odd angles in it, plenty of things no one else was doing in American films—in one wonderful shot, the camera tracks up a skyscraper's exterior, enters a window and reveals hundreds of workers at their drone-like toil in a vast office space. (The back rows were filled with dwarfs.) But still he was almost casual (excepting a few shots like the one just alluded to) in his devices. Sometimes you don't even notice what he's doing at first glance. It is masterful moviemaking. Perhaps most important, these people never become abstractions; there is enough specificity in their lives to keep us fully involved in them before, finally, they melt back into "the crowd."

The movie was widely acknowledged as something unique and important at the time, but it did not have much influence on Hollywood. There was no rush to imitate its style. It was one of the great one-offs of film history. Not that Vidor was done with his great run of the late twenties. He followed this film with a genial and expert comedy, *Show People*, in which a young woman comes to Hollywood intent on stardom, which she achieves. It is a tribute, perhaps slightly premature, to the early (or Mack Sennett) days of the industry. Who knew Vidor had a sense of humor?

His career would extend for three more decades and would include some fine films—or should we say some fine scenes? Somehow, sound pictures seemed to puzzle him. He had so much to say, but much of the time he was awkward with words. "He has created more great moments and fewer great films than any director of his rank," Andrew Sarris wrote—correctly, I think. I fully like his delirious late melodramas, *The Fountainhead* and *Beyond the Forest*, in which Bette Davis utters her famous "What a dump!" line and Vidor surrenders to his own hysteria. More typically, his sound films stumble rather earnestly along, until suddenly a great, essentially silent sequence spectacularly intrudes on them—the bringing of the water to the parched landscape of *Our Daily Bread*, the gathering of the hands to stop the railroad from intruding on their ranch in *Duel in the Sun*, the great battle sequence in *Solomon and Sheba*. And, for a few moments, Vidor is returned to the greatness of the late silent era. It is one of the strangest careers in the history of the movies.

Yet no stranger than the career of Josef von Sternberg, who was born in the same year (1894). If Vidor was a man of sometimes vague ideas, von Sternberg was a creature of shadows and fog, of a romanticism that was dour, sentimental and lyrical. He was also probably the most arrogant son of a bitch who ever directed a movie. You could not speak on his sets, or snack, or argue with the auteur, of course.

From roughly 1927 to 1935, he was an important force in American film, breaking in by making moody lowlife films like *Underworld* and *The Docks of New York*, then discovering Marlene Dietrich in Berlin for *The Blue Angel* (all legs and pout) as she brings ruin to the hapless Emil Jannings. For the next five years, von Sternberg's career and Dietrich's were inextricably intertwined. They made six more pictures together and were, of course, famous as lovers. There is no doubt that she was totally smitten, and perhaps he was, too. In his biography of von Sternberg, John Baxter prints a note Dietrich slipped into her lover's pocket after the first screening of *Morocco:* "You—Only you—the Master—the Giver—Reason for my existence—The Teacher—the Love my heart and brain must follow."

Wow!

Susan Sontag, in her "Notes on 'Camp,'" offers, among many definitions of the term: "Camp is the outrageous aestheticism of Sternberg's six American movies with Dietrich, all six, but especially the last, *The Devil Is a Woman*." That's pretty much inarguable. But with ironies attached. There's no question that whatever fame still attaches to von Sternberg rests on these movies. They are vivid in their way, and increasingly absurd, with the offscreen story of the great von Sternberg-Dietrich romance resonating somewhat with that dwindling band of people who care about ancient movie history. And there is this: Once the pair broke up, von Sternberg's career was essentially over, though he had thirty-five years of a leftover, increasingly irrelevant life to live. Dietrich, of course, continued on, almost until her death at ninety-one—never a wildly popular star yet always a purring force to be reckoned with, if largely, in the end, as a nightclub attraction.

But von Sternberg is sold short by this more or less exclusive concentration on the Dietrich films. They grew more and more exotic as the years wore on and achieved a sort of wacked-out perfection in *Shanghai Express* (1932). That's the one in which Dietrich murmurs, "It took more than one man to change my name to Shanghai Lily," and you don't know whether to laugh, cry or flip off the DVD. It's more or less about her turning to high-class whoring after some unexplained disaster in a love affair she has been conducting with the immaculately stiff Clive Brook, and then reencountering him on a bandit-beset train where their love is rekindled. Not that anyone gives much of a damn about that. The point is to let von Sternberg's camera caress (or ogle) his star until a happy ending is achieved.

People at the time took it as a mindless adventure story with lots of careless subplots. But in the whole history of the movies, no film has ever been as avid (to the point of unconscious comedy) in its adoration of a star—and her hats, though that's another story. We need simply say that we are made, at last, simply to surrender to the story, giggle and snort though we may at the transformation of Dietrich into a perfectly obscure object of desire. We talk sometimes of directors making "personal statements" in their films, but few, if any, make *erotic* personal statements as slavish as this one. The camera, manned by Lee Garmes, who won an Oscar for the film, is arrogant in the stillness of its gaze.

"Had von Sternberg made only *Shanghai Express* his position in the pantheon of filmmakers would be secure," Baxter writes, and that's possibly (if too enthusiastically) true, though for reasons Baxter doesn't quite get—he doesn't acknowledge the (mostly) buttoned-down hysteria of this enterprise. But there was another film, *The Last Command,* made four years earlier, that is the most important signpost on the road not taken by von Sternberg. The film has only a minor erotic element and is all sober fluff in its plotting. Yet it is, I think, a great film.

It stars Emil Jannings as Sergius, a Russian general, brought low as a result of the revolution and, somewhat inexplicably, working in Hollywood as an extra. Working there as well is William Powell, a former revolutionist now prospering as a director on an epic scale. He observes Sergius and hires him, in effect, to play himself—a tragedy-stricken Russian general, who dies in the film. Not enough is made of Powell's motives, but the actor's disdain for von Sternberg is manifest throughout the film. We don't know if Powell was simply trying to humiliate his former enemy or if something more complex is at work in his character. But Jannings, who seems to have been a rather childlike figure, was, at the time, everybody's idea of a great actor. (He was soon reduced by his inability to master English and, after retreating to Germany, a rather too comfortable relationship with the Nazis.) We can stipulate, however, that in this picture he did attain something like greatness in a performance, a blend of pride and pathos that earned him the very first Academy Award for acting.

The film itself had its fair share of steam and smoke—there

were trains crashing about in it. But it had an openness that was rare in von Sternberg's films. Its epic qualities dictated that, and Jannings's performance dictated a certain spaciousness as well, and audiences responded to it. Preston Sturges thought it was the most perfect movie he had ever seen, though one wonders how long he clung to that opinion. In any case, as I said, this was a signpost on a road not taken by von Sternberg, who reverted to more closeted and atmospheric films, many of which were written by that expert, cranky screenwriter Jules Furthman, who was as difficult a character as the director himself. By 1929 von Sternberg was in Germany for his fatal encounter with Dietrich, whose narrow gifts in those days required films of an equally narrow range. It is not too much to say that, in one way or another, he was trapped in his obsession with her for the next five years. Every one of their films together traced one aspect or another of his fixation on her. After that, it is mostly loose ends and minor or abandoned projects.

We are all, like it or not, auteurists now. It is, if nothing else, the most convenient path through the tangled and ambiguous history of the movies. Even Pauline Kael, though she never admitted it, was an auteurist. But aside from congruities of style—admittedly a huge exception—isn't it likely that the authorship of movies by their directors is finally a record of their obsessions? If that's even partially true, then von Sternberg is exhibit number one. We don't doubt his minor place in this peculiar pantheon, but his claim rests almost entirely on the seven movies he made with Dietrich. The face, the voice—never forget its hypnotic qualities—her form, slinking sometimes, direct at others, was everything to him. With her he was something; without her he was almost nothing. In the whole history of the movies, no director's reputation has been so thoroughly staked on one performer's image. It is something to contend with when, as sometimes happens in the circles I travel in, we get to debating the validity of auteurism.

6

Men with Movie Cameras

Here I want to reiterate the premise of this book. It's about pleasure. It's about the movies I would have you download tonight and watch with delight, and no sense of dutifulness. This does not mean that I am unaware of the huge number of omitted movies, or that I lack respect for them. Fritz Lang is a case in point. I think both *Metropolis* and *M* are overrated, movies that are running now on their reputations rather than on reengagement with their merits. Lang made a lot of routine outings when he settled into his long run as a busy director of genre films. The exception that tests this opinion is *Spione* (1928), that giddy, half-mad espionage drama that defies description and is impossible to turn away from. He is loose and free here as he only rarely is in his other pictures.

What's true of Lang is true, I think, of Russian silent movies as well. Their importance to a group of directors cannot be overestimated. Elia Kazan can speak for all of them: "God, that's it. . . . That's adventure. . . . Not just some friends of yours on the stage yelling at each other." He said that his flirtation with communism was based less on politics than on the films he saw from the USSR.

That was true of the next generation as well: We were taught to revere the Russian cinema, and justifiably so. There was, at least in the films exported to the United States, an epic quality—and a technical skill—that was largely unmatched in our native cinema. Yet I don't particularly want to see those movies again. My best critical academic friend, Jeanine Basinger, recently said to me, "I'm done with them." By which she means that they were vitally important when we were young and soaking up the knowledge that was vital to our becoming film historians, but less so now. We will, naturally, respond favorably to their great sequences (the Odessa Steps sequence, for example) when we encounter them in an anthology film. But, guilt-ridden as I am to say it, they are a slog when I sit down to watch them in their entirety. I hasten to add, however, that they will never be less than "historically important," and no one seriously interested in movies can afford to miss them.

That brings me to that huge stumbling block of the late silent era, *The Passion of Joan of Arc* (1928), Carl Theodor Dreyer's great film about the trial and martyrdom of the Maid of Orleans. Unlike most of the other movies in this book, I have seen it only once, and I doubt that I will return to it in the years remaining to me. In part that's because it is so vivid in my memory, and in part it's because it sets out a "story" that is so familiar.

It is a film that seems to be told mainly in close-ups, though that is mostly an impression. There are sequences of what I suppose might be called "action," though that's a peculiarly weighted word in this context, as we shall see. Mostly, Joan sits on a stool while a panel of judges questions her claims to sainthood. They are by and large grotesques, wearing a weird collection of funny hats, and they sometimes seem obsessed with the fact that she chooses to dress in male clothing, which must seem to us the least of her "sins." Dreyer covers them in a series of close-ups—some individual, some linked by tracking shots—which pause to study each face closely and then move on. Joan answers their questions softly and simply but remains convinced of her righteousness.

She quite correctly fears the flames of the auto-da-fé, so much so that the first time she is taken out to the stake she confesses that her claims of being in touch with God—that she is acting on His instructions—are false. By this time, the film has lost its static quality. The judges decide to torture her into confession and conduct her to that chamber of unspeakable pain. There is no doubt that they are lasciviously looking forward to seeing this girl naked and in pain—and here Dreyer abandons his stately manner. It is a sequence as quick-cut and horrific as anything in the history of cinema. Something similar may be said of the two outdoor sequences where Joan confronts the stake. They are not especially quickly cut, but they have a roominess and an attention to detail in the handling of crowds, for instance, that is exemplary. As viewers we are—perversely—somewhat relieved to be out in the open at last, freed of the claustrophobia of the courtroom. Joan's death in the flames is handled powerfully and simply, and the movie concludes not with her death but with the riots that ensue as the populace realizes that a terrible mistake has been made.

In a certain sense this is a perfect movie; there is nothing in it that strikes one as careless or miscalculated or excessive. A master is in control of its every shot. And that says nothing about Maria Falconetti's performance as Joan. She was "discovered" by Dreyer working in a boulevard comedy in Paris—pretty but not glamorous, a young woman of no particular piety but exuding a kind of common sense. And, I guess, patience: Dreyer said later that her performance was created shot by shot—look up, look down, turn here to the right, there to the left. It could easily have looked manipulated, but it does not. She has an ease before the camera that is transcendent. She worked without makeup and there is a scrubbed clarity about her that is heartbreaking in its seeming lack of calculation. There is near-universal consent among critics and historians that her ability to transcend Dreyer's finicky direction, to ease it back to simplicity and naturalism, constitutes one of the great performances in film history. They will find no disagreement from me.

Yet she never made another movie. She returned to the theater, as an actress and producer, and died during World War II as a refugee in Buenos Aires. One has the instinctive sense that she knew she had nothing more to prove.

The Passion of Joan of Arc is a film beloved by critics. That's partly because it gives those secularists an opportunity to prove they are not impervious to the religious impulse when it is presented soberly, without spectacle, as it so rarely is in the movies. More important, it is a great act of modernism. It tells, obviously, a very traditional story, which could have been a fusty bore, as all the other pictures about Joan of Arc are. But it is rich in shots and sequences that belie that intent in an unselfconscious way.

Passion does not *seem* like a great act of modernism, its stylistic innovations are so quiet, its narrative so traditional. It hides its hand very well. But there is a curious thing about modernism in the movies: They do not in their earliest years boast of a figure like Picasso in painting, Diaghilev in dance, Joyce in the novel or Stravinsky in music. Maybe that's because the movies were such a young art that no one thought to look for innovation in them. Maybe it is because many people could not see that it was an art form at all, so deep were its roots in popular nineteenth-century theatrical forms, as were its greatest artists (Griffith, Chaplin, et al.). There were gestures toward modernity, some of which I have alluded to here. But setting aside such oddities as Buñuel's *Un Chien Andalou* (which I adore, but it is not quite a movie as we understand the word), there is only one film that, from first frame to last, throws down a full-throated challenge to the movies' traditional understanding of what a film might (and might not) be.

When David Thomson was planning *Have You Seen . . . ?,* his book of a thousand short essays about movies that he loves and loathes, all important milestones in the history of film, he quite sensibly decided to include only fictional film. But then a friend asked, "What are you going to do with Dziga Vertov and *Man with a Movie Camera?*" Thomson reports wincing, writhing and worrying before finally including it in his book.

He made the right call. The film is not really a documentary. It is, perhaps, a poem. It is, assuredly, one of the few great modernist gestures in the history of the movies. And it is today as fresh, as stirring, as it was the day it was released in 1929. There was, in the late silent era, a little vogue for "portraits" of great cities—*Berlin: Symphony of a Great City* (1927), *People on Sunday* (1930)—and I suppose it fits in that cycle. But not really. For Vertov creates, without telling us so, a "city" composed out of parts of Kiev, Kharkiv, and Odessa—in other words, a fictional city. This city awakens in the morning, goes through its workday, indulges in its nighttime play and then goes back to sleep. What holds the film together is a cameraman (played by Vertov's brother, Mikhail Kaufman) clambering high, slouching low, as he seems to record "life caught unaware"—the events of a day, from the birth of a baby to visits to a beauty shop. The film also records the work of an editor—Vertov's wife, Elizaveta Svilova—fully accessing all the known movie tricks of the day to enliven a film that doesn't need enlivening, but profits from it. It is not the first film to take in the process of filmmaking—people were interested in how movies were made almost from their beginning—but this was the first to self-consciously explore the tricks of the trade in some detail.

Vertov had more in mind than just making a "city symphony." In a foreword, he says, "This experimental work aims at creating a truly international absolute language of cinema, based on its total separation from the language of theatre and literature"—which, of course, it does not do. The movies remain today, as they were then, a storytelling medium. Movies like *Man with a Movie Camera* are something of a dead end. Even a city wasn't rich enough to sustain a feature-length film—witness Vertov's need to resort to three cities to create one semifictional one.

Yet the film is a marvel. Our cameraman (whose activities were recorded by Vertov himself) is a heroic figure, a Stakhanovite of imagery, faintly comical in his tirelessness. Vertov even makes entertaining a sequence of people reporting for instruction to Stalinist seminars. And in his little way he is not unaware of sexuality—there are those shots of women dressing to go to work. There is not a moment in the film that is not exhilarating, alive to all the possibilities.

The movie is very quick. It does not linger long on any of its many subtopics. Yet it never feels rushed. It is always loyal to its pace, which can probably best be described as that of the observer wandering the streets, pausing to enter some shop or institution and then moving on, glimpsing, but not really studying, what he sees. Vertov wants to create an impression of something that is new in the world, and not in all its aspects benign, though Vertov takes no moral position on that. How it will work out in the long run is not his concern. It is an implacably jazzy, attractive place we want to be in. We want to do what Vertov does: find a way to respond to its rhythms with rhythms appropriate to it.

One wonders if, later in life, when he had sunk back to anonymity, Vertov regretted his total surrender to the city, buying into its seductions too much. I think not. The pall of Stalinism has not yet settled on this place that is not a place. It is fresh and new and, above all, hopeful. Seeing it today, we are hopeful, too—for a moment. How wonderful the spirit of modernism was in its youth—the old, the staid, the tragic washed away, the greater horrors to come not yet imagined. Released when Vertov was just thirty-three—still time for idealism and for the thought that anything is possible—maybe this is a film of youth. We don't know. And maybe we don't want to know.

In his consideration of the film, Thomson writes that all its tricks "are candid and innocent as someone warning you that he's going to cheat you." But he goes further: "It is the only silent film that needs no qualification or apology. It is perfect. It is new still. And it makes you love the world."

This is an important point. In our consideration of silent films—of all films, in fact—I am entirely aware that they contain conventions of editing, camerawork and, above all, acting that require of us, watching now, the suspension of disbelief. That's the way they did things in that foreign country that is, as the cliché goes, the past. We brush past these awkwardnesses, our eyes intent on the higher, more lasting values of the movie in question. This movie—with its quick cutting, its ironic (yet loving) portrait of its demonic cameraman, its frankness about what it is up to—obviates all that. I don't think you could make something like it today—the city no longer is the avatar of our poetic hopes for modernism. The ambiguities of *Sunrise* have already, as of 1929, intruded on that pretty, energetic fantasy. So *Man with a Movie Camera,* like most of the movies in this book, is, finally, in large measure, a lucky accident. There was a man with a theory of his art who had the wit and energy to make a film that demonstrated brilliantly what he was thinking about. He never repeated his triumph, which is a tragedy of sorts, but not one unique in the history of the movies. Just ask Orson Welles.

Maybe I'm just being self-consciously eccentric when I name this film as the one the entire silent era was aiming at. As I've said, it was something of a dead end, in that it was released so late in the silent era and because, of course, it is hard to imagine its techniques being used in the comedies and melodramas that ruled in the other realms of movie production. We know from the experience of our own eyes that the revolution made by the soundtrack was total, sudden and complete. Sound, so bulky and balky, cut off the slender stalks of innovation that had just begun to take root in the last years of the silent era. George Lucas once argued to me that the movies never really recovered from this abandonment of their pure visual element, and I don't have any serious disagreement with this view. It was trouble enough mastering sound. It consumed everyone's energies. But we did lose something. And the spirit, the promise, of *Man with a Movie Camera* is one of the several things that we lost and never found again.

7

A Studio's Way

One day, probably in 1928, Bill Wellman was making what was apparently a routine movie called *Beggars of Life*, a part talkie, when he grew impatient with the immobility of the microphone. William A. (for Augustus) Wellman was not a notably patient man. He had been an aviator in the Lafayette Flying Corps in World War I and had parlayed a friendship with Douglas Fairbanks Sr. into work as a movie director, which was fun and kind of adventurous in its way.

In those days, the camera was enclosed in a booth (to prevent its whirrings from being picked up by the microphone), which could only be somewhat painfully and briefly moved, a drag on the camera's former mobility. The microphone, inextricably linked to the camera, was the problem—that is why, in many very early talkies, actors are seen sitting around tables, talking into flowerpots in which the microphone is hidden. Briefly, the sound recordist became king of the set, infringing on the director's dominance of the moviemaking process.

So Bill Wellman, whose legendary "Wild Bill" demeanor belied the sweetness, even sentimentality, of his nature (I know because he was my good friend in his late years, when I made a documentary about him), decided to do something about this problem. He grabbed a broomstick, hung a microphone on it and had one of the grips hold it out of the shot over the heads of the actors. Thus the boom was born, and it had a vital impact in restoring movement to the movies.

As for Wellman, he made *Wings* and won accolades for making a real movie as Hollywood then understood the term—thrilling, sentimental, romantic and pure fun. Dissatisfied with a stuntman's attempt at a crash landing, Wellman hauled himself into the cockpit, executed an expertly managed crash, walked away and never flew a plane again.

Wellman is usually seen as not much more than a colorful footnote in the early history of the movies, an amusing, inventive guy, capable of making good, solid movies in virtually every genre, which he continued to do until his retirement in 1957. But I'm going to make a larger claim for him. By 1931, he was under contract at Warner Bros., and for the next four years he did more, I think, to establish the tone and style of that studio than any single individual, making it—to my taste anyway—tough, brash, funny in its brawling way, and willing, as no other studio was, to look life in the eye, before applying a little saving sentiment to the picture in its last minute (though sometimes it didn't even bother with that).

It's been noted that Warner pictures were—literally—dark, and people guessed that was because Jack Warner was saving on sets and the electricity bill, which might have been true. Its stars—Cagney, Edward G. Robinson, Bette Davis, Joan Blondell—were an odd-looking lot who probably would not have been stars elsewhere, and they were constantly aroil with rebellion, which was a matter of indifference to Wellman. The thing was, if you missed the logo, you still knew the picture was from Warner less than half a minute into its often brief running time. Maybe MGM had that kind of character, too, except, more often than not, your heart sank when you realized what you were in for, which was slickness without sharpness, sentiment without authentic tragedy (though, of course, MGM was far more successful financially than Warner).

One day, as Wellman strolled to the commissary for lunch, he was approached by two young writers, Kubec Glasmon and John Bright, who pressed upon him their treatment for a project called "Beer and Blood," assuring him that it was based in part on their own experiences hanging around the Chicago underworld. That appealed to him—he loved realism (or his own particular brand of it), and after reading the piece in his office that afternoon, he immediately took it to Darryl Zanuck, then the head of production at Warner Bros. Zanuck at first demurred to the project, thinking he had made too many gangster pictures lately. Why should he do another one? he inquired. "Because," snarled Wellman, "I'll make it the toughest one of all." "You got it," said Zanuck.

And, indeed, it was tough—but not until Cagney, originally cast as a best friend, replaced Edward Woods as the lead in the picture. "Eddie wasn't tough at all; small-town boy," Cagney later said. It made all the difference to Cagney's career and to the fate of the picture.

It's not just a matter of one of the most famous scenes in movie history—the grapefruit in Mae Clarke's face. It is, largely, the demonic energy Cagney brings to his role as the gangster, Tom Powers—that mixture of psychopathy and wild humor and, yes, charm that marks his rise and fall in the underworld. It seems to me, to this day, that the screen had never before seen anything like this performance—if only because it required a soundtrack to convey the full snarling nuttiness that Cagney unleashed and Wellman was smart enough to let unfurl in all its glory. It remains, to my taste, the greatest gangster picture of the genre's first era, all anarchy and wildness.

Wellman did not make many more gangster pictures over the course of his long career. He didn't have to. But yet, *The Public Enemy* (1931) was a kind of model for the pictures that would immediately follow it. This was not a matter of plots or stars. It was a question of spit-in-your-eye attitude, leavened by rough comedy sometimes, and rough sentiment, too.

"In any Bill Wellman operation," wrote the late, great Manny Farber, "there are at least four directors—a sentimentalist, deep thinker, hooey vaudevillian and an expedient short-cut artist whose special love is for mulish toughs expressing themselves in drop-kicking heads and somber standing around." It's irresistible not to quote from Faber; his writing is so colorful and jazzy, and records an impression that is accurate in its way. Alas, it's wrongheaded in its own way, too, though that is not Farber's fault. He was writing when Wellman's Warner Bros. pictures were not generally available and he had to focus on the longer, more striving films that were all right and sometimes better than that (see *The Story of G.I. Joe,* for example) but do not, in my estimation, match the power, and the plainness, of his best work at Warner Bros.

Wellman was not a director much interested in subtexts. What you saw was what you got, as in *Heroes for Sale.* Such "deep thinking" as the film contains centers on Richard Barthelmess and his confrontation with the Great Depression, at its depths in 1933. He gets out of the army after World War I a drug addict, cures himself, prospers with a laundry, loses his wife and business in the downturn, joins the army of the unemployed and is last seen living under a bridge with the anonymous victims of economic disaster. (No one could say the studio was afraid of unhappy endings.) The story was swift—the running time is a mere seventy-three minutes—but it leaves out nothing and is one of the comparatively few movies that directly address the effects of the Depression. Particularly fine is a riot of the unemployed, which is powerful, efficient and scary. I have no idea what Wellman's politics were at the time, but the movie drips with compassion—and outrage—about the victims of

national tragedy. And it does so without particularly sentimen-
talizing them. They are mute as they are hammered by a fate
from which there is no escape. Our sympathy for Barthelmess
and the rest of the victims is enlisted because no special plea is
made for them. *I can't go on; I must go on* is the tone.

Wild Boys of the Road, which immediately followed, is a
shade more sentimental, but somehow very powerful as well.
Zanuck, who was gone from the studio before it was released,
liked "ripped from the headlines" stories, and he saw a touching
one here: kids riding the rails, looking for work, food, a place
to rest their heads for a night, in the depth of the Depression.
Wellman's film simply follows a group of them on their travels. There are no big stars (his new and beloved wife, Dorothy
Coonan, was one of the gang), and much melodrama ensues,
including one of the most potent sequences of the era: a boy
losing his leg to an onrushing train as the kids run from railroad bulls. This leads finally to a hopeful ending, wherein a
Roosevelt look-alike promises better times ahead. But the main
thing about the movie—eighty-eight minutes long—is its mad
rush. There is nothing "mulish" about it, no "somber standing around" in it. Wellman was a director of surfaces in these
days—bright, hard, depthless. So it happens that this was the
first Warner Bros. picture that I saw of his, and I responded to
its pell-mell pace and rough sentiments.

This, I thought, was a man to reckon with. He told the
unvarnished truth, as he did in an inconsequential movie that
same year called *Central Airport.* A man and a woman enter
a hotel room, undress, and simply proceed to go to bed—no
questions asked. I loved that about the guy—the lack of dither
in those pre-Code days, simple behavioral truths offered without apologies or simpering. He went on to grander enterprises
(he made the first and probably the best of the endless *Star Is
Born* pictures), but I still think there was a match of man and
material in the Warner years that deserves serious study—not
that that will ever happen these days, when movie history is all
haste and half-knowledge.

We are not yet finished with Warner Bros., nor with several good directors bustling about on their lot. It is not too much to say that by the mid-1930s Warner was, of all things, an auteurist studio. Wellman was in and out of the place, of course, and Raoul Walsh had come over from Fox in the late thirties, and Howard Hawks was more there than anywhere else during this period. Hawks was a dry, rather affectless man, who spoke in a monotone, placed his cameras in spots that seemed in retrospect inevitable and, above all, dreaded "fuss." He was also a congenital liar, a dandy and a powerfully secretive man. I came to know him rather well in his late years and came to like him a lot, though I knew I was never going to solve the mystery of the man.

Of the directors who shuttled on and off the Warner lot in the thirties and forties, Hawks had by far the greatest range. Comedies, melodramas, westerns, even musicals—everything seemed to be his dish of tea. He had a spectacular relationships with Cary Grant and Humphrey Bogart and Lauren Bacall and, of course, John Wayne—among the many actors and actresses he worked with so effortlessly. He claimed he found his style in 1932 with *Scarface*. It was, he liked to say, everything but the kitchen sink, up angles and down angles until (to borrow his phrase) it "reeled the mind." (And he hated cutting it all together.) From then on his camera would be eye level, his cutting severe, his emotions understated. Above all, his manner worked for virtually every topic. We can name a few, together with their genres: *Twentieth Century* (romantic farce), *Bringing Up Baby* (ditto), *Only Angels Have Wings* (comedy-adventure), *To Have and Have Not* and *The Big Sleep* (romantic mysteries) and a slew of westerns starting with *Red River* and proceeding from there.

And we are far from done, regretting the absence from our list of such films as *His Girl Friday* and *Ball of Fire*. I might as well say it—with a gulp—that it is probably the best filmography in the history of American cinema. Even the semi-duds—*Hatari!* among them—have more spunk than a lot of directors' presumed masterpieces. Or to put it another way, there is scarcely a Hawks film that I would not happily pop into the DVD tonight and watch. Indeed, there is this interesting thing about most of his work: It doesn't date. The dialogue in some cases may be seventy-five or more years old, but it remains crisp and funny, and the situations that occasion it are plausibly farcical. You don't have to make many allowances for it.

Unlike his competitors, Hawks was famous for two themes that he worked endlessly. One was the functioning male group bickering as they bonded in pursuit of whatever adventurous goal they were jointly pursuing. They were funny guys most of the time, but they were also haunted by death, which was usually greeted if not with a laugh, then with a shrug. The temptation toward the lugubrious was sternly resisted. (See the passing of Thomas Mitchell in *Only Angels Have Wings* for the perfect example of gallantry under the ultimate pressure.) And then, perhaps more famously, there was the Hawksian woman. Putting it very simply, she was always one of the guys, bantering on an equal footing with men. (She always had wise-guy lines that matched in their insouciance what the boys were saying.) Hawks used to say that they were the kind of women he found most attractive, and we have no reason to doubt that.

There were plenty of funny ladies in the movies of this era, but it seems to me the radical simplicity of the Hawks style served these women as the works of no other director did; their ease, their directness, their appraising manner are really beyond compare. And you have to think that his radically simplified style was the perfect servant of his subject matter. I have no idea how self-conscious it was, but I think it represented that stream of modernism that aims at stripping down subject matter to its bare-bones essence—just enough and no more.

I'm not saying that Hawks is the greatest of all directors— I'm not saying that about anybody—but the body of work is superlative. The continuing freshness of his films cannot be denied, nor the sheer fun and tension of them.

And still we are not quite done with Warner Bros. Not when *Baby Face* has been ignored, and, for that matter, *I Am a Fugitive from a Chain Gang*.

Baby Face (1933) was directed by Alfred E. Green, who began directing in 1919 and didn't quit until sometime in the 1950s. He was a typically prolific studio director, making his share of all-right and not-so-hot movies, with his biggest hit, *The Jolson Story*, coming late in his career, in 1946. *Baby Face*, to which Zanuck made some story contributions, is quite brutal. Barbara Stanwyck plays a woman from a coal town, raped by her father and rendered frigid as a result. She makes her way to the big city, where she works her way to the top—actually frigidly fucking her way to the president's office—where, at the end, George Brent is rescued from ruin by her. (Among the men she uses in her rise is John Wayne.) It is, to say the least, a very cold film, and it is all of seventy minutes long. It attracted little attention when it was released, was re-edited when the Production Code was given teeth, and was then restored in recent years.

It is, I think, a near-to-great film—for its speed, its bluntness, its complete lack of hypocrisy. It says people, some of them, are like this—more of them, perhaps, than the studios liked to contemplate. And also that the studio system, when it just didn't give a damn about particularly pleasing the public with saving, sentimental gestures, was capable of really brutal truth-telling. And that says nothing about Stanwyck, who is simply great in her hardness and heedlessness. The fact that her best friend is a black woman, beautifully played by Theresa Harris—and that her race is never overtly commented upon—is one of the many felicities of this film. At this time, Stanwyck was the finest of screen actresses, working often with directors like Wellman and Frank Capra, who responded to the directness of her address, how she failed to sue audiences for their sympathy yet somehow attained it. She was often, or so it seemed to me, radically alone in her pictures, yet she never gave in to that quality. She later made more famous films *(Meet John Doe, Double Indemnity)*, but her essence is here in this increasingly well-regarded little movie. The film also had an unintended consequence: It caused some sort of row between Harry Warner and Darryl Zanuck, which caused the latter to leave Warner and become head of his own company, which quickly became Twentieth Century Fox in 1935. But the important thing is this: When a place like Warner Bros. wasn't trying too hard, when it was just banging them out, it was capable of casual greatness, generally unrecognized at the time.

Sometimes, alas, the opposite is true. Witness *I Am a Fugitive from a Chain Gang* (1932), which is based on an allegedly true story. The title tells it all. A heroic, down-on-his-luck war veteran is standing around rather too near a robbery, is sent to a chain gang, escapes, builds a decent life, is lured back south, where his name is supposed to be cleared—a trick, of course—and back he goes to prison, from which he escapes again, only to be doomed apparently to a perpetual life on the run. The movie's concluding line is immortal. He visits his wife one dark night. She asks him how he lives, what's to become of him? He replies, "I steal."

The picture was directed by Mervyn LeRoy, half-forgotten now but at the time the producer and/or director of some good pictures *(Little Caesar, They Won't Forget)*. His star was Paul Muni, at the time considered—not least by himself—a great actor, though in fact he was a great ham, often hiding out in heavy makeup and accents and playing noble historical figures.

That said, I think you have to enter an exception for *Fugitive.* Muni is perhaps a little too well-spoken in it, but there's a naturalness in his playing, a simplicity and directness, that is very effective and quite rare in his career. You can make the case that his fugitive is the unluckiest man in the world (or, anyway, the most naive), but he makes you believe he is an everyman, you or me but for the grace of God. The movie, long by Warner standards (ninety minutes), rattles along at a one-damn-thing-after-another pace that is utterly compelling even now. It was for Warner Bros. a self-conscious attempt to make an "important" movie, an ambition at which it admirably succeeded. It has the pace (if not quite the verve) of its more routine productions.

Except I wonder about that word "routine." There was so much at that studio that only looked routine. There was that little raft of Cagney pictures—smart, fast-talking, usually comic, occasionally striking a brief serious note. They were made so quickly, so cheaply, with seemingly so little regard for his enormous talent; he loathed them, though actually they were often pitched perfectly to his freewheeling gift for something like anarchy. There were no less than fifty movies that starred Joan Blondell, who should have attained parity with Cagney, but Warner was such a boys' club, mostly impervious to her never-ending world-weariness. (See *Blonde Crazy* or *Three on a Match* for examples of her rough magic.) Bette Davis and Humphrey Bogart came a little late to this party. She didn't make an impression until she made *Of Human Bondage* at another studio and then was misused, if not abused, until the studio finally acceded to her demand for chin-up tragedies in the later thirties; he took a long time to recover from his miscasting as the brooding gangster in *The Petrified Forest,* which played like a limp parody of a Warner gangster film.

But we cannot leave this studio without referring to its most spectacular directorial star. That, of course, was Busby Berkeley. I think it's fair to say that in his way, he was among the most unique—if limited—talents in the history of the medium. We all have some idea of what he did. In essence, he set hundreds of dancers in motion in a fashion that was at once militaristic and erotic, in settings as exotic as he could imagine, photographed from angles that literally no one had ever seen before (or, for that matter, have seen since). He could be parodied, but he could not be equaled. There was once "a hall of harps," there were waterfalls, of course, and girls arranging themselves as violins for spectacular overhead shots. He once did a swell number featuring rocking chairs. His method, often, was to sit around brooding while his cast of hundreds stood idle, waiting for inspiration to strike the master—which, eventually and reliably, it did.

He was expensive talent, no doubt about that, and seemingly ill-suited to the frugal Warner style—except that for a few years he was a sensation, well worth his price, mostly because his work was so strangely sexy. Never did so many cameras track through so many invitingly open thighs as they did in his production numbers, never did so many scanty costumes invite our fantasies, while hoping against hope that the censors were nodding. The best of Berkeley was generally of the so-called pre-Code era, when censorship was lax and, in fact, his chorines were sometimes actually naked beneath, say, their flowing hair or other covering.

I've never made my mind up: Did the military precision of many Berkeley dances somehow defuse their sexuality, or did it enhance it? We generally want women to flow gracefully in their movements, and these routines often locked them into antisexual poses and postures. I guess the most we can say is that there was, quite often, a tension between the sexiness of the numbers' intent and their means of arriving at that goal. Or maybe it was simply the sheer number of women involved that carried the day. We were used to seeing relatively few dancers in movie production numbers; Berkeley tended to overwhelm us with pulchritude.

It is impossible to name a single movie of which he was dance director as a "best." In those days he did not take a credit as director, a task that was assigned to staff directors, among them Mervyn LeRoy. Their stories were generally cheerful and inane, just excuses, really, to make a movie. But there are two numbers I might single out as outstanding, because they are so dark and risky within the context of musical movies. The first, "Remember My Forgotten Man," occurs in *Gold Diggers of 1933*. It's a plea for men who fifteen years earlier had fought for their country, but are now among the legions of the unemployed. Uniformed, carrying rifles, they are seen marching on a gigantic wheel, which keeps turning and turning but never disgorges them from their hopelessness. It is a powerful image, accompanied by a lugubrious song. It is a genuine shock to find it in the midst of a lightsome musical.

Where the idea came from is not recorded so far as I can determine. It is certainly a tribute of a sort to the social consciousness of Warner's nonmusical offerings of the time. But, more important, it is an act of high creative daring. There is nothing else quite like it in the musicals of its time. Possibly we could cite as comparable the ballets of the MGM musicals that began appearing a decade later, but their pleasures were of an aesthetic nature and more or less fit the overall design of the picture, and, of course, they had no "message" whatsoever.

Berkeley was by no means finished. Two years later, in *Gold Diggers of 1935*, he was back with what I think is his masterpiece—in my opinion the greatest number in the history of the genre. "Lullaby of Broadway," by Harry Warren and Al Dubin, was instantly recognized as a great song, but it puzzled Berkeley; he had no ideas for staging it. Finally, he told Al Jolson he could have it for a movie he was planning if he could not come up with something himself in twenty-four hours. Under that pressure, he came through—a dream sequence in which a "Broadway baby" comes to a tragic end.

She is played, beautifully, by a singer named Wini Shaw. She is introduced as a careless young thing, disporting herself with Dick Powell on a typical night among the bright lights of the big city. Eventually, with dawn beginning to break, she decides to go home. Time passes, and the next night she is back to her careless rounds, at which point something like a hundred chorus boys and girls, who have been innocently deployed to this point, start to form themselves into smiling but somehow menacing lines, surrounding her, starting to harry her. This leads to a wild montage—all quick cutting and raked angles—

and Wini finds herself in a tight space, crowded by the dancers, who seem, as does Powell, unaware of the menace they pose to her. She seeks to escape. They are still, ostensibly, having fun, though the underscoring is beginning to grow threatening. She registers something near panic and escapes onto a balcony— where she trips and plunges to her death. The music becomes hushed. Berkeley's camera moves back through his images of Broadway and settles in Wini's now vacant apartment, concluding with an overhead shot of her face, which fades from view.

There is nothing like this piece in American cinema. To say that it is haunting radically understates the case. I said earlier that the coming of sound cut movies off from the further development of their visual poetry; to some degree, this sequence argues against that point. But the poetry is different— harder-edged and, like the "Forgotten Man" sequence, much more socially conscientious. Berkeley is saying that we are, to adduce the cliché, "dancing on a volcano." Or maybe he was just a desperate choreographer, looking for something to save a number that he liked before giving it to Al Jolson. We do know that he never went in this direction again, though there was no retreat in the matter of visual splendor. He, of course, affected innocence, saying, "In an era of breadlines, Depression and wars . . . I wanted to make people happy, if only for an hour."

Which he basically did. It's just that it's hard to resist this little asterisk.

By 1935 Warner Bros. was a somewhat changed place. Zanuck had been replaced by Hal B. Wallis, a smooth, soft-spoken expert executive moved up from the publicity department. His taste was different from Zanuck's. Or maybe the world was changing. Or maybe it was a combination of the two. The studio did not entirely abandon its hard-bitten ways, as we'll have occasion to see later. But the romantic Errol Flynn arrived—the first Warner leading man who might have succeeded at other studios—and Bette Davis was at last more or less placated with the aforementioned doomy romances (like *The Letter*) that she deemed, often correctly, were best suited to her talents. Under Wallis, Michael Curtiz became the studio's leading director and its most prolific one, too. He made a lot of lightweight stuff (with great conviction) as well as immortal pictures like *Casablanca, Yankee Doodle Dandy* and *Mildred Pierce* (which perhaps suggests the studio's expanded range of interests) and drove Wallis to produce reams of memos complaining of time spent laying out the tracking shots Curtiz adored. But, along with the much more dashing Raoul Walsh (who came to the studio in 1939), Curtiz kept the place flourishing until television, in the late 1940s, almost killed the golden goose for everybody.

Here is a measure of Wallis's executive skills: On the one hand, he was capable of solving the vexing question of Flynn's ill-fitting wig in some movie or other. On the other, he was capable of ordering the spectacular push-in, worthy of Curtiz, that brings *The Roaring Twenties,* that late, great gangster film, to its heartbreaking climax. I am of the opinion that Wallis, virtually unknown to the general public, is the greatest production executive in Hollywood history.

I am also of the opinion that Warner Bros. was, in this period, the greatest studio in Hollywood history. But, there's "sophisticated" Paramount to consider.

8

"The Son of a Gun Is
Nothing but a Tailor"

L ove Me Tonight begins with a standard opening shot of Paris: the Eiffel Tower thrusting up over low rooftops. Then there are quick cuts to the quays along the Seine, of shutters opening, of a worker digging in the street with a pickax, of shopkeepers setting out their wares. Two shoemakers start hammering out a beat as they repair some boots—one, two, *three,* one, two, *three.* Soon a whole district stirs itself into musical wakefulness. There's a cut to Maurice Chevalier's famous straw boater hanging on a nail. The star is then revealed pulling a turtleneck over his head. He grabs his chapeau, tilts it at a rakish angle and sets off jauntily down the street, greeting and being greeted—in rhyme—by everyone.

It is, or was, a justly famous set piece, but it is by no means the end—or the greatest—of this 1932 film's pleasures. It occasions two immediate thoughts: that Rouben Mamoulian sure knew how to get a movie off to a dazzling start, and that maybe by now this genius of the early sound era deserves something more than his rather patronizing footnote in the movie histories. "Mamoulian's tragedy is that of the innovator who runs out of innovations," Andrew Sarris wrote of him, not entirely unjustly.

But it might be fairer to say that he was an innovator who was inimitable. That's partly because he made only sixteen films over three decades, choosing to divide his time between Hollywood and Broadway, where he directed the original productions of three touchstone musicals: *Porgy and Bess, Oklahoma!* and *Carousel.* He was, as well, a difficult character who was fired from or quit *Laura,* as well as *Cleopatra* and *Porgy and Bess.* As a Russian émigré (he was born in Tbilisi, Georgia, in 1897) he was never entirely comfortable with dialogue or the conventions of American-style narrative. *Love Me Tonight* tells a pretty banal story—humble Parisian tailor falls in love with neurasthenic princess—though Mamoulian didn't give a hoot about that. Or, it would seem, about acting: Let Chevalier's vaunted French "charm" cloy, let Jeanette MacDonald's double chins quiver cluelessly in a role that needs spunk and irony.

Mamoulian was primarily a shooter and a cutter, a man who preferred to communicate in purely visual terms—someone who had rather obviously learned much of his art by studying Eisenstein and the other masters of "Russian montage" and vividly applied their manner to American commercial kitsch instead of Soviet political kitsch. Such borrowed means are often weirdly discordant with his ends, if you stop to think about it. But the bedazzled eye doesn't really care about that. It is simply hypnotized by Mamoulian's self-excited daring.

Love Me Tonight has no great aspirations. What it has is a shimmering Rodgers and Hart score, which it is Mamoulian's primary business to stage intoxicatingly. For example: "Isn't It Romantic?" Chevalier starts the song in his tailor shop. It is picked up by a customer who passes it on to a cabdriver, then to a group of French soldiers in a train carriage. Next thing you know, the *poilus* have switched the rhythm to a march tempo, to which they tramp happily through the countryside—where, apparently, some gypsies overhear them, for we find them singing it in their encampment outside the great castle where most of the film's action will take place. Has ever a movie story made a transition from point A to point B more delightfully? It's imitation Lubitsch, of course, made at the same studio—Paramount—where the great man was also, at the time, making his delightful musicals. (Apologies for introducing the great man after his imitator, but so be it—*Love Me Tonight* can stand on its own.)

That opening is a superb beginning for a director at the top of his game. He stages the movie's title song in exactly the opposite way, as a melody sung off camera, haunting the dreams of Chevalier and MacDonald as they toss and turn in their separate beds. He even essays some split screens in the sequence. Toss away a big number with a few intercut single shots? Are you kidding? But Mamoulian knew what he was doing. His simplicity in this passage is powerfully effective, especially because it is followed by two great montage rampages.

First Chevalier's true identity is discovered and the denizens of the castle start a *sprechstimme* number—"The son of a gun is nothing but a tailor." The swells in the drawing room begin murmuring it, and pretty soon (cut, cut, cut) the whole place—the cooks, the chambermaids, the footmen—have joined them in mock shock.

Now, however, MacDonald comes to her senses. She really loves the tailor, who has boarded a train for Paris. She flings herself on a horse and into a heroic montage—galloping hooves intercut with churning wheels. You'd think an empire instead of a silly love affair were at stake. That irony is clearly not lost on Mamoulian, who caps the sequence with heroic low-angle shots of MacDonald standing on the tracks and the train screeching to a halt inches from her.

You can't quite believe your eyes. Or Mamoulian's luck. He was at a studio that, like Warner Bros., had a house style—as light as the other studio's was dark, and also witty and, as people said at the time, "continental." It didn't particularly fly with the public; the studio suffered ignominious bankruptcy in this period, and Mamoulian suffered a quick descent into handsome, but rather staid, historicism *(Queen Christina, Becky Sharp, The Mark of Zorro).* He had his moments, notably with *High, Wide, and Handsome* (1937), a musical western of supreme goofiness, and in his last film, *Silk Stockings,* a graceful musicalization of *Ninotchka* (1957). But he lived on for thirty marginalized years thereafter, making no more films.

He was not an auteur. He was too restless and cranky for that role. So he has slipped down film history's page to something like footnote status. One has to think that, either shrewdly or accidentally, he took advantage of the panicky confusions of the early sound era—when no one quite knew what the talking picture should or could be—to impose a uniquely cinematic vision on the medium. Like Busby Berkeley, he created an electrifying set of stylizations for the musical, which never achieved camp status and therefore was not ripe for the revival that Berkeley's numbers achieved. We will never speak knowingly of a Mamoulian masterpiece of high silliness. The musical's later masters, Vincente Minnelli and Stanley Donen, integrated song and story more wittily, more lovably. But they were directors who liked long takes and flowing dance numbers, which Mamoulian didn't do in his early days. Nevertheless, his admittedly intermittent capacity to wow us remains, giddily, gloriously undiminished—at least in a couple of instances—despite the passage of seven decades. You just have to know where to look for it. And forgive him for making a near-perfect Lubitsch picture before Lubitsch fully invented his mature manner. It's an accident of history and of release schedules.

9

A Touch of Lubitsch

Venice. A pretty canal. A gondolier's song. We are primed for romantic enchantment at the outset of *Trouble in Paradise*. Until it is revealed that the gondolier is not poling a pair of embracing lovers through the languid waters. What he's propelling is a garbage scow. And his song underscores a sequence in which a second-story man KOs a victim in a hotel room and scuttles over the balcony.

The camera then tracks across some Venetian facades as the gondolier's song is picked up by an underscoring orchestra. It comes to rest on another balcony, where it finds a "baron" (Herbert Marshall), who is planning a seductive dinner for a "countess" (Miriam Hopkins). It is causing him a certain distress. "Beginnings are so difficult," he complains—ironically, considering that the sequence in which he is participating is one of the most famous and justly admired beginnings in movie history. The obliging waiter proposes cocktails as an icebreaker. The baron agrees, though why such an obviously practiced roué does not automatically think of a nice, dry martini as the ideal choice for such an occasion is not explained.

Somehow the cocktails silently mutate into champagne—mostly, one imagines, to accommodate this inspired dialogue: "And waiter," the baron says, "you see that moon? I want to see that moon in that champagne."

"Moon in champagne," the fellow solemnly notes on his order pad.

"As for you, waiter," the baron adds, "I don't want to see you at all."

We now settle in for what is surely the wittiest seduction scene in movie history. What with one clue and another, we're already pretty certain the baron and his inamorata are not what they're pretending to be. Now we learn that he's the notorious society thief Gaston Monescu, specializing in jewels but not averse to lifting cash and, for all we know, bearer bonds and fur coats. His inamorata is just plain Lily (no last name given), and she, too, is a thief, every bit Gaston's equal, except in the strong-arm department. For it is, in fact, Gaston we have just witnessed bonking the conk of a rich ninny—Monsieur Filibia (Edward Everett Horton)—and making off with his overstuffed wallet, an act that will have consequences further down the plotline.

Before the pair reveal their true identities, they practice their skills on one another. She has stolen his wallet. He shakes it out of her. He then gallantly returns her pin to her. "It has one very good stone," he observes. She asks him for the time. He gropes for his pocket watch, which she then retrieves from her purse. It was five minutes slow, she says, "but I regulated it." He confesses to having her garter, which he has no intention of returning. She clutches at her skirt. He removes the garter from a pocket and kisses it lightly. Whereupon she hurls herself into his arms. "Darling!" she cries. A moment later we see his arm hanging the DO NOT DISTURB sign on his suite's door. Fade out.

Ah, the Lubitsch touch, as it was then and as it will forever be known. It was not a very complicated thing, a blend of more or less genial cynicism and tart sentimentality, executed with compulsive detail. It was Lubitsch's habit to act out for his actors their movements and their line readings and for them simply to imitate him. There was not, to say the least, a lot of improvisation on his sets. He had, after all, been an actor in Germany before he turned to directing, and he had made some thirty pictures there before Mary Pickford brought him to America in 1923. That relationship did not work out, but he made something like ten more films in the late silent era, among them, rather amazingly, a silent version of *Lady Windermere's Fan* that was quite delightful, given that Oscar Wilde's epigrams were, perforce, confined to the intertitles.

His early sound films were largely musicals, set in Europe and marked by rather more sweep than was common in the genre at the time. He had, of course, done dialogue pictures before *Trouble in Paradise,* for instance, but I think it's fair to say that this is the film in which he found his main line, from which he would deviate only occasionally for the rest of his career.

At the time *Trouble in Paradise* was released (1932), some earnest souls thought of its opening as a sort of Depression-era comment on the movie that was to follow—wasn't romance among the well-heeled and well-spoken "garbage" when millions were out of work? Some considered it more narrowly, as a very extended example of the Lubitsch touch, in this case virtually a full-body massage—all grace, lightness and ingratiation.

But however you analyzed the opening of *Trouble in Paradise,* you could see that the director and the screenwriter, Samson Raphaelson, continually grounded its deftness in a harsher reality. Besides that garbage scow, there was the fairly brutal robbery and a phone call to the baron's suite, in which a friend or relative of Lily is shown to be distinctly déclassé. You also had to admire the fact that they extended its deliciously ambiguous tone for a breathtaking fifteen minutes.

Lubitsch and Raphaelson could not, of course, sustain that tone for the movie's entire running time (which was just under an hour and a half). This is not to be taken as criticism. It is more sensible to be grateful for what we have received, especially since the rest of the movie is very good indeed.

They make the transition to Paris, where the movie will settle down, jarringly—a shot of the Eiffel Tower, with animated radio waves emanating from it, introduces a slightly lame satire on radio commercials and advertising signage. The tone of this brief passage signals a general shift in the movie's mood—it becomes just slightly nervous, a trifle too busy and somewhat digressively developed. It seems to have too much on its mind.

Lubitsch would have disagreed with this judgment. In his marvelously detailed study of Lubitsch's American movies, William Paul quotes him thus: "As for pure style I think I have done nothing better or as good as *Trouble in Paradise.*" Paul buttresses this comment with a rich sampling of critical writing that echoes the notion that this is a near-to-perfect comedy.

To see why it doesn't quite fit that description, it's necessary to undertake that most boring of critical tasks, a plot summary. I'll try to be brief. The advertising sequence takes us to Mariette Colet (Kay Francis), heiress to the Colet perfume empire, whose products the ads are satirically promoting. We meet her as her board of directors proposes wage cuts. She is more interested in her luncheon engagement and rejects their idea. But on her way to lunch she pauses to buy a purse, which is her most interesting moment in the movie. The clerk shows her something undistinguished for 3,000 francs. No, she says, it's too expensive. She spots something exquisite. Its price is 125,000 francs, but she snaps it up. This is possibly one of the clearest statements of value Lubitsch ever made. Junk is always overpriced; something beautiful is always a bargain.

In any event, the purse moves the plot. Gaston, now in Paris with Lily (and not doing terribly well), steals it at the opera and brings it to the living room of Mariette's very elegant deco house, which is crawling with poor people, among them a left-wing radical who keeps crying "phooey" to Mariette's wealth. Gaston dismisses the radical (with some blunt comments in his native—possibly Romanian—tongue), returns the purse and is rewarded with a job as Mariette's private secretary.

He proves adept at straightening out her tangled affairs, all the while supervising what seems to be a superfluous diet-and-exercise program for Mariette. He even brings Lily on as his assistant and they begin planning what could be their best score. But Gaston has fallen in love with Mariette. Lily finds out and, driven by jealousy, attempts to go through with the robbery by herself. Mariette discovers her, but forgives her. In the movie's last scene, they reprise their earlier pickpocket competition and we see that they have made off with 100,000 francs, a pearl necklace and, yes, the purloined purse that caused all the trouble in paradise.

And, you ask, what's wrong with that? To which I reply: nothing. But in parsing the movie's main line, I have left out a few details. Mostly these involve Monsieur Filibia and a character known only as "the Major" (Charles Ruggles). They are Mariette's suitors, but the former is silly and the latter is rather stiffly British. Both are highly conventionalized comic figures of their day, and both are unfunny. Indeed, they are straw men. One can't imagine Mariette having the slightest interest in either of them, and indeed, she is dismissive, almost rude to them, throughout the movie. Filibia at least has a function—he has eventually to remember who it was that knocked him out and stole his money in Venice, which, with many a furrowed brow, he finally does.

The relationship between Gaston and Adolphe J. Giron (C. Aubrey Smith) has a little more bite. He's the chairman of the company's board, whose claim to competence is based largely on his forty-year relationship with the Colet family. Each instinctively understands the other to be a crook (Giron is an embezzler), and a nice tense scene of recognition and accusation is played out between them. Recounting the encounter to Mariette, Gaston allows a certain class resentment to show. He has worked his way up from nothing, he's "a self-made crook," but that cuts no ice with the upper classes. As he observes, membership in the social register allows you to escape jail. It is what the movie has in the way of social commentary, but the observation is scarcely original, and it is, perhaps sensibly, rather thrown away by Marshall.

He and Mariette also rather throw away their romantic possibilities. This occurs in another famous sequence, one that is the movie's emotional center. Their rooms in Mariette's palatial home are adjoining. There is, as far as we know, no internal door connecting them. There comes a moment when she has to go out for a boring dinner party at the Major's. She would rather stay home and, at last, go to bed with Gaston. He thinks, however, that she should go to the party and return early. Their positions, however, shift in the course of a discussion to which we are not privy. What happens is that one or the other of them emerges from time to time to instruct the befuddled butler to either let her car go or let it stay. What's funny—and never explained—is that sometimes he speaks to this functionary from her room, while sometimes she speaks to him from his room. And vice versa. Romantic confusion has rarely been so wittily emblematized as it is in this sequence.

The sequence concludes yearningly—with shots of his chaste bed, first seen in a mirror, then with their embracing silhouettes projected onto it. She says there's no need to hurry their consummation—they have days, weeks, months to enjoy themselves. But Gaston—and we in the audience—are beginning to suspect otherwise. Lily is on to them. Monsieur Giron awaits below, prepared to unmask Gaston. And at the party, Filibia will finally make the connection between Madame Colet's secretary and the man who robbed him in Venice.

But it is a beautifully designed and perfectly paced bit of moviemaking, dryly witty yet touched by romantic loss. Despite our fondness for Lily, we really want Gaston to attain his heiress—at least for a night. And we want Mariette, at last, to have a man worthy of her. Much as we like Lily, we can't help suspecting that Gaston and Mariette are in some ways better-matched souls. Let me put that another way: They hint at the possibility of transcendence, of a respectable life for him, of a life less sunk in boredom and social irrelevance for her. Gaston and Lily are bound only for the criminal margin, for lives lived perpetually on the run.

That, naturally, is a subject for debate. So is Gilbert Adair's contention (in *Flickers*) that *Trouble in Paradise* is "a masterpiece of delivery, the most mellifluous, the most perfectly spoken film in the history of the American cinema." I think it does not quite achieve that status. Mariette is supposed to be a somewhat careless, even ditzy rich lady who is brought to common sense by Gaston, rather as Claudette Colbert would be by Clark Gable in *It Happened One Night*. But that kind of lightness was not in Kay Francis's range. She's rather a sober presence in the movie, better at yearning than she is at brittle exchanges.

Something similar could be said of Marshall. Bright, brisk Miriam Hopkins draws the incisiveness out of him. So do the minor characters who suspect his bona fides. But when he's around Francis, he tends to moo his lines, suggesting a weltschmerz to which his character is not, perhaps, entirely entitled. I prefer the smart, edgy *knowingness* of Hopkins's performance, and I feel, putting it simply, that the movie's Francis-Marshall nexus is just a bit softer, creamier, than I'd prefer.

One could, however, as easily argue the opposite, namely that the Gaston-Mariette romance is from the start foredoomed, and that they know it. Seen in that light, their relationship gains a certain poignancy from their implicit acknowledgment that the social distance between them is too great to bridge more than temporarily.

But if Lubitsch was, in this, his first talking picture comedy, just a little more jittery, a little less sure of himself than he soon would be, it is unimportant. Indeed, the movie I—by no means alone—consider Lubitsch's masterpiece, *The Shop Around the Corner* (1940), is actually more sentimental. That film is really quite a simple romantic comedy, with James Stewart and Margaret Sullavan as employees of a small shop, bickering in love in a movie that seems perfectly written, perfectly paced. It has heart, too, principally located in a character played by Frank Morgan. But the thing I like best about it is the calmness of its formalism—it's a movie of impeccably edited medium shots, and also one that observes the unity of place rigorously, which somehow dries out its potential for sogginess.

You eagerly forgive the occasional insecurities of Lubitsch's work, particularly when you realize that the main line of American moviemaking was already veering away from him. This was 1932, the year of *The Public Enemy* and *Scarface*, of *I Was a Fugitive from a Chain Gang* and *Red Dust.* The movies were embracing a grittier realism, a more wisecracking, more "American" style of dialogue.

Lubitsch, though, stuck to his path. He would never make a full-length movie set in contemporary America. (He did, however, make a great, brief contribution to the anthology film *If I Had a Million.*) He would also cling very largely to the Mittel-European playwrights he loved to adapt, to the French settings—or rather the backlot versions of them—that he loved to explore. Interestingly, he would be fired by Paramount because, as William Paul tells us, only two of the pictures he made in his eleven years on the lot made money.

It was probably the critics, adoring his elegance, who kept him alive, and bless them for that. Without their efforts— Lubitsch is one of the few directors who seem never to have suffered a "reconsideration"—we would not have such other timeless delights as *Bluebeard's Eighth Wife, Ninotchka, Heaven Can Wait,* and *Cluny Brown* to light our weary way. Indeed, it is only lately that one has begun to fear for his posthumous reputation. The anonymous (and historically ignorant) studio lords of the DVD have ignored him. We desperately need his films—for their own delicious sakes, but also for the reminder they offer of a witty and romantic imaginary world that never was but surely should have been.

10

Two Cheers for Mr. Muckle

M r. Muckle may be the crankiest man in the history of the movies. He is a customer of a near-moribund grocery store presided over by W. C. Fields in *It's a Gift* (1934). He has purchased a package of gum. He wishes to have it delivered to his home. Fields does not wish to do so. In addition to his congenitally foul temper, Mr. Muckle (the superb, virtually unknown Charles Sellon) is deaf and blind. Naturally, he and Harold Bissonette (Fields) fall to squabbling. It is, I think, possibly the greatest quarrel in screen history.

There is a plot, of sorts, to the film. Fields wants to relocate. No one else in the family wants to. But that's purely nominal. Mostly the movie is an excuse for Fields to reflect and riff on topics that occur to him as he makes his way through the days of his life. For example, he is trying to get some shut-eye on a porch in the early-morning hours. But there are noisy neighbors, a nagging wife, Baby LeRoy and an insanely cheerful insurance salesman in search of someone called Carl LaFong—a name he insists on endlessly spelling out ("capital *L,* small *a,*" etc.). All of them, naturally, conspire to rob Fields of sleep. To say that herein Fields is harassed almost beyond human endurance radically understates the case.

In his desperation, he at one point cries out in the grocery store, "Mr. Muckle, honey," trying, in his way, to break through the man's intransigence. It is a cry of the heart at once poignant and hilarious, and, of course, unavailing. Yet somehow he fumes his way through.

In some ways *It's a Gift* is a careless movie. There are some sequences that would have been much better had they been more thoughtfully worked out. But the film is not about elegance. Its slapdash qualities are what it is most essentially about. If you want elegance, see Lubitsch, to take a convenient example. Sometimes—rarely, I must admit—movies need to be loose and shaggy, just out for a good time. That's what's happening here. Though I think it's fair to say that *It's a Gift* also holds true to its dim view of human nature in general. Fields would go on to appear in movies a little more carefully plotted and directed, but not, I think, funnier. In its way, it is a perfect package.

11

Shrieks, Freaks, Geeks

Horror films always exist on the fringes of the movies. This is not to say they are unpopular. It could be argued, for example, that Lon Chaney's *The Phantom of the Opera* (1925) is one of the true glories of the silent screen, the most elegantly realized of the several screen versions of Gaston Leroux's sort of trashy, sort of wonderful tale of the romantically macabre—at once touching, rueful and, if nothing else, beautifully designed. We must also mention *Nosferatu* of 1922, a Dracula story, and a masterful one at that, also beautifully designed.

These films have, however, two salient defects: They cannot speak, and they cannot offer sound effects, those chilling offstage noises that, at their best, hollow at the marrow of your bones. It's often the sound of one hand clapping.

Dracula, in 1931, was something else again. Bela Lugosi had played the title role on Broadway and was recruited to the role after the death of Lon Chaney. He was a weird little guy, basically a lifelong recruit to horror, which turned out to be an extended and tortured path. He had an occasionally incomprehensible accent and—possibly—a somewhat ironic attitude toward his roles (it's hard to tell). For instance, offstage, the wolves howl, and he pauses to reflect on the commotion: "Children of the night," he muses. "What music they make," the stresses falling oddly in the two lines, the rhythms uniquely his own—and unduplicable.

Dracula is an odd job, scarcely more than an hour long, badly acted by players taking long pauses between words so we can hear each one, and finished in haste. There may be a good print of it somewhere, but I've never seen it; it's all murk and dimness in the prints we have. But under Tod Browning's direction, it had something. It's camp now, but at the time it was enough to start a trend that has never really died.

Frankenstein, a year later, was something more. James Whale was the director, and the picture has a grace and gravity very far from the rather slapdash manner of *Dracula.* This is due very largely to the performance of Boris Karloff in the title role. He has his fears, particularly of fire, but the film depends on his innocence for its effectiveness. He literally does not know what he's doing. He is, I think, conscious that he's a sport of nature, and he's angry about that, without being able to articulate what's bothering him. Yet he's also capable of great tenderness. It would have been easy for Karloff to rip and tear at this role, but he doesn't. There is nuance in his puzzlement. We feel for him. And we are perhaps reminded that, of the classic horror films, this fairly loose adaptation of Mary Shelley's novel has the best credentials. It is literate, it has a solid structure and it is given a well-acted, well-mounted production. This is a monster who is somehow not monstrous. Of the pioneers of this revived genre, it is a film that needs few apologies. There are others.

For instance, *King Kong* (1933). I think it is one of the greatest works in the history of popular culture, for a lot of reasons.

Most important, it is wholly original. Co-directed by Merian C. Cooper and Ernest B. Schoedsack, it alone of the horror films of the classic era has no literary roots—except, of course, the "beauty and the beast" story. Indeed, though it has plenty of scary sequences, it is not really a horror movie at all; it is, if you will, a romance, the story of the greatest misalliance in the history of movies.

Withal, it is a sexy story. Simply put, Ann Darrow (Fay Wray) is a stowaway on a voyage to Skull Island. In short order, she is staked out to placate the mighty Kong, who pretty much rules the place and has pretty much never seen so toothsome a wench as this. She writhes prettily and screams mightily, which only has the effect of enhancing her fair, blond form. He is an innocent, seduced by her incomprehension. You could also say that eventually there is some kind of attraction between them, though the movie never overtly speaks of this. Mostly the great ape, for all his thumping around, is a complete gentleman with Ann. What is on our minds as we watch is—how to put this?—a question of scale. He's so big, you see. And she's so tiny. We are not entirely unaware of the possibilities.

No point in dwelling on this, of course. You know the rest anyway. Kong is captured, is put on display in New York, escapes and meets his famous fate atop the Empire State Building. He is so tender with Ann at the end. And the sequence remains a masterpiece of stop-motion animation by the great Willis O'Brien and one of the most masterly romantic conclusions in the history of film.

And that's not the end of its gifts. Its score, by Max Steiner, is the first fully symphonic score in the history of the movies—just as O'Brien's work pioneered imagery we had never seen before—and it is a good one, at least by the nonexistent standards of the day. This is, to evoke the cliché, pure movie magic, yet it is hard to take it entirely seriously. I mean really—an ape and a girl. It's preposterous. If you come right down to it, it's B picture stuff, isn't it? But the spectacle is overwhelming, even today. You don't have to make allowances for it. Against all the evidence of your eyes, it works. That heart beats true, even after eighty years and many bad imitations. The movies, of course, are many things above and beyond *King Kong*. But some of their giddy essence is in it, too. The sheer joy of the thing, the fun of it and the sobriety, too, are things we do not find as often as we once did at the movies. And we are the poorer for it in so many ways.

As we are the richer for *Bride of Frankenstein* (1935). It had taken Universal (and director James Whale) something like four years to come up with a sequel to *Frankenstein,* for reasons that are, to me, at least, unknown. But it was worth the wait. *Bride* is, I think, close to being a great film—if only for its wit. It was written by a couple of anonymous studio types, and it is impossible to say whence sprang the bickering tone of the thing. But it is palpably there, and the actors are responding to it, straight-faced, but with humor and self-awareness. Especially Elsa Lanchester as the title character, who is the great addition to the cast. Apparently, she learned her hissing speech pattern by studying the swans in London parks. But the sources of her shroud-like costume and her frizzed-out, erratically dyed hair seem simply to be inspirations of the moment.

It's a wonderful performance by an actress who never quite got her due, full of weird energy and waywardness. You never quite know what's coming next with her, but whatever it is, it is always a surprise and a delight. It's not too much to say that she is a sexual hysteric. She's drawn to Karloff's monster, and also fearful of him. He, on the other hand, is more soulful than he was in the original film. He is facing a life of utter loneliness. Put simply, he needs a bride, and for him it is love at first sight of her. He is also somewhat more civilized than he was in the first film—he can speak a little, is capable of friendship and loves music. The film is not screwball, but there's an element of comic wariness in the approaches and withdrawals of their relationship that goes down well—a weird but palpable sexiness that is a little bit like the way the people in romantic comedy at first hate each other before they hook up.

As for Karloff, this is a very rounded performance. He is, of course, capable of anger and outrage, but the most interesting thing about him is his innate gentleness. Quite literally, his character did not ask to be born, or created, or whatever. He is forever puzzled by his ambiguous status and doing his best to come to grips with it. In life, the actor was a kindly man, and here he was operating under huge physical restraints—tons of makeup and painful prosthetic devices, all designed to enhance his hugeness, his essentially grotesque qualities. At the same time, his innocence, his sense of cruel victimization, had to be maintained.

But this is a horror film. For all the admiration that has been heaped on it—especially in recent years—it is an outlier, not taken entirely seriously by cineastes. There is no disposition to value genre pictures highly. "Yes, but . . ." attaches itself to films of this kind almost automatically. So the performances of Karloff and Lanchester (and others in the fine cast) tend to be overlooked. In retrospect, we want to snicker at them, to see them as guilty pleasures, rather self-satirizing. But these were—no other phrase for it—serious artists. Probably, at the time, it was just a rather silly job for them. But they were skilled professionals, and they were working at the top of their game. We need to remove all the asterisks from this film, to see this as a serious enterprise, beautifully made by actors, directors and writers and featuring performances that are, quite frankly, unimprovable. "It's only a movie, Ingrid." But, by damn, it is in its way a great one—its appeal somehow close to the heart of what the movies can be in their giddy, corrupt, commercial essence.

The Invisible Man (1933) is another success in the genre, its conceit carried out with high spirits and real élan. A fellow learns the secret of not being visible to his fellow citizens, which gives him obvious advantages, criminal and otherwise, over his fellow citizens. It was the talking-picture debut of Claude

Rains, and at the relatively advanced age of forty-four, it made him something of a star, which was odd in itself, in that only on those rare occasions when he put some clothes on did he become visible to the audience. Mostly his is a vocal characterization, and a great one—Rains had one of the most flexible and elegant voices in the history of the cinema.

He had, for many years, been a reliable stage actor—at one point he had been Charles Laughton's teacher—and he got this part because Lon Chaney, who had been scheduled for it, had died in 1930. Rains was alive to all the role's comic possibilities—and is superb. Under James Whale's direction, Rains is particularly alert to the befuddlements of ordinary citizens confronted with a character they cannot see but who is manifestly, mysteriously present in their lives. I'm going to go out on a limb here and propose that Rains may be the best character actor in the history of the movies.

He was slight of stature, so he could never aspire to the heroic. He was known to have a taste for the bottle and for the habit of marrying unwisely, and with some frequency. He was often paired with Bette Davis, and they were apparently chastely, inordinately fond of one another. He acted prodigiously, relentlessly, effortlessly, and his range was astounding.

We remember him best as the merrily cynical Captain Renault in *Casablanca*, but there is so much more—corrupt senators, lovelorn Nazi agents, mean-spirited district attorneys, father figures by the yard, possibly best of all in the title role of Mr. Skeffington, a Jew hopelessly in love with Davis in the severely underrated wartime romance of the same name. I truly believe there was nothing he could not do—except, as I said, be a flat-out hero. (Naturally, he never got an Oscar, though he had four nominations.) He never gave a bad performance. On such careers is the routine magic of the movies built. You almost never notice players like Claude Rains until they are gone. You simply expect the excellence that he routinely delivers, without fuss or feathers.

With these classics, horror established itself as a genre in a few short years, and it would never again be absent from our screens. It would, however, for many years be a B picture genre. Not until the 1970s would it once again become a major film form. Until then, it was pretty much Lon Chaney Jr. as the Wolf Man, paired now and then with the delightfully incomprehensible Maria Ouspenskaya. She had once been a leading member of Stanislavsky's immortal company but came to the United States in the twenties to work on the stage and to Hollywood in 1936, where she won Oscar nominations and the delighted regard of audiences enjoying an acquired taste. Chaney profited from that, too. His transformations into the hirsute antihero were touched with a sort of sadness. Poor guy, he couldn't help what happened to him when the moon turned full and his beard began to grow.

12

What's Funny About That?

Sometime in the 1970s, working occasionally as a writer and producer on television documentaries, I met Frank Capra. I liked him. A little later I made a film about him for my series *The Men Who Made the Movies*. From time to time we appeared together on television and in other public forums.

In the decade or so before World War II, Frank had been arguably the most famous movie director in America, and one of the most prominent. Oscars were his, as well as the good opinion of decent mankind. He said, with a certain false modesty, that what he made was "Capracorn," but his films were cheerful, and suited to the somewhat forced optimism of the media landscape of the time. He served honorably in the war, making propaganda films, and came home to Hollywood expecting to pick up his career where he had left it a few years earlier.

That, however, was not to be. By and large, his movies now

seemed merely corny and out of touch. He was felled often by "cluster" headaches and by commercial failure. He made his last feature film in 1961, *Pocketful of Miracles,* and retired without making an announcement to that effect. He was trotted out on state occasions, and the rest of the time he lurked in La Quinta, near Palm Springs, full of restless energy and seeming good cheer. You would never see Frank Capra down in the dumps. In time, an autobiography, *The Name above the Title,* appeared, relentlessly upbeat and, some people said, not entirely truthful, but a good read nonetheless, which he obviously enjoyed promoting.

Whereupon good luck played a decisive hand in his life. In 1946 he had made a film entitled *It's a Wonderful Life.* It starred James Stewart, Donna Reed and a wonderfully malevolent Lionel Barrymore. It is, as you doubtless recall, the story of a small-town savings-and-loan operator, eking out a living and dreaming of far-darting travel and adventure, but pretty much stuck in the quotidian. It has a fussy angel, and it shows what would have happened to his little town and his loved ones—all of it grim—had he not stuck it out in Podunk.

It is a fairy tale, and it did not do much business when it was released. But then—a mighty Capraesque touch here—someone forgot to copyright the thing and it became free programming on television in the 1970s, Christmas cheer all around. There was no money in it for Capra, but that didn't matter. It was widely—no, universally—understood as a masterpiece of sentiment. And it completed one of the unlikeliest comebacks in the history of show business. I don't know if the film is brilliant or far less. It simply is, for better or worse.

I entered Frank Capra's life again. His sons talked NBC into doing a documentary about Frank, and I was asked to write it, working with a prince of a fellow, Carl Pingitore, who signed on to direct it. The idea was to create a warmhearted portrait of a man who created warmhearted films, good-natured and chucklesome, but with strong, liberal-minded messages.

Capra's films are superbly written, mostly by Robert Riskin, but with a fine contribution *(Mr. Smith Goes to Washington)* by Sidney Buchman, and they are wonderfully played by the likes of Barbara Stanwyck, Jean Arthur and Gary Cooper—people who can make dialogue sound witty (or at least perky) even when it's not. Critical opinion, such as it is, has turned against Capra. David Thomson states the most negative case: "a hypocrite. A careerist and credit grabber, a rearranger of the facts, a liar. A reactionary, a bogus liberal, an anti-Semite, a self-serving fabulist and an informer. And a big admirer of Mussolini."

This indictment is based largely on a biography subtitled "The Catastrophe of Success," by Joseph McBride, who started out an admirer and went over to the dark side in the course of writing his book. To put it mildly, Thomson's is a "yes, but" proposition. And one that could be applied in large part, I would think, to the majority of movie directors, a breed not known for being shrinking violets. Who among them are not, for example, careerists and credit grabbers? And fabulists, too. Who, among a much larger segment of the population, do not, alas, grow more conservative as they age (though I do not think Frank ever became a full-on reactionary)? As for his liberalism, I do not for a moment distrust it, particularly during Frank's glory years. He was a man of large and simple passions. He was never a director of secret subtexts. What you saw on the screen in those days was what you got. And when it comes to Mussolini, well, there was a time when George Bernard Shaw, among others (including the saintly D. W. Griffith), thought well of him, too.

Even so, the single-mindedness and animus of McBride's book is astounding. It is a book rendered stupid by a kind of bigotry that is rare in modern biography. And no one is going to issue a corrective—not at this late date, not on behalf of a director slipping down history's page. I can only say that McBride's Capra bears little, if any, resemblance to the Capra I knew.

Which brings me back to the film we were making back in the seventies. We had a lot to work with. *It Happened One Night* (1934) remains a first-class romantic comedy—Gable grumpy,

Colbert ditzy and full of a kind of wayward (and ageless) charm. Pictures nowhere near as famous (*The Miracle Woman,* about evangelism, and *American Madness,* about a hard-pressed idealistic banker) were more powerful than anyone except Pingitore and I knew going in. The *Deeds-Smith-Doe* trilogy was as strong (and troubled) as I had remembered it. *Arsenic and Old Lace* (1944) was a slightly hysterical farce, with Cary Grant at his best and—what the hell—we had *It's a Wonderful Life* to top the whole thing off. Ours was scarcely a great film, but it seemed to us entirely respectable.

The network disagreed. They said the film was not, you know, funny. We pointed out the simple truth: Capra was not, for the most part, a funny guy. He could be a charming guy, but his themes were deadly serious. Edward Arnold's fascist in *Meet John Doe* (1941), for example, was a truly menacing figure, who should alone give the lie to the notion that Frank was sending secret, admiring messages about men of corrupt and corrupting power.

Frank's passion for his work remained palpable. He never faltered in his commitment to it. There was not a slack frame in any of it, at least in his finest period, and I reveled in his intensity. There was greatness in the work. You could not turn away from it.

That did not entirely have to do with his themes and ideas. The main thing I observed during this passage was that his films were masterfully directed. For a decade he was, I think, one of the two or three great American directors—sequences like the concluding wedding scene in *It Happened One Night* and the great rally in the rain in *Meet John Doe* are, I think, among the most privileged moments in American cinema. Working on the TV film, I found myself increasingly lost in such bravura filmmaking—though, interestingly, audiences didn't seem to notice that, so lost were they in the sentiment and idealism of the pictures. You had to get some distance from their immediate impact to appreciate their craftsmanship.

In its little way, our film was a troubled production. I didn't get on very well with one of Capra's sons, and the network's lack of confidence in the enterprise grew apace. We all tried hard, I think, and the film was by no means a catastrophe. It was just mildly disappointing. Eventually, we turned it over to the network and moved on to other matters. I have no doubt that Frank was disappointed by this result, but on those rare occasions when he put in an appearance, he was resolutely upbeat.

I lost touch with almost everyone I worked with on the show, though I remained friends with Pingitore and Capra. The show remained notably absent from the network's schedule, and I assumed that it would never be broadcast. Two or three years slipped by, and to be honest I pretty much forgot about the thing. It was no more than a minor disappointment. But television shows—even ones that everyone loses confidence in—do cost money, and networks understandably want to recoup some of their costs. So, of all things, the show was scheduled on a Christmas Eve, when the potential audience for it was about ninety-seven people, all of whom were shut-ins. To my knowledge, it was never announced in the press, let alone reviewed. It was not repeated or sold overseas or otherwise exploited. It is, I venture to say, one of the most thoroughly ignored programs in the history of television.

But I was not finished with the Capras. Frank died, at the age of ninety-four, in 1991. His passing was by no means ignored, though the obituaries were more guarded than they would have been some years earlier. I wrote a couple of pieces that attempted to redress the balance in his favor. I was also asked to appear on another television show about him, produced, once again, by his sons. It was a happy experience, lengthy and leisurely, and it offered some pretty good insights into the man and his films.

I think *Meet John Doe* was his finest work. There are so many things wrong with the picture, which begins as a kind of comedy and veers, at the end, very close to tragedy, from which it is rescued at the last minute by a not entirely persuasive happy ending. It was at the time (1941) neither a critical nor a commercial success, this story of a sore-armed baseball pitcher (Gary Cooper) who is promoted by the marvelous Barbara Stanwyck to become the head of the John Doe club, which sees him, eventually, as the figurehead of a national populist movement, at first supported, then betrayed, by Edward Arnold's fascist rich guy. Cooper is very far from being his usual self. He is, as David Thomson says, a neurotic figure and, in his innocence, an easily exploited one. In time, he is betrayed by his followers and dissuaded from suicide by an outburst of desperate populist sentiment. It is an ending that was much argued over by Capra and his colleagues.

There are desperate improvisations that don't really add up in the film. Yet, at another level, there is that rally in the rain, a masterful construction in its shooting and editing. And in its meaning. It starts out to be a celebration of Cooper as a heroic everyman. But it ends up as a terrible indictment of the volatility of the crowd. Gone is the sunny optimism of Capra's early years. His people are now "a great beast," and Capra fully embraces their volatility. They have an infinite capacity to be misled for reasons they cannot understand (which is an important reason why the desperate attempt at an upbeat ending does not work—it is too little, too late).

This was (at the time at least) an unacknowledged crisis for Capra. The war, of course, intervened. He was a long time away from the movies, and when he returned to them he could not return to his former ways, except with *It's a Wonderful Life,* which was, as I said, a failure when it was released in 1946. It is a far darker and more dangerous film than we care, even now, to admit. Having tasted the forbidden fruit of seriousness, he could not return to the comic, though he tried in ways that were generally rather wan and listless. But sobriety was not, it seemed, an option, either.

For roughly a decade, Capra was a great filmmaker, an almost perfect exemplar of the American spirit in his time. I think Frank was puzzled by his fall from favor. There is something that endures in his work, something that transcends his moment.

13

Greatness

A case can be made—probably I'm in the midst of doing it—
that the period between 1935 and the onset of World War II
was the greatest era in the history of American movies. But I'm
naturally resistant to such ultimate superlatives. Good movies
are made all the time—though obviously not as often as bad
ones. What we can say is that by the mid-1930s, Hollywood
had settled down. Most of its best first- and second-generation
directors were working steadily, as were the most important
stars of early talking pictures.

But what are we to make of *Cimarron* and *Cavalcade*—now
basically unwatchable—as best-picture winners? Or, for that
matter, of *Grand Hotel* and *The Great Ziegfeld*? Surely, the
Academy could have done better than these safe, sane and comfortable pictures? Officially speaking, it was a mediocre period,
especially among directors—the names we now revere were

scarcely mentioned then. But, of course, history grinds along. Balances are redressed.

The problem was, to a large degree, one of critical standards. Most of the people reviewing movies at that time—a notable exception was the sharp and graceful Otis Ferguson—were not cineastes. They had the impulse to pass judgments, but they were borrowing their standards from other media. They did not fully (or even halfheartedly) grasp that movies were a unique means of expression. For example, they could see that film had about it aspects of the theater, that it was by and large a dramatic medium. So the standards of the play were imposed on it—especially in American film. (Europeans were permitted somewhat more leeway in this regard.) We must not forget that D. W. Griffith was basically a man of the theater, and rather hangdog at first about making movies. It wasn't until he enjoyed inordinate success with *The Birth of a Nation* that his problem became the opposite—one of grandiosity. I hold that his most enjoyable movies of this era were rather unpretentious little movies, on the order of *A Romance of Happy Valley*. He didn't despise these movies, but he didn't think much of them, either. He was convinced that his future lay with the epic exertions of *Intolerance* and *Way Down East*.

His films were "cinematic" all right. They could not have been accomplished in any other medium. The same was true of the novel as a source for movies. And I think (we're speaking in broad generalities here) it was perhaps a more useful model. It had a range, a looseness of structure, that granted film a waywardness that suited it. In fact, you could argue that the movies had before them a model—in the work of Chaplin, Keaton and the other silent comedians—wherein their future could be read. But they were set apart. They were so odd. People could not see in them models of behavior and dramatic structure that were generally applicable to the medium. Also, of course, they needed to talk. Until they could, the silent film, for all its felicities, was a crippled medium.

Some of the movies discussed earlier in this book obviously triumphed over these defects—like *The Crowd*. But the victory of the talking picture in the marketplace, when it arrived, was simply overwhelming. In 1927, *The Jazz Singer* opened, and by 1929 silent film was dead. In the entire history of culture, no technology-based revolution was accomplished with such speed and completeness. And lack of apparent regret. Only Chaplin held out for a while—he did not speak on-screen until 1940.

There was about the sound movies of the early years an undeniable rough magic. It was enough for a brief while that dialogue and songs issued from the screen. It seemed like some kind of minor miracle—and never mind the quality of what was said or sung. Of course, there were wonderful pictures in this era, ranging from *Duck Soup* to *Camille*. But I think we probably ought to risk a generality: The roughness was, almost unconsciously, being smoothed out of them. They became, by 1935 or 1936, much slicker, particularly the comedies and the romances. Not many of them were "great" movies, but a certain standard was attained. The average inched higher.

As with, for example, *Dodsworth,* in 1936, directed by William Wyler, from a script by the playwright Sidney Howard, based on the Sinclair Lewis novel. Wyler was shortly to become everyone's idea of a great director, a man largely devoted to "important" adaptations of plays and novels, culminating in *The Best Years of Our Lives,* about which I am more dubious than most. (Never mind—we all have our blind spots.) Wyler was a sober and earnest craftsman, whose preferred pace was rather stately, but he also had a very fine eye for performance. His best films contain yards and yards of very good naturalistic and unfussy performances. None more so than *Dodsworth*.

The story is, in its way, quite linear. In his early fifties, Sam Dodsworth (the sublime Walter Huston) sells his automobile manufacturing company for no particular reason, largely at the behest of his wife (Ruth Chatterton), for an idle life in Europe. She occupies herself with "playboys"; he occupies himself with nothing very much. He's bored and restless, totally at loose ends. Huston, who originated the part onstage, is befriended by the young and vibrant Mary Astor (as Edith Cortright), who offers him what amounts to a new life. He is, however, a good and faithful man. The idea of setting aside even the charade that his marriage has become does not sit easily with him, especially as he is a man who must also find meaningful work to achieve fulfillment—not easily accomplished at his age. We fear for him, for the real possibility of misery, fecklessness, a wasted, petering-out sort of life.

That, however, does not happen. Sam rallies. The restless, entrepreneurial side of him cannot be entirely stilled. And Astor's character keeps turning up—patient and willing to wait for him to sort through his many issues. By the end of the movie he is considering a new business (aircraft manufacturing) and is devotedly committed to her. *Dodsworth* is that comparatively rare thing, a serious movie that ends happily for the people in it we care most about. "Love means never having to say you're sorry," goes its tagline, and we believe it.

It is a very elegant movie. Wyler's direction seems to me perfect in its understatement, and the playing is the same. It is a calm movie, but it is also intense without ever raising its voice. When people talk about it—which they do not do as much as they should—the word "adult" is often used. I have no objection to that. It is definitely a film for grown-ups. But it is more than that, I think. In a period when romantic drama tended to be somewhat overwrought, the tone of the picture seems to me exemplary. It is just so steady, so lacking in fuss and feathers. It draws you in without ever seeming to beg for your attention. At a time when the movies tended to be somewhat frenzied in their bid for our attention—though, on the whole, there is nothing wrong with that—*Dodsworth* spoke, quite uniquely, in my judgment, to our yearning for something more "refined" (I guess that's the word I want) and delivered it without misstep. And, it seems to me, without any true competition.

14

Ornaments of the Age

Romantic comedy. Screwball comedy. You know: *The Thin Man. My Man Godfrey. It Happened One Night. The Awful Truth. Bringing Up Baby.* And so on. In the latter half of the 1930s, it set the tone for the period. Which is slightly perverse, I suppose; these were, after all, grim times. But that may be the reason the screen was so giddy: We needed these pictures, perhaps more than we cared to admit.

A case in point: the sublime *Twentieth Century,* written by Ben Hecht and Charles MacArthur and based on a play. It has Hawks directing John Barrymore and Carole Lombard on a train—very confined but not giving a damn about that. He's a producer, she's a star (and ex-wife). He needs her for what sounds like a truly terrible show he's trying to produce. She's probably still in love with him but doesn't want to admit it. In the course of their antics, he is called upon to recite the story of his play, which includes, among other things, a solemn imitation of a camel. This is one of the great comic monologues in the history of the movies.

Hawks claimed he had to settle Lombard down. After shooting for a day or so, he took her out for a walk and told her she had already done enough acting for the entire movie. She was perhaps overawed by Barrymore, who actually was always an amiable and unpretentious presence on his sets. It seems to me that screwball comedy, in its full glory, begins here, in 1934. It has it all—attractive people, smart dialogue and, as Andrew Sarris acutely noted, leading players who did not offload their wisecracks onto the supporting players. They damn well did it all themselves.

There were obviously all kinds of other films in this era, including those featuring Bette Davis, Humphrey Bogart and Errol Flynn. But I do think comedy set the tone for the period; it is the first thing I think of when my mind turns to it. This does not mean—as we've already had ample reason to see— that wonderful movies were not made prior to that more or less arbitrary 1934 date. Or that pretty bad ones weren't routinely released in the latter half of that decade.

Let's consider Cary Grant. There's no particular reason to do so, except that in my fanboy way I adored him from the first time I clapped eyes on him, probably in *Arsenic and Old Lace.* He was just so damned funny in that. More sophisticated appreciation arose later.

Of his past I at first knew nothing. I later learned that he had known hard times in the familiar patterns of show business: a lost mother, a stern father, work in a boy acrobat troupe, that sort of thing. In his apprentice days he had been a stilt walker, and then an appealing and apparently quite expert, if more or less minor, musical comedy player, who was making quite a nice living in the theater—on Broadway, on the road—in the 1920s and early '30s. He was not yet a great star, but he was likable and nearly always had work. In those years, I do not believe anyone predicted the greatness that was soon to be his. He would have been a star of some sort—he was too good-looking, and too easeful, to have avoided that fate. But until perhaps 1937, there were far grander star careers.

Yet here we have David Thomson writing in his *Biographical Dictionary of Film* that Grant is "the best and most important actor in the history of the cinema." He is almost casual in his assertion. *Really?* one thinks. *Can that be so?*

You pause to think it over. On reflection, you come to believe it is likely true. He was not an actor of huge range—high hero-ism was mostly beyond him. But, as Thomson writes, he could be "attractive and unattractive simultaneously; there is a light side and a dark side to him, but, whichever is dominant, the other creeps into view."

Not that that came easily to him, though he had the gift of making it seem so. He came to the movies in 1932 playing minor roles in minor films—a rather recessive fellow standing around with his hand thrust in his pocket, as he himself said. He admitted imitating the likes of Rex Harrison. He debuted in April *(This Is the Night),* but by the fall he was with Dietrich in *Blonde Venus* (a second lead), by no means making any grand assertions. He followed that, however, with the best of his early films, *Hot Saturday.* (Seven Grant pictures were released in his first year at Paramount.) It is his first lead, and you can see in the film a little bit of the actor who would emerge in the next few years. He plays a young man who keeps himself rather apart from his peers, the better to live in a free-spirited way, avoiding the hypocrisies of small-town life. It's minor, but in its way it is rather smart, too. There is something hard and glittery about him; he was, oddly enough, showing his dark side on the screen before his charm was allowed to surface. And it led directly to his first "prestige" production, the role of Pinkerton in *Madame Butterfly,* opposite Sylvia Sidney, produced by her lover (and the studio's head of production), B. P. Schulberg. The film was a creaky flop, but it brought Grant to the avid attention of no less a personage than Mae West, who provided him with the notoriety around the studio, around town, that he had thus far largely lacked.

She put it about that he was an extra she had spotted around the lot (not true, of course), but he was her kind of hunk. He played agreeably, but still recessively, with her in *She Done Him Wrong*, which was a studio-saving hit, full of Westian zingers and zappers. Within a year he was thrown into a sort of sequel *(I'm No Angel)*, also a hit.

Whereupon he suddenly became Cary Grant—that is to say, the Cary Grant we came to know and love. The unlikely instrument of his deliverance was a flop called *Sylvia Scarlett* (1935), wherein he plays a feckless fellow known as Jimmy Monkley, a con artist and swindler. The audience at the premiere hated the thing—so much so that some of the cast, which included Katharine Hepburn (who plays something like half the movie in drag, which I guess gives you some idea of its slightly desperate quality), Brian Aherne and Edmund Gwenn, offered to make another picture for producer Pandro Berman without fees to make up for the disaster (or so the story goes). He rejected them. ("I don't want you . . . ever to work for me again.")

But for Grant—although he does not appear to have recognized it at the time—it was something of a miracle. And an unexplained one. According to George Cukor, who directed, the actor who until then had no particular identity—was, indeed, rather awkward—had suddenly "flowered." "He felt the ground under his feet." He was both mean-spirited and cheeky, both a sparrow and a hawk, in the words of the script. It is a performance, at last, thought out and colored both in darkness and in light.

There is no explanation anywhere on record of how this transformation occurred. Perhaps Grant had just finally grown up. Maybe something in his morally ambiguous character spoke to something in his past experience, something he could identify with. All we can say for certain is that he abandoned his passivity and attacked the role in the highest spirits.

He now entered upon a period virtually unprecedented in American movie history. *Topper, The Awful Truth, Bringing Up Baby, Holiday, Gunga Din, Only Angels Have Wings, His Girl Friday, The Philadelphia Story, Suspicion, The Talk of the Town*—from 1937 to 1942 there is no actor's filmography to compare with Grant's. It lies at the heart of Thomson's admiration and my own. And we have yet to consider *To Catch a Thief, Indiscreet, North by Northwest* or *Charade.*

He was obviously fortunate in his directors. In addition to Cukor, he worked in this period with Howard Hawks, George Stevens and Alfred Hitchcock—the best of the best at that time. Since he was a persnickety sort of man, we have to believe that he had a lot to do with making those choices—especially Hitchcock, who did him the favor of making Grant's first real venture into darkness with *Suspicion.* It is a film that ends happily—preposterously—and should not. But it is important as a venture into territory that is significant for the rest of his career. It showed that he could go to the dark side—especially with this director—without totally abandoning his charm. It added greatly to his available range, putting, for example, *Notorious* (which may be my favorite among his films) within his grasp. There were films he was offered and for whatever reasons rejected *(A Star Is Born*—the Garland version—and *The Third Man),* but career management is a field rife with error.

Around his eightieth birthday, I wrote a little book about him. He was by then many years into his unannounced retirement. He was happily married and he had, at last, an adored child—his daughter, Jennifer. He liked to go to baseball games and putter about. He read my modest book and liked it well enough. He occasionally, for no apparent reason, called me up and we would chat pleasantly, nothing world-shaking. He was likable and leisurely. We talked much of the time about his peers, some of whom I also knew slightly. These chats were modest ornaments to my days, and I hope for his.

By this time he had taken to doing little shows for charity— film clips, anecdotes, that sort of thing. In the summer of 1986,

I was planning to move from New York to Los Angeles, and I judged that we were good enough phone friends that I might call him up and meet him face-to-face when I settled in L.A. That was not to be—he died of a stroke in November, in Davenport, Iowa, of all places, as he was preparing for one of these appearances.

The obituaries were all about his "charm," of course. And why not? It was, for the casual reader, his most salient quality. What did they care about—if they even noticed—his darker side?

Movie stars—a rare few—enter our lives unbidden. For some reason we take a shine to some of them, and our belief in them remains unshaken, no matter what the fates deal out to them. So it was for me with Cary Grant. I liked and admired him. He rarely disappointed me on-screen, and I know nothing of his life away from the camera that would give me pause. He must, of course, have had a dark side, else he would not have been the actor he was. But on that we will not dwell. The image is what we have. And we are—in this instance anyway—right to cherish it.

15

"Up This Hero Goes"

And to complete the phrase, "down this zero goes." We speak now of Preston Sturges, and his strange, enchanted, foreshortened career. For a very few years (1940–1944) his was among the great Hollywood rides. But yet, there were so few films—perhaps a baker's half dozen of them—between *The Great McGinty,* which started his merry run, and *Hail the Conquering Hero,* which was his last great comedy. Rarely in film history has a career blazed so brightly and ended in such sudden disarray. But for those few years, he was the comic master of all he surveyed. With him, I believe, screwball comedy reached its apotheosis.

Except that the comedy was not really and truly screwball. It was rather too literate—verbally very playful—for that characterization to fully apply, and too rich, as well, in eccentric characterizations and ideas. You will not find too many comedies in our movie history that revolve around a virgin birth, as *The Miracle of Morgan's Creek* does. It seems to me that the most potent impact on his style derived from the weird force of Americans talking and squawking when he encountered them on his more or less permanent return from Europe in the late 1920s. Put simply, he had never heard anything quite like that slightly mad babble. No one among his competitors had the ear for it, or the slightly odd personal history that alerted him to its comic possibilities.

He was, I suppose, something of a mama's boy. His mother was an intimate of Isadora Duncan's, which meant, among other things, that the oddities of human behavior held no terrors for him. He had a hit play, *Strictly Dishonorable,* soon after he returned to the United States, which was made into a movie a couple of years later. Thereafter, he wrote (and, of course, later directed) about two movies a year until near the end of World War II. He quickly had the itch to direct, but it was not satisfied until *McGinty,* in 1940. That said, the majority of his films were successful, and in some instances they attracted more than the usual buzz in Hollywood—none more so than *The Power and the Glory* (1933), which starred Spencer Tracy and Colleen Moore in a story that people would eventually come to realize prefigured *Citizen Kane,* as it told the story of the rise and fall of a powerful business magnate (in this instance, C. W. Post, of cereal fame). It was eccentrically structured and rather gloomy, and many in its audience could not "follow" its story. But for its time, it was not quite like anything else coming out of Hollywood. It was, to be sure, a flop, but it did Sturges no harm. Rather, it marked him out as talent to watch.

He fulfilled his promise at least twice in the years ahead— with *Easy Living,* in 1937, and *Remember the Night,* two years later. The former was a comedy starring Jean Arthur, Edward Arnold and Ray Milland. It's about the romantic adventures of a young woman after a fur coat thrown out of an apartment house window falls on her head. It's kind of a screwball farce, full of pizzazz and romantic energy—about as enjoyable as any picture of its time and genre. *Remember the Night* was more ambitious and, I think, more successful. In it, Fred MacMurray is a Manhattan district attorney who for some reason has to take Barbara Stanwyck, who is being held on shoplifting charges, home to the Midwest with him for the Christmas holidays. It's a long trip by car, and it achieves predictable romantic results, which are worked out in surprising ways. It is a very original conceit. And one of the best films directed by Mitchell Leisen.

Therein, however, lay the rub for Sturges, who didn't much like the man. He thought his directorial "improvements" were spoiling the rhythm of his work. It's hard to say, really. Leisen, a former art director, was perhaps something of a fusspot. Or, putting it another way, he liked his movies to be smooth and graceful, while Sturges liked them to be rough and ready. But his greatest sin was that he was a director, and Sturges was not. Sturges made it very clear that he would become one or he would leave Paramount. In 1940 he attained his ambition with *The Great McGinty*, which was a success and for which he won the writing Oscar.

Sturges followed this film later that same year with *Christmas in July*, probably the mildest in his string of hits, but still quite a winning little film. It features Dick Powell as an insanely optimistic jingle writer and Ellen Drew as his very realistic girl-friend. He loses the jingle contests he keeps entering, which, perversely, only enhances his belief that he is drawing closer to a victory. He achieves that with this punning lulu: "If you can't sleep, it isn't the coffee, it's the bunk."

The picture was a success, and fully established Sturges as a genius, Hollywood style. It prepared the way for what many regard as his greatest film, *The Lady Eve* (1941). He had truly major stars for this one, Barbara Stanwyck and Henry Fonda. Stanwyck, with her enthusiastic professionalism, was a particular delight for him, but Fonda stole the show as Charles "Hopsie" Pike, one of the great dimwit performances in movie history. He is the heir to a great brewing fortune ("The Ale That Won for Yale"), which is of no importance to him. His passion is herpetology. It armors him against her designs on him, in what is surely one of the great romantic comedies ever.

Fonda's is a great performance. It takes courage for an immoderately handsome man, best known up to that time as a romantic, occasionally heroic lead, to play a dope so convincingly. But he did it with quiet relish. And Sturges kept the film on a tight rein; it could so easily have deteriorated into farcicality. It is played soberly, and it is all the funnier for that. It was a great success. At this point the director could do no wrong. He was ready for *Sullivan's Travels* (1941).

And for the beau ideal among his leading men, Joel McCrea. He was good-looking, rather than overpoweringly handsome, and an agreeably relaxed presence on-screen. You were always glad to see him turn up there. He represented for Sturges an essentially rational figure who was moved, at times, to slightly irrational impulses from which he had to be rescued, which he always was. We meet him in *Sullivan's Travels* as a successful comedy movie director who wants to do a serious movie entitled (perfectly) *O Brother, Where Art Thou?* He has a vision for it ("death gargling at you from every street corner"), but he concedes that he really doesn't know much about life as most Americans live it, so he embarks on a journey to discover the true spirit of the country. Along the way he meets a girl (Veronica Lake) who instinctively understands what he doesn't. ("There's nothing like a deep-dish movie to drive you out in the open.")

But he has a long road to travel, including a stay in a prison work camp, where he at last learns (watching a Mickey Mouse movie) that the world wants (and needs) laughter more than it wants tragic drama. Until that point, I think *Sullivan's Travels* is something of a masterpiece, a brilliant blend of the sober and the hilarious. But the ending doesn't work. It's too pat, too easy, too comfortable and comforting. Which somehow doesn't reduce my affection for it. It's not Sturges's best movie, but it has great heart and high ambition.

And some other virtues. Sturges was beginning to put together his stock company and here, for example, we find the splendidly choleric William Demarest working for him for only the second time. There was also Franklin Pangborn, Porter Hall, Eric Blore and Jimmy Conlon—a group that is one of the glories of Sturges's career.

So far Sturges had enjoyed only one solid hit, *The Lady Eve*, but otherwise everything was coming up roses for him. He was the critics' darling, the most talked-about director of the moment and, in this period, a well-rewarded one—one year drawing the third-highest salary in the United States. He had a restaurant, The Players, which was a money pit but also, for a couple of years, the place in Hollywood everyone wanted to see and be seen in. His relationship with the studio was quarrelsome at times, but what could they do? Virtually every other studio would have signed him the minute he showed signs of restiveness. Best of all, there is nothing in the record to show that he was denied any project he proposed.

He followed *Sullivan's Travels* with *The Palm Beach Story*, in 1942. It is a cheerful and frenzied movie, in which a delightful Claudette Colbert takes off from New York for the title city in search of a husband, although, in fact, she already has one of those in the form of McCrea, an inventor in desperate need of capital for a visionary airport he wants to build. Much merriment is supplied by Rudy Vallee, as a prissy millionaire, by the Ale and Quail Club (don't ask) and by the vagaries of a deliciously surprising farcical plot. It's not, finally, top-of-the-line Sturges, but it'll do. Its largest pleasures take place alongside the plotline, not directly in it.

Take, for instance, the Wienie King, gloriously played by Robert Dudley. He's an accidental millionaire, inventor of a variant on the hot dog, a product he refuses to eat. Mostly, he is sort of a freelance philosopher-poet, immortally reciting this poem (of Sturges's devising) to Colbert, who cannot restrain herself from genuine, unscripted giggles as he intones:

> Cruel are the hands of time—
> that creep along relentlessly
> Destroying slowly,
> But without pity
> That which yesterday was young.
> Alone our memories
> resist this disintegration—
> And grow more lovely
> with the passing years.

Of the hundreds of funny, poignant lines Sturges wrote, none are funnier, I think, yet more oddly touching, than these. The sequence always gets a big laugh in the theater. But there is something authentically sad and sobering about it as well. It bespeaks the seriousness of purpose that underlays much of Sturges's work, which he was quick to get out of with a joke or a diversion of some sort.

Except when he didn't. That is more or less what happened when he forged ahead with a seriously intended enterprise called *The Great Moment,* which became the first disappointment of his directorial career, though one that, at the time, did not particularly waylay it. If people thought about it at all, its lessons seemed more salutary than discouraging.

It is based on a book called *Triumph Over Pain,* by René Fülöp-Miller, a biography of W. T. G. Morton, the discoverer of ether as a pain killer. One is somewhat at a loss as to why Sturges was drawn to this material, but he began sketching out scripts for it as early as 1939. It's said by some that an accident requiring fourteen stitches, administered without anesthetic, had focused him on the boon of pain relief. There is also the possibility that Morton had not particularly prospered, a situation that Sturges could relate to. Controversy clouded Morton's claims about the material benefits of his work. The possibility that the great comic genius wanted to be taken seriously for a change cannot be entirely dismissed.

The studio didn't much like the project but was reluctant to deny its leading director his heart's desire—especially since Sturges was willing to insert into his script some comic riffs. So the mess proceeded, to some kind of dubious glory. Sturges insisted on Joel McCrea for the Morton role—the studio wanted a weightier presence—and he played the role essentially as a doofus, or possibly as a very lucky stiff. Conventional heroism was beyond this actor. His portrayal of Morton is sloppy. He basically stumbles to glory in his dimwit way. But he did start mankind on the road to one of its greatest boons.

Everyone was puzzled by the result, when *The Great Moment* was finally released, after a long delay, in late 1944. Where had their funny Preston gone? He was only occasionally on view here. And when he was, his comic passages fit uneasily with the more sober ones. The critics and the public—such of it as saw the film—were kind as they could be. But it was unquestionably a flop.

Yet I think we come close in this movie to the essence of Sturges. He thought, I believe, that the human race was stupid—good-natured, but really kind of dumb. His leading characters proved it time after time by sacrificing the better angels of their nature for some high-blown passion from which they were rescued, before the final fade-out, by the assertion of common sense, more or less uncommonly arrived at.

He has considerable compassion for his ordinary Joes and Janes. There's not a mean or grasping bone in their bodies. They are likable lunkheads, doing their best to navigate life not only as it is, but as they think it might be in their most idealistic dreams. Life, of course, is armed with a huge supply of banana peels, which it scatters heedlessly in their paths.

This thought is not a critical commonplace in Sturges studies. At his best, he builds his comic worlds very reasonably and peoples them with seemingly sensible folks who act like lunatics but never once indicate that they are anything but completely normal. Other filmmakers dabble in this kind of thing, of course. But Sturges was unique in his total commitment to this—er—worldview. Maybe that's why his career as a certifiable—another *er*—genius was so short, his fall from grace so sudden.

But not quite yet—not with two masterpieces, *The Miracle of Morgan's Creek* (1944) and *Hail the Conquering Hero,* on his agenda. The former is, of course, his comedy about virgin birth (and could anybody but Sturges get away with that premise in Hollywood's prissy early-forties climate?). The latter is about a fraudulent war hero who just the same proves to have the highest virtues—the ones we were supposedly fighting for—in the small-town context that was already beginning to disappear when the film was made, in 1943.

Miracle is something of a literal miracle. When it finally went into release, James Agee thought the Production Code office had been "raped in its sleep." For, yes, Betty Hutton, playing its heroine, Trudy Kockenlocker, has somehow gotten pregnant by a soldier named Ignatz Ratzkiwatzki, in circumstances she can only dimly recall. Eddie Bracken, playing Morgan Creek's hapless 4-F, Norval Jones, is recruited to marry Trudy, which he eventually does after much farcical milling around. What he—and we—don't know until the end is that Trudy is going to deliver sextuplets.

That's about it for plot. Or maybe it isn't a plot at all—just an endlessly complicated situation, a very frenzied and funny situation that ultimately very satisfactorily resolves itself. For all its fast-paced comings and goings, *Morgan's Creek* seems to me a neat and trim farce, worked out, when you come to think of it, with no loose ends.

The picture's release was delayed for something like a year while censorship hassles were worked out. But one of the minor miracles of *Miracle* was that Sturges delivered the picture he had set out to make, essentially without compromise. It has many felicities: Bracken is a great bumbler—he should have had more of a career—and Hutton is superb as Trudy. She, too, deserved more than she had in the movies. She was, to be sure, a troubled, rebellious person (she ended up in a Catholic rectory, apparently content at last), but at least this once there is a freedom and freshness in her playing that is a revelation—not that she was all that bad in, say, *Annie Get Your Gun* or *The Greatest Show on Earth.* Her career lasted only about a decade. Yet she might console herself with this: According to David Thomson, she was Ludwig Wittgenstein's favorite actress.

I do not know what to make of that.

Miracle turned out to be, of all things, a smash hit. The reviews were only all right, but the public took it to heart. It was Paramount's biggest hit of the year and the biggest hit of Sturges's career, grossing some $9 million and earning a few Academy Award nominations as well. Sturges's relationship with the studio was by this time deteriorating, but he owed them one more picture on his contract, and he pressed ahead with it.

Hail the Conquering Hero is really quite a simple film. Eddie Bracken is Woodrow Truesmith, 4-F but not telling anyone, working a modest job and getting servicemen to send letters home attesting to his valor in foreign fields. One night he meets a group of marines (led by William Demarest) and confesses his hoax. The marines present him as a hero to his hometown, and he gets away with his impersonation for a while. Eventually he is found out and temporarily disgraced, but he recovers his standing by the simple expedient of telling the truth. It is a sweet, lovely and quite modest little film that everyone liked. It was not a great hit, but it did all right. Sturges received simultaneous Oscar nominations (for writing) in 1944, losing to Lamar Trotti for *Wilson.*

And then, as I said earlier, as suddenly as his career had begun, it went into decline. He left Paramount and partnered with Howard Hughes to make *The Sin of Harold Diddlebock,* a mostly witless disaster that required three years to reach the screen and didn't get a proper release until 1950, in a re-edited version. Sturges was at the time a comparatively young man (forty-eight when *Diddlebock* was released), and he still had a few films to make, of which *Unfaithfully Yours* (1948) and *Les Carnets du Major Thompson* (also known as *The French, They Are a Funny Race*) (1955) are the best, having from time to time some of his old cheekiness.

But from 1946 until his death, in 1959, times were hard for Sturges. One anecdote seems to sum up his story in those years. The director Richard Brooks was having lunch one day in Paris (where Sturges passed much of his time in his later years), and he saw the latter through the restaurant window. They acknowledged one another, and it became clear to Brooks that his colleague was in need of a meal. Which he provided. That's the way it was with him in those years. The sudden success and the equally sudden failure are almost without precedent in Hollywood history—quite a number of good directors go on working past their best years—and one searches for the reason without reaching firm conclusions.

Perhaps his range was more limited than he understood it to be. Since his films were unique—nothing quite like them—it's possible that he just ran out of steam sooner than he'd expected. His was a tight little world, dependent on a relationship with the larger world that was in perfect comic adjustment for a few years and then suddenly was not. Everything—the restaurant, the instinctive if fractious relationship with the studio—just went south.

Yet he hung in there. He was a gallant man. He didn't feel sorry for himself. One night at the Algonquin Hotel, in New York, he lay down with a touch of what he thought was indigestion and died before the night was out, not exactly forgotten but yet robbed of the acclaim that would accrete around him beginning a decade or so later. Would he have fashioned a full-scale comeback had he lived out a full life? I simply don't know.

His best film was probably *The Lady Eve,* the trimmest of them, the one with the fewest errors of execution. But all of his major works—there were only seven of them, between 1940 and 1944—have their felicities. The mystery that abides is the sudden disappearance of most of his gift after *Conquering Hero.* He had a short run, but as the years wear on, the strength of his best comedies does not weaken or grow frenzied.

By the time Sturges was running out of steam, screwball comedy was winding down as well. It was the war that mostly did it in, I suppose. Under its impress, we lost our taste for intricate romantic tangles. We settled for Bob Hope and his ilk—strings of gags (good, bad and indifferent) that were okay but were hardly high wit. He tended to play cowards, and the image I retain from his career is from *Caught in the Draft* (1941), wherein he repeatedly jumps off a piano in an attempt to flatten his feet to 4-F status. You can, I think, see what I mean.

There was, however, one certifiably great comedy to round out this period: *His Girl Friday* (1940), with Cary Grant and Rosalind Russell, under Hawks's direction in a remake of *The Front Page,* with a matchlessly befuddled Ralph Bellamy as the hopelessly square guy she somehow thinks she loves in preference to Grant. At times—dare I say it?—I think it is my favorite comedy. It's so mean-spirited, so breathlessly paced, so brilliantly written (by Charles Lederer, working off the Hecht-MacArthur play). I've seen it a bunch of times, and still it remains full of surprises for me. It is a masterpiece, but because it's a comedy, it is mostly dismissed as "a nice little picture," as if comedy were easy to do. Do not be deceived. And don't you dare miss Billy Gilbert in one of the great, if brief, comic turns of all time.

16

Getting Serious

Since this book is primarily about pleasure, it follows (for me) that comedy has some sort of pride of place in its reflections on movie history. But that, obviously, places a serious limitation on its scope, not to mention on its definition of pleasure. So I need to play a little catch-up. I'll begin with Bette Davis.

It is 1989. The phone rings one day. "Mr. Schickel?" a secretarial voice inquires.

"Speaking," I reply.

"Miss Davis is calling."

I don't know any Miss Davises, but I'm willing to play along.

There's a brief pause and then an unmistakable voice, somewhat cracked by age. It is her very self.

I had recently written a little appreciation of her, which she had read and liked. She was calling to thank me for it.

She wondered if we had ever met. I said we had. There was an afternoon in 1960, at the summer home of Robert Rossen, the movie director—she was visiting nearby and breezed over (they had known each other at Warner Bros. in the old days), full of energy and good cheer. It was probably the first time I had ever been in the presence of both a director and a star, and, putting it mildly, I was bedazzled, though trying not to show it, of course. A few years later, I did an interview with her for a television show I was working on. Naturally, she had no reason to recall either occasion—she'd had, after all, a lifetime of such forgettable encounters.

I had, in fact, come at her career in a rather backward fashion. I was aware of her as a presence in my early moviegoing years. I surely saw her in pictures like *Now, Voyager; In This Our Life; Watch on the Rhine*. And, of course, *Jezebel* (1938), which I actually prefer to *Gone with the Wind*—it's so much more hysterical, so much more intense in performance. Such energy, such attack. There were other female stars I liked for one reason or another, but there was something about her I could not define that drew me to her.

"Fasten your seat belts," "What a dump"—that sort of thing sealed my deal with her. And let's not forget *The Old Maid, The Star* or *Mr. Skeffington*. They were, relatively speaking, latecomers in her career, but their energy was boundless. You couldn't (anyway, I couldn't) turn away from them. And that says nothing about *What Ever Happened to Baby Jane?*

She faltered in the 1950s. She was really quite young—only forty-two when she made *All About Eve*—yet already beginning the slide toward the grotesque, which preoccupied her in her later years. She had never been a looker, and instinct instructed one to turn away from the spectacle she sometimes presented. But she fascinated even in decline. It was a great career for a while, and then something of a shambles. And, come to think of it, really sort of a masculine one—tenacious, giving no quarter and asking none. At the end, her best work was on television. It was what was on offer, and she did it with a full and still hungry heart. You can't ask for more. I imagine she was dreaming of a comeback. Possibly on her deathbed.

Anyway, here she was on the phone, her voice pretty much cracked by booze and cigarettes, but somehow gallant, overpowering in its way. She was still a star, bad pictures and all. Then she said a great thing: "We ought to have a date."

I don't know how I responded—probably with "Absolutely" or some such banality. And then she was gone as quickly as she had come. We never had that date. She died that autumn, at age eighty-one.

Bogart is an entirely different matter. He was a success of sorts on the stage, made some inconsequential movies in the early thirties, then retreated to Broadway, where he found something like stardom as the gangster Duke Mantee in *The Petrified Forest*. It's a dreadful movie. But thanks largely to Leslie Howard, he got to repeat his stage role on-screen and, as a result, received a Warner contract. From 1936 until 1941 he worked steadily at the studio, but to little avail. He was nominally a star, but he did not do much of significance—the one exception being *Black Legion* (1937), a very tough and absorbing story about a sour factory worker who becomes involved with a Ku Klux Klan–like organization, which to this day has not received its due.

People think *The Maltese Falcon* (1941) was his breakthrough film, and it is the first faithful adaptation of the famous Dashiell Hammett novel. But, aside from its delightful supporting cast (Sydney Greenstreet, Peter Lorre, Mary Astor), John Huston's first film seems to me not very good. It is cramped and static. Actually, it was another 1941 film, *High Sierra,* that was Bogart's true annunciation. Released before *Falcon,* co-starring Ida Lupino, it is about a paroled gangster "rushing toward his doom," as Henry Hull puts it, in the territory of the title—under Raoul Walsh's expertly paced direction. Taken together with *Falcon,* it granted Bogart, after five wilderness years, authentic stardom.

Which was sealed forever in 1942 with *Casablanca,* about which far too much has been written. Of it I think simply this: It has everything. It is jam-packed with incident and paced with relentless fervor, including weltschmerz and wisecracks. And absurdity. Its success derives from the fact that it omits nothing. Lots of people have noted that it is full of nonsense. But in some sense, that's its glory. You could say, perhaps, that it's the perfect bad movie. But, of course, perfection of any sort is rarely attained in the movies. That's why we remain hopelessly in thrall to them.

There was much more to come from Bogart, which we will arrive at in due course: *To Have and Have Not, The Big Sleep, In a Lonely Place, Beat the Devil, The Treasure of the Sierra Madre.* But this much we can confidently say: He had, in the forties and fifties, as great a run of pictures as anyone ever had. And even, at last, some happiness in a life that had previously not been notable for that quality.

Which brings me to my favorite movie star of the time—Errol Flynn.

Say what?

Hear me out.

Offscreen, a trumpet is sounding "Boots and Saddles." On-screen, George Armstrong Custer is bidding farewell to his wife, Elizabeth. This, the central scene of *They Died with Their Boots On* (1941), is doomy with portent. Ostensibly, he is about to ride forth on what seems to be a fairly routine scouting mission to, of course, the Little Bighorn. They could as easily have parted with something like "See you in a couple of weeks." But Flynn as Custer is edgy. And so is Olivia de Havilland as his tremulous wife. This final farewell is beautifully played in a very understaged way. They wish to make nothing of it—there has been a lifetime of farewells, after all. But at a certain point something must be said, and Flynn does so with a perfect line: "Walking through life with you, ma'am, has been a very gracious thing." It's one of the best romantic lines in the history of the movies, I think. And on it he exits.

She swoons. Frankly, I swoon. For me, the final battle, well staged by Raoul Walsh, comes as an anticlimax after this.

This is a lovely and romantic film of only dubious historical veracity—as if, in context, anyone gives a hoot about that. In it, Flynn was everything a romantic leading man was supposed to be—graceful, gallant, humorous, athletic, with the lightest possible hand with the ladies. As he was in *The Charge of the Light Brigade, The Adventures of Robin Hood, Gentleman Jim, Objective, Burma!* and a little-seen but lovely wartime vehicle called *Uncertain Glory* (1944), an intricate story of underground life in Europe, in which, quite possibly, he did his best acting.

His director, as he so often was in these days, was Walsh, whom Flynn habitually called "Uncle." Raoul thought him to be a wonderful, instinctive actor, a complete natural. There was, of course, much trouble in this life—drink, women, a notorious statutory rape case, a career's waxing and waning, and an early death at a mere fifty—but with some of his best work coming in his final years in character roles. By then, "in like Flynn" was a national joke. But the acting was not. His last role, in *Cuban Rebel Girls,* with his sixteen-year-old girlfriend playing opposite, was, yes, a bad joke. But if you balanced this career's length against its accomplishments, there was much to be said for it, not least the grace and ease of a man who was never caught acting.

Forced to choose my favorite Flynn picture, I guess I'd have to pick *The Adventures of Robin Hood* (1938), because it's just so playful and action-packed. It follows most worthily in the tradition established by the Douglas Fairbanks silent film and seems to me—all nostalgia aside—every bit its equal in charm. It's not at all harmed by the fact that Flynn and his co-star, de Havilland, were in love during the film's making. Claude Rains was a superb villain, and the rest of the supporting cast was fine, too. Michael Curtiz directed. It is great pure entertainment.

Which brings me to Greta Garbo, to whom I always seem to come belatedly. As a kid, I'm not certain I saw her at all. Her specialty—doomed romance—was not something that held much appeal for little boys. She was more a vague presence to me than a living one in those days. Naturally, I had heard of her—who had not? But she was a mystery that I assumed would be revealed to me someday. Actually, it remained a matter of considerable indifference to me.

I'm pretty sure I first encountered her in the lugubrious *Anna Christie* (1930)—that stuff about not being stingy with the whiskey. These were not exactly ideal circumstances for our introduction. God, it's a stiff. Or to put it in a slightly more high-toned way, it lacks, shall we say, a certain elegance?

Mildly puzzled, I did not see another Garbo movie until I was an adult. It turned out to be, thank God, *Ninotchka* (1939), which I think is the only great movie she ever made—no gloom and doom here—though a case can be made for *Camille, Queen Christina* and, yes, the supremely goofy *Mata Hari*.

Ninotchka is a marvel. Directed by Lubitsch and written by (among others) Billy Wilder, it contains this marvelous passage: "Comrades! People of the world. The revolution is on the march. Bombs will fall. Civilizations will crumble. But not yet, please. Wait. What's the hurry? Give us our moment."

Who could resist? It is such a perfectly judged film. I suspect that its perfection played a role in her subsequent withdrawal—what else did she have to do? There was only one more picture, *Two-Faced Woman,* which is not as bad as it is made out to be, but is hardly a great work. There was also a lot of teasing about other projects that never came to pass. She could afford to be idle—she would leave an estate of some $32 million—and didn't have a damned thing to spend her wealth on. So she wandered about the midtown streets—people were always catching glimpses of her—saw a certain circle of friends (she was not a recluse) and gave no evidence of being unhappy or even particularly lonesome.

It was at this point that I briefly entered her life. At the time I was keeping company with a lovely woman who was friendly with the nutritionist Gayelord Hauser, with whom Garbo was in the habit of staying for a month or so every year. He groused about her—not the easiest of houseguests, we gathered. But

everyone's a star fucker. He called one day and invited us to
join him for an evening with "Miss Brown" and a few others.
Needless to say, we did not—could not—refuse.

There have been many learned studies of Garbo's refusals
and withdrawals. Therefore, I'm going to make a deliberately
simple one. I think she was fundamentally a very shy person,
who by some lucky-unlucky chance—it had a lot to do with her
great beauty—found herself in a profession not entirely suited
to her nature. She did the best she could with that circum-
stance, but, at some fundamental level, I don't think she was
ever entirely comfortable—not for long anyway—with being
an actress, let alone a star. She was lucky that she made enough
money to live her life in ease and pleasantness, teasing people
with the possibility of a return to the screen, though I don't
believe she ever meant to do so.

On the evening in question, at ease among friends, she
turned out to be pleasant, quite talkative, a full participant in
the evening's conversation—always as "Miss Brown," of course.
You would not have known—though of course you did—that
she was anything but a lightly lined and handsome woman. She
might have been the owner of a boutique or some such enterprise.
At some point I found myself engaged in talk I couldn't entirely
follow about finance, and my attention wandered a bit—to her,
inevitably. She caught my glance, smiled and winked at me. I
winked back. For a second I was Armand or Vronsky, a whole
generation of males caught in that all-knowing glance—our
otherness, our waywardness, our peculiar devotion to plot
and ploys at the expense of the infrangible moment exposed,
accepted, indulged. She had the gift for imparting this gift. It
saddens me that she made it difficult for the future to find it.
Yet I imagine her not especially caring about that.

Her career on-screen seems to me, in retrospect, not very
distinguished. For a star of her sometime magnitude, there are
not many movies that we would today seek out—too many
of them are soppy, rather doomy romances, directed by Clar-
ence Brown, who apparently got along well with her but obvi-

ously did not press her any more than the studio did. It was essentially a lazy enterprise. George Cukor, who directed her in *Camille,* once surprised me by remarking that she might have been slightly stupid. I think that's probably not the case. I think she had a pleasant gig and saw no reason to press her luck with vaulting ambition. She was valuable to MGM, because her pictures did well abroad, until World War II interrupted that run.

So she idled her life away. She simply had very little ambition, as the rest of us understand the term. But she was, in the end, quite likable. Imagine that—after all the kerfuffle that had for so long surrounded her! I'd have been happy to see her again. I never did.

It seems to me from the foregoing that I come off as some sort of junior genius, full of firm and more or less advanced opinions on movies at a very early age. Nothing could be further from the truth. I am distilling here ideas and opinions that are the result of spending far too much of my life thinking about this stuff instead of reading the great books or whatever. In fact, at the time, I was just a doofus like everyone else of my age, liking just about everything that moved and spoke from the screen. I had no taste whatsoever.

One of the theaters I attended most regularly as a kid was the Times, about ten blocks from my Wisconsin home. Oddly, it had rear-screen projection. That's to say the projector was behind the screen—no beam flashing over our heads from the back of the auditorium. Seething with restlessness (no sensible adult would attend the Friday night show or the Sunday matinee), we knew the double feature (plus a newsreel, cartoon and "prevues") was about to begin when the projectionist appeared at the top of the left-hand aisle, newspaper folded under his arm, and strolled to the front of the theater to start the show. Such aplomb! We talked about that. Imagine reading the paper as marvels unfolded, unattended, on the screen before him. How cool was that? Except, of course, the word "cool" was not in our lexicon at the time.

Well, he was just an IATSE guy doing his job. He didn't

necessarily have to like the movies. But still, we wondered, how could he resist them when we could not? In my later life I have known only one other person—the late writer Elizabeth Jane Howard—who was so supremely indifferent to the charm of the movies. We did many things together, Jane and my wife of the time and I, but I don't suppose that in the course of a long period when we were, I think, best friends we saw more than three or four movies together. I do not know how our friendship prospered as mightily.

By 1939, I was pretty much seeing movies on my own recognizance, with or without Danny and Kenny, which is in itself a remarkable thing, come to think of it, as I was just six years old. My parents were hardly careless people—rather the opposite— but they thought nothing of parking me in a movie theater for the afternoon. Ushers were legion. I was never once "interfered with," as the saying went. I just gnawed my Milk Duds and blissfully watched the movie (or sometimes it was a movie and a stage show starring Ozzie and Harriet or Spike Jones and His City Slickers).

It was a glorious era. A few years back there was talk about— even a book or two—dubbing 1939 the movies' greatest year. I'm okay with that—the case can be made, not that it makes much difference. Movies ebb and flow in no pattern that I've ever been able to define. There are just cycles (or fads) that mysteriously come and go: westerns in, westerns out; film noir all the rage, then, briefly, out of favor; you know how it goes.

Mr. Smith Goes to Washington, Destry Rides Again, Only Angels Have Wings, Wuthering Heights—all were made in 1939, all of them worthy movies, still eminently watchable. But the alert reader will have noticed some omissions—*Gone with the Wind, The Wizard of Oz* and, straying a little further afield, *The Rules of the Game.* Can you imagine?

GWTW seems to me a faux epic—a great movie because its producer, David O. Selznick, kept insisting it was. And because it was so goddamn long (running time around four hours), everybody read the novel on which it was based and everybody was in a dither about Gable saying, "Frankly, my dear, I don't give a damn." I guess maybe you have to have been a grown-up to have appreciated all that, but of course, I wasn't. I think I might have liked it better if Bette Davis had played Scarlett O'Hara. It needs her kind of lunacy to work. Vivien Leigh is too kittenish for my taste, too intent on ingratiating herself with the audience. The thing is finally too ponderous with Selznick's ambitions for it. Anyway, that's my minority report.

Wizard is a bit better, I think—wonderful character roles, a very good score, and I loved it when the Wicked Witch melted into a puddle. What's not to like? Nothing, I guess. When my kids were little, I reveled in their fondness for it. But that's finally the problem with it: It wants so desperately to be liked, it pants with its need to be adored. And to me the film grows tiresome in the process. *Ease off*, I keep silently crying—to no avail.

Finally there is *The Rules of the Game* to contend with. I came to slightly know, and to enormously like, its director, Jean Renoir, late in his life. Again, it was my Griffith book that brought me into the presence of this dearest of men. (He gave me the key elements of its ending.) He had enjoyed great, deserved success with his previous films, *La Grande Illusion* and *La Bête Humaine,* but this one, on release, was a disaster. It is a sort of romantic comedy, with many felicities—notably a central piece of a particularly brutal hunting sequence that quite transcends the lightsome air of the rest of the picture. It was cut and recut as war impended, then banned as, of all things, "a threat to morals" during the hostilities and wasn't released until after the war. It was, indeed, thought to be lost. Elements, however, were found, and from what I'm told it was restored from eighty-eight minutes to its intended release length of close to two hours, its reputation kept alive by critics like André Bazin. Finally, a restored version (with one sequence still apparently missing) was presented at the 1959 Venice Film Festival, where, at last, it was belatedly acclaimed.

Shortly thereafter, I began wrestling with it. I still don't get it—a state that I am not the least bit proud of. I have never felt so lonely in critical dissent. *The Rules of the Game* is ostensibly a romantic comedy, very well played by a cast that includes Renoir himself as a character who fussily interferes in the love lives of others, to make up—I think—for the emptiness in his own existence. It is a perfectly good premise. But the movie is, to me at least, distinctly unmerry, because, I believe, it keeps veering off toward an unwonted sobriety. I have tried so hard to enjoy this movie. I am aware of its several virtues. I take full responsibility for my failure to embrace it.

Meantime, there is *Gunga Din* to think about. Which still seems to me among the best adventure spectacles ever made. Cary Grant, Thuggees on a rampage, Sam Jaffe as the title character—and pretty much the whole kitchen sink of action tropes. It's masterfully directed by George Stevens and full of badinage about marriage that threatens the palship of Grant, Douglas Fairbanks Jr. and Victor McLaglen. It's bliss.

Then, from the same year, there's *Stagecoach,* the first western John Ford shot in Monument Valley and the film that finally made John Wayne an authentic star. It is a very shapely western, well written by Ernest Haycox and Dudley Nichols, and well played by a cast including Thomas Mitchell, Claire Trevor and John Carradine. The coach is loaded with types, but they're played with great conviction. When we first see Wayne, he's twirling a rifle, flagging down the stage. In his hands the weapon looks like a toothpick. In what seems like about ten seconds, the Indians are attacking, and the fight between them and the coach riders is about as well staged as any such movie encounter—equaled, but not exceeded, in the future.

Some wise guys were later heard to wonder why the Native Americans didn't simply shoot the horses as they thundered along in pursuit of the stage, which is the kind of question "realists" are always asking at the movies. But, of course, carried along by the action, we never thought to raise it. Probably the Indians didn't either, what with all the excitement. John

Ford's thoughts on this matter were of the practical variety. He conceded that, in reality, the Native Americans would probably have plugged the ponies, but that would have left him with a movie about two reels in length, which would have been absurd.

Decades later, I met Ford. He had taken to his bed for his last illness, but he had known D. W. Griffith, and he agreed to discuss him with me. He had been instructed by his doctor to cut down on his cigar smoking, and he was doing so by cutting the stogies in half—and chain-smoking them by lighting the second half from the stub of the one he had just finished. He recalled falling from his horse, being knocked unconscious and awaking to find himself cradled in Griffith's arms. There were other anecdotes, which I judged quite believable. It was too late in his life for him to gild any lilies. At one point he asked me if I had any ambitions to direct. At that point I did not, and told him so. He glowered at me, perhaps thinking of other writers, like Peter Bogdanovich, who were then being bitten by the directing bug. "Why not?" he groused. "Everyone else wants to."

Eventually, I did begin to direct—documentaries, not features. But he was the first person to propose to me this slightly ridiculous idea, which, I must admit, would gnaw at me from that day forward. To him, I think, it was not a silly idea. Directing was in the range of human possibility, so why not have a go at it, if you were so disposed? I never pass his house without thinking of him—and of the hats on the coatrack in the front hall, waiting for the old boy to come downstairs, grab some headgear and go out to make a picture, which, of course, he never did. He died in 1973.

I cannot leave him without mentioning what I think of as one of his best pictures, *Fort Apache* (1948). It stars Henry Fonda as Owen Thursday, an angry and permanently ambitious cavalry officer shunted off to the eponymous military base, his career in shreds, but not his ambitions for a return to past glories. It is, I think, one of Fonda's best performances—unbending. He is meant to be a version of George Armstrong Custer, but harsher, more ruthless. He refuses to treat the Indian tribes in his vicinity with care and understanding, despite John Wayne's amelioratory efforts. We gradually realize that he is a man seeking immortality through martyrdom, which he gets, while Wayne and a wise old Indian watch the slaughter from a nearby bluff.

I want to pause a little longer over Fonda, who may be the best actor of the movies' Golden Age—not the most beloved, just the most expert in his astonishing range. Consider: the sobriety of *The Grapes of Wrath,* the lunacy of the herpetologist Hopsie Pike in *The Lady Eve,* a variety of presidents and cowboys, his beloved *Mister Roberts,* about whom he came to blows with John Ford, who threatened the film's integrity with cheap jokes and sentimentality. This says nothing of his stage work, or of the soft-spoken integrity of, say, *Twelve Angry Men,* or the long-delayed Oscar for *On Golden Pond.*

I met him a few times, and he seemed to me a hard man— reserved, ungiving, perhaps caring deeply for nothing except his art. Let's think again about that ramrod in *Fort Apache.* He sits while the Native Americans are forced to stand. He wears a stupid kepi to keep the sun from burning his delicate neck. In the history of the movies, there is no more unyielding a figure than Owen Thursday, nor one more foredoomed. We know he must die; it's just a question of when—pretty much quickly and ignominiously. It is one of the most abrupt massacres in the long history of bad movie endings.

Whereupon the movie takes a surprising turn. John Wayne is addressing a gathering of journalists gathered around a painting of Owen Thursday's last stand, assuring them that it is authentic in every detail. They buy into this lie, because by this time Wayne has decided to buy into it as well. The film ends with the cavalry riding past the camera in a permanent heroic review. "When the truth becomes legend . . ." and all that crap.

Ford believed it, though. He believed, that is, that this country requires its heroic myths to survive. At some level it is an appalling thought. But such is the skill with which the picture is made that you can accept it, as just an ordinary western, especially if you are fifteen years old when you first encounter it. (You didn't expect to find moral complexity in westerns at that time.) You are left wrestling with it—mildly—for the rest of your life. It doesn't exactly haunt you, but it stubbornly sits there—John Ford's not inconsequential contribution (he would go on to make similar ones) to the ongoing debate about how much truth we can stand when faced with the question of what lies we need to sustain to keep our ambiguous American democratic faith alive.

17

Masterpieces

You may well ask, "Where's Disney?" Good question—especially since what is probably my best-known book is about Walt and his works. This period was, I think, the highest of his studio's times. I mentioned that the first movie I ever saw was *Snow White and the Seven Dwarfs*. There was some anxiety in our household as we set forth one Saturday night for the Parkway Theater to see it. This tension was not shared by me. My father wanted to make sure I would not be frightened by the big, potentially scary images projected from the screen.

Fat chance. I loved them. What could be better than this? As it happened, the next movie I saw was *Rulers of the Sea* (1939), which starred Douglas Fairbanks Jr., who much later in life became my friend. (I even helped him write a sketchy book.) The film was about a trans-Atlantic steamship race, and I thought it was the cat's meow, though on mature reconsideration a few years back, it turned out to be a pretty thin and underproduced movie, the sort of thing Fairbanks Jr. made too many of in his on-again, off-again career as a second-class matinee idol. (He really liked idling about in London, involving himself in mysterious enterprises that never seemed to amount to much.) He was a genial, dapper and well-met fellow, and I passed some happy times in his company, though he frequently pretended that I was somehow hard to find; nothing could have been further from the truth. It was just that he sort of mislaid me from time to time, only to reappear, with a merry cry, after an absence of a few months. In his later years, I sometimes thought, he had all the pleasures of being a movie star without having actually to bother to do much work at his nominal trade.

Pinocchio is the first great movie I ever saw, though I didn't know it at the time (1940). No one did. Everyone seemed to like it, this story of a puppet who wants to become a real boy. It has lovely Harold Arlen songs and a genial Jiminy Cricket who acts as his conscience, but it was received basically as just another Disney movie, having just enough comedy to get away with that misunderstanding.

That, however, doesn't reckon with the movie's darkness: Among his many misadventures, Pinocchio is swallowed by Monstro the whale, for godsake. Throughout the film he is in constant peril. I seem to remember that at the time there were complaints about its lack of fidelity to Carlo Collodi's original story, about which I cared nothing, since I had never read it. I could see the darkness of the story—not just the whale, but the escape from Pleasure Island, to name just one other powerful example. There were lightsome touches, of course, but the picture was laden with doom—or, more properly, I suppose, constant threat. Disney would never return to that level of menace. The coming of war had something to do with that, and maybe other distractions (the theme parks and so forth) played a role, too. Or possibly the thing in some way scared the master. There were hints here of a darkness to which animated film might aspire, but which could be dangerous to the form, not to be lightly undertaken. *Fantasia* (of the same year) was safer, prettier, and with some exceptions ("Night on Bald Mountain," for example), it would not scare the little pants off Disney's prime audience of children.

As the years have worn on, my regard for *Pinocchio* has grown. There is in it a beautiful balance of the light and the dark, a confidence in its pacing that is near to sublime—no sappiness. It is, I believe, the studio's masterpiece. I'm sorry there have been no other films from Disney that have aspired to this one's felicities. But I'm very glad this one exists, if only as a signpost on a road not taken.

Which brings us, for no reason other than the calendar, to the greatest movie ever made. I speak here of *Citizen Kane*. And I speak with a degree of irony. It is a very good movie, of course. It has never failed to reward me over the many years I have seen and reseen it. It is surely better than *How Green Was My Valley*, which won the best-picture Oscar that year, though in its way that was not at all a bad film.

Is *Kane* really the best film ever made? You would get some arguments about that in the foreign territories, I imagine. I think to some degree we are still playing catch-up ball with *Kane*. It was well received critically when it opened in 1941 (a strange, notable exception was James Agee), but it was not a great success at the box office, and though it received a number of Academy Award nominations, it won only one—deservedly—for the Herman Mankiewicz–Welles screenplay, one of the most intricate and elegant ever devised. Of course, the film deserved so much more. I think we should have recognized its greatness more fulsomely at the time; it remained a kind of rumor until it came out of hiding in the 1950s and '60s. At that point people started calling it the greatest movie ever without thinking too much about it. They also placed it at the center of the Welles legend. He had stumbled so badly (or so it seemed) in the intervening years—so much promise unfulfilled, so many promising deals down the drain, not to mention those wine commercials, or the weight, or the nonsense with Merv Griffin. It is possible to see Welles as the most legendary failure in modern American culture—one of them, certainly.

Citizen Kane is simply the faux rise-and-fall biography of a man who owned a chain of newspapers, scandalously based on the life of William Randolph Hearst, all denials to the contrary notwithstanding. It is very funny (we tend to forget its wit), wonderfully acted by Welles's Mercury Players and wonderfully stylized visually by Gregg Toland's great deep-focus photography. It is a film whose visual snap fully matches the dance of its dialogue. Pauline Kael famously called it "a shallow masterpiece," and I suppose there's some truth in that. But which of us would not prefer that to the ponderousness of movies that lose their breath and fall limp upon the ground? Besides which, how many movies are "deep" masterpieces? It's a status to which quite a few aspire, but few attain.

The world was Welles's oyster as of, say, 1942, more or less. Hollywood did not much like him because, it was thought, he had not paid his dues, eaten his humble pie. The Oscars were payback. Perhaps the writers, traditionally the odd men out in the town, could afford to be more objective about this matter than its grandees—you know, not give the kid all he was due. People were saying that the movie he was finishing, *The Magnificent Ambersons,* was pretty good. Welles needed just to settle down and finish it. All would be forgiven at next year's Academy Awards.

Instead, Welles—famously—blew town. He would complete post-production long-distance, from Rio, where he was on some sort of goodwill mission that Nelson Rockefeller had set up. Welles's editor, Robert Wise, sent him cuts by mail, with Welles calling and writing his responses while he was having fun in the sun. To say that he was distracted is a wild understatement. He needed to be in Los Angeles, getting his fingers dirty, but try telling that to a twenty-six-year-old genius, which he believed himself to be.

Wise toiled at his task and fought the fight for the picture as

hard as he could, but he was young, too, not yet the major director he would become, and the previews were not successful. It's
an oddity about *Ambersons:* Unlike *Kane,* it does not announce
itself as a radical departure stylistically. It is just an adaptation
of a rather conventional Booth Tarkington novel, well enough
liked by readers, and in Welles's version a well-made movie,
too—the story of a prominent small-town family's snotty scion,
played by Tim Holt, getting his comeuppance.

It's possible that the film meant more to Welles than *Kane*
did. He saw in it elements of his very recent childhood. It suffers
from what we might term unearned (or premature) nostalgia,
but that's only a slight flaw. Another was not Welles's fault—it
was just not what people were expecting from him. There was,
as I already implied, nothing visionary about it. It was just a
solid film, of a kind that has always been something of a staple
in American movies, though rendered here with much more
than customary genre intensity. I don't think it could ever have
been a great hit, though the reviews were quite good and it
received a number of Oscar nominations.

At some point, I think, Welles smelled a flop from far-off
Rio and began disassociating himself from it. And the studio
backed off of it. Besides, there were many distractions: He was
writing a newspaper column, doing his magic show, acting a
bit and, in general, wishing to be understood not merely as a
genius of the cinema but as a genius in pretty much all things.
It took a toll. His film was radically cut, whole sections were
lost and, finally, it was playing in some locales as a second feature to a Lupe Velez movie. It's possible to argue that no one in
the history of the movies suffered a mightier fall than Welles
did between his first feature and his second.

Yet, even in the damaged form in which we now know it,
Ambersons comes close to being a great movie—and at the least
it is a very good one. It has good nature and a genuine feel for
the not-too-distant past. It has great sequences—the ballroom,
for one. And Tim Holt's character is really a fascinating little

shit. This was not enough for Welles, of course, and I think it took something permanent out of him; "vaulting ambition" is one phrase for what went missing. The rest of his filmography is essentially split between genre crime pieces and Shakespeare adaptations, which were on the whole not particularly inspired. There was never to be another film with the go-for-broke spirit of *Kane* or the fullness of spirit that animated *Ambersons* at its best.

It's possible that this is a case of "too much, too soon." It might have been better if he had worked himself up to *Kane* instead of leading with it. There are, of course, felicities in the later work. But so much of it was routine. In the end he was, I think, a great talker about movies, but only rarely a great maker of them. He became lost in his own mythology, and in his own vast weight, which rendered him a disembodied voice, intoning the banalities of voice-over, speaking to his acolytes, who helped him keep the dream of comeback alive when the hope of that was clearly lost. The genius had become, to be brutally frank, just another jobbing actor, and more than a bit of—yes—a ham. And kind of a blowhard.

John Ford once called himself "a career man." He wanted to be judged on the whole vast body of his work, which was brave of him, I think, considering how many pictures he made, among them some terrible turkeys. That was not the case with Welles. When in 1952 the British film magazine *Sight and Sound* began taking an international critics poll every ten years of the best films ever, *Kane* was not mentioned. By 1962 it had begun to top the list, and it has remained near that spot ever since. *Ambersons* began appearing near the top in 1972, and *Vertigo* has taken over for both of them in the most recent balloting.

I'm a career man, too. Not wishing to take anything away from *Kane,* I'm inclined to judge directors by all their work, where Welles comes up short. Hawks, Hitchcock, Renoir, Bergman, De Sica, Ford and on and on—their contributions to film history are far larger than those of Welles. All of them have given us pleasure (and greatness) over huge spans of years. Careers require management, of course, and patience, and the ability to recover from downswings. And a bit of luck. But at the end of the day, I think the contributions of someone like Hawks or Hitchcock are more important than *Citizen Kane*. Their films set the tone for entire decades. Pleasure, multiplied a dozen times in some of these cases, needs to be reliable, something we can count on, inching us forward to setting genre standards, for example, while at the same time keeping a grip on the slippery pole in good times and bad.

We don't have to choose, of course. *Kane* and *Ambersons* are both great movies. They will endure and prosper. But let me pass a harsh judgment here: There is something wrong in Welles's career path. With all his gifts, he should have done more. Not a dozen more great movies—that's asking too much—but he should have done something more consistent, more challenging overall. It's as if he somehow shrank back from the greatness that was within him, frittered it away. He was, in the end, flighty, wasteful, careless. There is such disparity between what he accomplished at his best and what he actually achieved over so many heedless years.

Laurence Olivier once said that "genius"—if that's what afflicted Welles—is a terrible waste of time. You spend too much time serving its primps and poses, not enough time doing the hard work required to serve its demands, its exigencies. Eventually it eats at your soul, hollows you out. You become spin-driven by your own pomposity. You become, finally, fatuous, a joke everyone but you is in on—though they dare not speak of that to your face. The possibility that Welles was not a genius at all presents itself. Maybe he was just a very talented guy self-deceived by too early success, running endlessly to catch up with an inflated image. In which case he becomes a very American tragedy—a spellbinder for those who wish to be spellbound. Leave him at that—this careless, infuriating fellow.

But note this, too. I have devoted as many words to him as

I have to nearly any other figure in this book. Looked at hard, he's a two-movie talent. He doesn't deserve all the books about him, when his competitors, and equals, are given such short shrift—if they're lucky, one or two hasty, skinny volumes by nonentities. He keeps getting the last laugh.

And somehow, we let him have it. Somebody left the door open once when he was voicing a commercial about canned goods. The mask slipped and we heard the self-loathing in the backchat he had with the guys making the recording. It was far from pretty. But it was what querulous truth he was capable of at that late date. This is America—we will go on selling the product when it is long past its due date, which is roughly when unadmitted farce turns into what can conveniently be termed some sort of tragedy.

18

___

Don't You Know There's a War On?

Oddly, almost all of the best movies of the World War II period were only inferentially about the war. I think the exceptions would include Ford's *They Were Expendable*(1945), that somber, excellent hymn to dutifulness, though it was not released until hostilities ended. And perhaps *Air Force*, Howard Hawks's drama about a Flying Fortress that takes off in peacetime and flies smack-dab into World War II. The script was by Dudley Nichols, and it has the distinction of being perhaps the most civilized war film ever made. There were certainly good movies made between the end of 1941 and the summer of 1945. But they were mostly musicals and melodramas. (If nothing else, film noir takes root in this period.)

Air Force (1943) was apparently made at the behest of "Hap" Arnold, a famous flier and commanding officer of the air corps, who wanted a celebration of, well, yes, the Air Force. The specified service was then just a branch of the army, and the Hawks-Nichols notion was simply to have a Hawksian group go airborne. The biggest name among the actors was John Garfield, playing a malcontent who can't wait to muster out, which is due to happen within days or weeks. Before the picture is over, he naturally becomes a full-hearted, not to say gung-ho, member of the team. The rest of the cast is composed of good character players (Harry Carey prominently among them), and their dialogue is crisp and brisk in the Hawksian manner.

The airplane keeps being waved on across the Pacific, finally seeing action in the Battle of the Coral Sea, in May 1942. Two scenes stand out (in my memory at least). In one of them, two American aviators are shot out of the sky, as they dangle helplessly from their parachutes, by a grinning Japanese in his Zero. We thought: Was there no depth to the depravity of this enemy, commonly referred to as monkeys and similar terms in the movies? (The Japanese in our war movies were almost universally—and racistly—portrayed as subhuman.) The other, longer sequence is the death of John Ridgely, pilot of the plane, and a sort of near-miss star. He is laid out in a hospital bed, and his dying is couched in terms of takeoff procedures ("wheels up," "into the sun"—that sort of thing). It's a weirdly effective scene—tight-lipped dialogue in the manner Hawks preferred, and there was more to it than we knew.

For it was written by William Faulkner. His only Hollywood credits were for Hawks pictures—they shared a love of hunting and other manly pastimes—and the director conceived the idea that Faulkner was just the man to write this scene, despite the fact that he had returned to Mississippi. Faulkner agreed and knocked the thing out quickly enough. (Once you've got a metaphor, writing is easy.) A little later, the writer and the director were on the phone, and the former flushed the toilet for the latter—it was the good use to which he had put Hawks's money. Up to then his plumbing had been strictly of the outdoor variety. The Nobel Prize was only seven years in Faulkner's future.

It is possible that my fondness for *Air Force* is based simply on the fact that I was ten years old when I saw it—ripe for the picking. But it's a well-made, if highly improbable, movie. If you return to it today you'll probably like it—and somehow Faulkner's ghostly presence in its mix does give it a certain weight.

I will digress for a story that I find somehow irresistible. Faulkner, Hawks and Clark Gable were heading out for a weekend's hunting, and the talk turned somehow to writing. They started listing the greatest living American writers, and Faulkner added himself to the group. Gable pretended ignorance—"Oh, are you a writer, Mr. Faulkner?" To which Faulkner deadpanned this response to one of the world's most famous human beings: "And what do you do, Mr. Gable?" I can't guarantee the truthfulness of the story—my source for it is the ever unreliable Hawks—but I want it to be so. Let's let it stand, shall we?

They Were Expendable is based on a best-selling book by William L. White, which records the devastation of Motor Torpedo Boat Squadron Three in the months immediately following Pearl Harbor. It is about John Bulkeley, renamed Brickley in the movie and played with great restraint by Robert Montgomery, with John Wayne as his number two, fuming his way impatiently through the snafus of war. They have a mission: to prove that their fast little boats can be used as offensive weapons in the war, instead of being confined essentially to picket duty. This they amply prove, particularly in ferrying General Douglas MacArthur out of the Philippines to command the entire Allied war effort in the Pacific.

But there is more to this story than routine military adventure. Ford met Bulkeley in England, rode around with him in his little boats and conceived a story of larger dimensions, which was written by the veteran Frank Wead. In essence, the movie is a hymn to dutifulness, as I said earlier. By its end, every PT boat in the squadron is destroyed. Their sailors are all, as it were, unhorsed. We see some of them taking up rifles, determined to fight on as foot soldiers in a war that, at that time, seemed a lost cause.

The movie is notable for its refusal of sentiment, which is fairly rare with Ford. There's a restrained love affair between Wayne and Donna Reed, pretty much tossed away, and there is very little badinage of the kind that was endemic in war movies. It is, as these things go, tight-lipped. I think its best sequence comes at the end. Wayne and Montgomery are ordered to Australia, and they must board the last plane bound for down under, which means that two other fighting men will have to decamp, possibly to their deaths, certainly to a long stay in a prison camp. Their fate sealed, the two soldiers exchange only a few words before deplaning—Wayne and Montgomery are simply given a number to call, a letter to deliver. We get it—no words need be wasted.

That's the way it is throughout this movie—no big speeches about war aims, very few corny songs on the track. We see, in the distance, Japanese ships and planes, but we never get a close-up of the enemy. That's not what this film is about. It's about sticking to your guns, about doing your best when supplies are short and hope is nonexistent, except in the longest possible term. The movie is simply a marvel of restraint, in a genre in which that quality was the rarest of commodities.

But if ever a movie was ill served by history, it is this one. The war was suddenly over as it was about to go into release— the atomic bomb, you know. It was instantly old hat. In the fall of 1945, no one wanted to see a war movie, though the reviews were not bad. It had—and has—its champions, but essentially it was ignored, as it still is. Do not count on a rediscovery.

Do not count on a discovery, either, for what I think is the best film dealing directly with the war, André de Toth's *None Shall Escape* (1944). It had a re-release a few years back on DVD, but essentially it is a lost cause, as much of this director's work is. He operated in what I suppose we might call the A-minus range—pretty good actors, decent scripts and taut production values, but nothing that caused a studio to enthusiastically get behind his films. This one was written by Lester Cole, later to be one of the Hollywood Ten, and it starred Alexander Knox (most famously of *Wilson,* a year later). The film is set at a post-war war crimes trial (a rather imaginative stroke, that), and it records Knox's career as a Nazi officer. He serves rather decently in World War I but is rendered restive by Germany's postwar difficulties—inflation and the like—so he becomes, in time, a hardened Nazi, unsalvageable by Marsha Hunt as his lover. By the end of the picture he exhibits no redeeming qualities.

In the film's most powerful sequence, a group of Jews are awaiting transport to virtually certain death in a concentration camp. To my knowledge, this is the only vivid, visual reference to the camps in a film of that era—though they were sometimes alluded to, rather mildly, in dialogue set well away from the front. (In Frank Borzage's *The Mortal Storm,* Frank Morgan is imprisoned in a camp, but it is shown as no harsher than a medium-security American prison. In *Mr. Skeffington,* Claude Rains is an American Jew imprisoned in a German camp while visiting there and losing his sight as a result, but that happens offscreen.) In his autobiography, Cole is prouder of the fact that he slipped into this sequence a couple of lines from La Pasionara's famous speech about it being better to live on your feet than to die on your knees. The film was nominated for the original-story Oscar. Harry Cohn, the head of Columbia, which produced it, was alarmed that the movie seemed to be "controversial," but he was pleased enough by its good reviews. Within its low-budget limits, it is a good movie. As Fats Waller immortally put it, "One never knows, do one."

De Toth, whom I came to know many years later when we served together on a Directors Guild committee, was, by then, long since retired from directing (his last movie—as producer—was released in 1970), and he was probably best known for *House of Wax,* the best 3-D movie ever, though this is not saying an awful lot. He was a Hungarian émigré and one of several one-eyed directors (John Ford and Raoul Walsh were among the others). How the eye was lost is in some dispute—maybe in a skiing accident, maybe in some sort of political incident. He was a cranky old guy and a lot like his best films, in that there was no bullshit about him. "Sardonic" is the best word I can find for him. I came to like him a lot. I never asked him why he stopped directing prematurely. The most I ever got out of him was that every year until Ford died, the great man called him on his birthday, a gesture André appreciated.

He made a bunch of movies, none of which are bad—a tougher trick than you can imagine—and three of which are superb. In addition to *None Shall Escape,* there is a little masterpiece called *Pitfall* (1948), with Dick Powell as an insurance investigator—and, yes, he's sardonic, not to mention depressed (Powell was expert at this kind of heroic flaw), toying with Lizabeth Scott while defending his home and family (his wife was played by the lovely Jane Wyatt) against the depredations of Raymond Burr's truly spooky private eye. It finally comes out okay, but not full-heartedly so. It was among the first to bring film noir style (and substance) to the suburbs, and it ends on an ambiguous note. We are left wondering if, in the long run, the Powell-Wyatt marriage can be saved. (I'd say don't bet on it.)

19

Children of Paradise

I t is 1945. The war is over. You wonder if the movies have a future to match their past. You know—television coming on, whole new patterns of leisure announcing themselves. But we have a movie to match the moment, *Les Enfants du Paradis,* which is almost never referred to by its completely serviceable English title, *Children of Paradise.*

It is, by any standard, an amazing film, beginning with the fact that it was made at all. Marcel Carné directed from a script by Jacques Prévert. It was shot in Paris and Nice toward the end of the occupation. Its principal set was a quarter-mile-long street (built from scratch), which was peopled by at least 1,500 extras (some say there were 1,800 players at work some days). It is over three hours in length and required eighteen months to shoot. It is an epic by any standard—though it does not take up an epic topic; it merely tells a sublime show business tale (the "children" of paradise referring to those who occupy the cheap seats, in the furthest reaches of the balcony).

The picture was plagued by problems political as well as logistical. It employed Jews and anti-Nazis, who literally had to mail in their contributions, and its star was the sublime Arletty, playing a fictional *"grande horizontale"* called Garance, involved with three men based on true figures and portrayed by Jean-Louis Barrault, Pierre Brasseur and Marcel Herrand. As it happened, she was, offscreen, in love with a Luftwaffe colonel, though she remained committed to France. She was intended to characterize the very spirit of French theater, but when the war ended she was jailed as a collaborator and was unable to attend the film's premiere. She said, in effect, that she had always been true to France, but the heart has reasons that transcend mere politics, and she was forgiven—not least, perhaps, for her insouciance. And for her eyes—so wise and perhaps slightly mocking. She did not work often, and then at least as frequently onstage as on-screen. She played in *A Streetcar Named Desire* in the theater (and worked with Sartre, too), became blind, wrote a memoir and lived to be ninety-four. To me, she is an immortal, and this film is her masterpiece.

The picture is slow to get started, but it gathers complexity and power as it develops. Arletty, as she negotiates the complexity of her several relationships, gives an enormously subtle performance, one of the great female parts in all of cinema, never sacrificing wit to the sobriety of its intentions. It is at once a gay and utterly serious movie, impeccable in its development—wise and reserved, sometimes slyly so. It is a signpost on a promising road not often taken in postwar film.

There is something else I want to say about *Children of Paradise*. It was finished and released in 1945, when I was twelve years old. I imagine that it made its way to the United States within the year. That was of small consequence to me. Other movies loomed much larger in my life, and within the critical community. It did not have any international stars like Jean

Gabin to help it along its way. At that stage, none but the truly devoted cinephiles had heard of Arletty. I guess Barrault was a little bit better known, but mostly as a kind of distant rumor. Consulting my various collections of reviews, I find no mention of the film at the time, except for a brief, enthusiastic burble by James Agee.

Yet I kept hearing about it, especially after I attended college and fell in with a group of cineastes who had seen it somewhere or other. Their enthusiasm fed my desire to see it, though I have no memory of where I finally caught up with it. It was probably in New York, when I was working my first jobs, had no television set and was haunting the Greenwich Village revival houses, for want of anything else to feed my eyeballs.

I was by this time not a total zero about movies. I was reading the reviews and noting pictures that I wanted to see. Some intentionality crept into my moviegoing—I was seeking out movies—though the supporting literature was surely scant and not very inspiring, a cult sort of thing at best.

But *Children of Paradise* and a few other movies became grails of a sort. My quest to see them symbolized—without my being entirely aware of it—my commitment to film as an art form that was going to become central to my life and, ultimately, of course, to my profession. I was stumbling toward something or other, but not daring to admit to this quite improbable desire.

Well, you have to do something to pass the time between the cradle and the grave. And note this: It cost me nothing to become "expert" in the field. It just sort of happened (there wasn't much competition). I wrote my first book about film in 1962, became a reviewer shortly thereafter and essentially never looked back. And only occasionally and briefly regretted what I had become.

20

Crime Waves

From the sublime to the absurd. Why not? I think it may be the best one-sentence history of the movies. *Crime Wave* (1954) featured Sterling Hayden as a police detective gnawing on a toothpick as he tries to quit smoking while helping a young couple (Gene Nelson and Phyllis Kirk) evade the clutches of some small-time crooks with big-time ambitions for a bank robbery. (Charles Bronson is in it, playing under his real name, Charles Buchinsky.) It is essentially a mean little movie, which was a specialty of André de Toth. He was a nice guy in his way, as I said, but he had a truly bleak spirit underneath his bluster that he did not necessarily hide, which is why he never got the recognition he deserved.

I was left wondering, after he died, about the mysteries of Hollywood careers. He made some very good movies; so why is he, at best, a footnote? I think there's the matter of genres to consider. He made a few pictures, and they were all right, but the standard references talk of him largely as a maker of westerns and crime stories. In his heyday, those did not get you mentioned among the big boys. The fact that they were always well made got noticed by the likes of me, but we did not make this connection—that other movies, of similar budget and ambition, did not often compare in competence to his. In the waning days of the studio system, when he was most active, there was a place for him; people in the business knew his work and liked it, but only occasionally did they give him shots above his station. And then, after a while, the studios weren't making many B pictures; if they got made at all, they were "indies," forced to scramble along the margins of the industry, often enough shakily financed and distributed. You can see why André just sort of said the hell with it and picked up his sculptor's tools. In an earlier Hollywood (or a later one), he would have fought his way in from the margins—lots of guys made their debuts in series films, Nero Wolfe among them, and moved quickly on to solid careers in the thirties and forties. Later, from the sixties on, they didn't have to apprentice at all; they wrote a screenplay or two, heard their genius proclaimed and skipped Nero Wolfe entirely—not that those often agreeable little films were being made much, either.

There are, of course, other careers like André's, and by paying modest tribute to him I hope to pay tribute to all of them. Talents of this kind were once something like the backbone of Hollywood, a significant source of its stability and profitability. And fun. That André achieved such solid results so consistently is a tribute to his professionalism and to a sort of ease with his craft that nowadays is missed perhaps more than we know. I'd like to see a festival of his work—complete with an unreadable monograph. Or maybe not. Maybe he should lurk forever on the fringe, waiting to be discovered, one picture at a time, by folks with nothing better to do than find good forgotten films. They would discover that low-budget moviemaking is not always a problem; that it can be, indeed, part of the solution.

21

Why We Fight

Britain had a history dating back to before the Magna Carta—a sustaining tradition. Other Allied nations had something similar to see them through the war years, to buck them up when the going got tough. But American history was comparatively short. We had suffered the Civil War, but that experience somehow did not seem entirely relevant to the present crisis. We had recently endured the Great Depression, but the harsh lessons learned from it did not seem particularly applicable to the war years, either. It was all well and good to bleat on about democracy and the glories of the American way of life, but there wasn't much fun to be found in speechifying. We needed something more cheerful, more innocent and sentimental, to keep us up and hopeful as the war wore on. We found that chiefly in nostalgia. During the war years, and for a while after them, movie after movie took us, among other places, back in time to the "Gay" Nineties and its songs—some authentic to the period, others pastiches of their manner.

Twentieth Century Fox had the best routine lot in this line of business. Betty Grable, famous for her legs and a pert presence on the screen, was from 1942 to 1951 absent only once from the annual list of the top box office stars. She could sing a little and dance a little and be sexy a little in a distinctly nonthreatening way. She seemed to be a nice girl; she was rather good in *Mother Wore Tights*—a showbiz life recalled—and persuasively scared in *I Wake Up Screaming*. Best of all, she was parentally approved, which could not necessarily be said of more dangerous-seeming rivals like Rita Hayworth. Fox had some nonthreatening guys like Don Ameche on their payroll, too. (It was quite late in his career before he proved that he could actually act.) The truth of the matter is that the studio's standard was routinely good-natured and genial—their musicals and comedies were okay, but rarely challenging. I think that was all right with the wartime audience. They were not looking for trouble. A bland biopic about a pair of songwriters, say, was just fine.

It was not until Darryl Zanuck came back from the war and started making more hard-hitting movies that the studio came into its own for a few years. He made tough movies— twists on his old Warner Bros. style. *Kiss of Death* (1947) is a good example, and Richard Widmark madly giggling his way to glory was, for a time, something new and definitely strange to the movies. He would not have been more than a character man before the outbreak of hostilities. When many of the major male stars were in the armed services, many of the older guys and the 4-Fs took up the slack, with, it seems, no notable diminishment in the movies' quality.

One Saturday night in 1942, there was an uncommon stir at 1721 North Sixty-eighth Street. We were going to the movies as a family. That didn't happen very often. This night, we were all going to see the early show of *Yankee Doodle Dandy*.

I had heard of its star, James Cagney, of course, but I don't think I had seen him in anything as yet, with the possible exception of its immediate predecessor, *Captain of the Clouds*, which was not so hot. I had also heard of the movie, which was wildly popular with ladies of my mother's generation. It struck me as kind of a dim proposition—a biopic about George M. Cohan, an apparently legendary song-and-dance man much beloved by older folks, though unknown to me, except by way of the publicity for this movie. But a movie was a movie, and besides, there was talk of ice cream sodas afterwards—"if it isn't too late." So off we went, toward transformation, in my case.

The story is quite simple: Cohan is running in a play called *I'd Rather Be Right*, which mildly satirizes Franklin D. Roosevelt, when he is summoned to the White House for what he imagines will be chastisement for his cheekiness. Not so, as it turns out—the president wants to give him an award, some sort of civilian equivalent of the Congressional Medal of Honor. The two men get to talking, Roosevelt asks Cohan to tell him his life story and he proceeds to do so, in a series of flashbacks that are highly fictionalized. In essence, they recount the history of the entire Cohan family's trip to vaudeville and legit stardom, which does not contain many setbacks but does contain many Cohan favorites, like the title tune, "Yankee Doodle Dandy," and "Over There," then being recycled as an anthem for the U.S. involvement in World War II. The recital over, Cagney taps his way down a preposterously long White House staircase and emerges into a parade of soldiers who happen to be marching past the White House and happen to be singing "Over There." He joins in that rousing chorus as the movie ends.

There are a couple of versions of how Cagney became involved in the project. He told me, decades later, that Fred Astaire had been mildly interested in doing Cohan's story—that would have been a disaster; Astaire was a genius of elegance, whereas the film needed someone more raucous and sentimental—but he dropped out and Cagney dropped in. There was also talk that Cagney needed a flag waver just then; he was, at the time, close to being a fellow traveler (he ended his life as a Reagan conservative) and needed to prove his all-American credentials. That's plausible, I suppose, but he was an enormously beloved star at the time; very few people would have held his personal politics against him in the early forties.

Anyway, it was done—in black and white, of all things—with the mysterious Michael Curtiz directing. He was a great, fecund filmmaker (*Robin Hood, Casablanca, Mildred Pierce,* etc.) about whom we know next to nothing biographically, except that he was a Hungarian given to fracturing English, staging elaborate tracking shots (which drove Hal Wallis crazy) and expressing no known opinions about the pictures he made.

What my family saw that night was, in essence, a pretty straightforward musical, which occasionally broke with the convention of staging its musical numbers within the confines of some theatrical setting and soaring off to do routines that could not be pulled off within any theater known to man. Normally, I would have hated that; the first aesthetic little boys embrace is stern realism. In this instance, though, I didn't give a hoot about that. The whole damn thing was a fantasy, and in a way I understood that instinctively, though I could not articulate the thought clearly at the time.

Cagney never had a dance lesson in his life. He and other kids taught one another their steps—and also the panoply of gestures that constituted a good share of his screen character—on the streets of New York. What emerged with him as a dancer was a style all his own—all strut and manic energy, nothing held back. There was in *Yankee Doodle Dandy* something heedless and demonic about his presence. There comes a moment, for instance, when he simply hurls himself at the proscenium's side wall, seemingly halfway up it, bounces merrily off it and proceeds with his number. There are dancers of more elegance, like Mikhail Baryshnikov, who are in awe of him because of the naturalism of his movements, though you can be sure everything he did was carefully choreographed.

It is, finally, a wonder. Cagney, who won one of history's most deserved Academy Awards for the film, was careful to downplay it. He liked to pretend a sort of improvised ease in what he did. But that kind of madness in him when he dances is unique to him. I had never seen anything quite like it. And I have never seen anything like it in the decades since—all the sweat hidden, yet clearly expended. And all the while, Cagney remained a nice guy in the public's estimation—a lovable scamp, if you will, with a sentimental and even genial side to him. Norman Mailer, who had a role in Cagney's last feature, *Ragtime,* said the man was as tough as they come, but, at heart, he was a very decent guy—because, as he put it, "there's nothing more depressing than finding a guy as tough as nails and as mean as dirt."

Cagney more or less agreed with this estimation. "I understood that type perfectly well. No strain." Interviewing him for a book and TV show I was doing on him, I objected. After all, *Ragtime* was not exactly a gangster film. But there was a hunk of hoodlum in almost everything he did, he said—"There really was. Oh, sure." He chuckled to himself as he remembered deviltries past.

Objections to the pictures Warner Bros. had forced him into in his early days were more or less forgotten, though they contained some of his best work. He was at last ready to be easy on himself. We stayed in touch a bit as my film came together, and one night in 1981, when he was in New York for the premiere of *Ragtime,* I received a call from his people. Could I possibly bring my film up to the Carlyle Hotel, where he was staying, and show it to him?

I could and I did. It was a very odd screening. He laughed at the sad bits in the film and teared up at the funny stuff, but on the whole he seemed to enjoy the picture. I got the impression that he had not seen the early films since he had made them—

and found them to be better than he remembered them. The next night we went to the *Ragtime* premiere and to a dinner at Lüchow's, then in its final days. He was sternly ordered not to eat the cheesecake (he was a diabetic), but he did, taking sly little bites of it when he thought no one was looking—a hint of deviltry in his demeanor, which no one had the heart to deny him.

I never saw him again. Still, he was an ornament of my life, a man who couldn't remember where he had lunch yesterday but had total, amused recall of the long-past past and was more than happy to share his memories, though pretending surprise that anyone was still interested.

Aside from the explosive talent of Cagney, *Yankee Doodle Dandy* was a pretty conventional backstage musical, and I would guess no more than a marginally "true" story—not that anyone cared very much about that. Its energy just blasted away whatever doubts the spoilsports grumbled into the ether. But a year later there was another musical that, in its unpretentious way, was unlike any previous venture in its genre.

First, perhaps a little cultural history is in order. In the spring of 1943, the musical *Oklahoma!* opened on Broadway. It was a game changer. There had, of course, been other shows that at least occasionally focused on ordinary people leading ordinary lives, but Rodgers and Hammerstein did so with an ease and thoroughness that was extraordinary. It had a shimmering score. It had ballet. It had a cheerfully comic subplot ("I'm just a girl who can't say no") and, balancing that, a dark side ("poor Jud is *daid*"). It had Jewish jokes—not so hot in retrospect. Most of all, it changed forever our expectations of what we wanted to see in a "musical play," as this one came to be called.

There were precedents for it—*Show Boat* and *Pal Joey* spring to mind. And the timing was perfect, feeding into the wartime nostalgia market that we have previously noted. It ran for five years, a record, and during its run imitations of its spirit had been mounted. More important, perhaps, MGM was an investor in the production. A novelty was on the way to becoming the new standard for this kind of film enterprise. I am talking specifically about *Meet Me in St. Louis* (1944).

It was based on a collection of autobiographical *New Yorker* short stories by Sally Benson, recounting the mild adventures of a typical American family, the Smiths, as they await the opening of the World's Fair in the title city in 1903. There is a running joke about the tiresome song that gives the movie its title. But it's a genial joke, in a film that, in its way, is a masterpiece. The tension in the film comes from a crisis: The family's father (Leon Ames) has been offered a promotion that would require them to abandon their idyllic life in St. Louis and move to New York, which no one, save him, wants to do.

Judy Garland, as everyone knows, is the picture's star—falling in love with Tom Drake and singing most of the songs, some of which became standards, by the relatively minor songwriting team of Ralph Blane and Hugh Martin ("The Trolley Song," "Have Yourself a Merry Little Christmas"). These are situated in the Irving Brecher–Fred F. Finklehoffe screenplay, and the film is impeccably directed by Vincente Minnelli.

I think a case can be made that this is Garland's best work ever. It's a relaxed and free performance, absent the tensions that marred so much of her work. She seems to be finding fun in it—she's not pressing, but she is not resisting the sentimental side of the role, either. There is real happiness in this work, when so much of the rest of her career was a thing of firings and suspensions and general misery. Is it possible that for the brief time of this film's making she was authentically happy? I really don't know. I do know that she had a grace and charm here that was mostly absent elsewhere in her troubled life.

Partly that's because she does not have to carry the whole picture herself. Most prominently, Margaret O'Brien was there to help out—at age seven. She was the one child actress who was allowed to be as neurotic as she wished—though we never knew if she was the least bit troubled in reality. (We do know that, while playing an English child shipped to America for the duration of the war in *Journey for Margaret* (1942), she carried a live hand grenade around with her for what seems like half the picture. We also have Minnelli's claim that he told her that her dog had suddenly died in order to elicit the tears that were required for one scene in this movie.)

What is remarkable about this performance is that this child carries the entire weight of the film's darkness. Without her presence, the movie would simply be a genial little slice of old-timey life with a few pleasant songs. But Tootie is a case. She is obsessed with death, she attempts to derail a streetcar, she accuses Garland's boyfriend of striking her and, in the film's grimmest sequence, she sets out to "kill" a harmless old neighborhood gentleman, Mr. Braukoff, whom she has come to see as an ogre. At the end of the film, during what appears to be the Smiths' last St. Louis Christmas, while Garland croons "Have Yourself a Merry Little Christmas," she rushes into the backyard and destroys a snowman family, symbolically destroying the whole idea (ideal) of the family.

Today, this kid would be in therapy five days a week. But the Smiths treat her as no more than an eccentric, as someone who is perhaps "just going through a phase." Maybe so, though her attack on the snow people finally leads Mr. Smith to abandon his New York dream. (The closing shots of the film show the family happily enjoying the fair the next summer.) The only faint hope the film holds out for Tootie is a cakewalk musical number with Garland, "Under the Bamboo Tree," a joyous, yet faintly hysterical, comic turn that hints that this kid may turn out all right in the end.

I've worried about Tootie, off and on, for the rest of my life. I'd really like to know what became of this troubled child. Of *Meet Me in St. Louis* I have no worries at all, though it is ambiguous about the pieties of American family life; in reality, I think Papa Smith, especially in that time and place, would have told the kids to quit their whining and start packing. But you can't have that, can you? You can only suggest the subversion of "family values," not destroy them, even now, almost seventy years later.

The film has grown in stature with the passing years. It is, I think, one of the few truly great musicals, hiding behind its mask of innocence, possibly because the people who made it did not know entirely what they were doing. Yet I also think they had a dim idea of what they were, in their careless, show-bizzy ways, questioning. Only Minnelli, himself the product of a wandering family of players, may have guessed at that. But he was an instinctive director, not at all good at analyzing his motives. In my acquaintance with him, his mask of innocence never slipped. He kept his own counsel about this—about everything he did. He married Garland, of course, around this time. They had a child—Liza with a *z*. He was ever an amiable, inarticulate man. His autobiography was called *I Remember It Well*—when, in fact, he remembered next to nothing.

22

Muse of Fire

I came late to *Henry V,* and I came with one of those annoy-ing little-boy grievances. I think it was around 1946 that I caught up with the film. It was a classroom assignment, and off I trundled to see it—on a school night, no less. I was wary of the thing. I imagined a lot of high-toned palaver, of which, of course, there was plenty, but which I quite liked. It was clearly spoken and, to my relief, entirely understandable. I felt very grown up "appreciating" it and expounding on it in the days that followed.

Better still, I noticed a mistake in the picture. There is a big old hell-for-leather cavalry charge in it, which was very gratify-ing to the kids in the audience, who needed some relief from all the high-flown talk. Anyway, down this valley Olivier's horse-men splendidly thunder—right past a whole bunch of power lines.

Yikes! How come Olivier didn't notice them? Or maybe he did and was locked into his sequence and couldn't move his horses and men elsewhere—it's a big damn series of shots. Maybe he just thought that with all the action nobody would notice. Except possibly gimlet-eyed youth, and what did he care about them?

I was naturally pleased with myself, being so observant. What adolescent does not like to see adults screwing up? But for once I didn't run around bragging. It was my little secret—and Olivier's, of course. I think my silence was a measure of my respect for *Henry V.* Or maybe my respect for a self-evidently distinguished movie. By this time, I think, I was just possibly starting to see how movies worked, how the Hitchcock and Hawks pictures sort of sneaked up on you and were acknowledged by some process of secret sharing. You didn't want to be caught out taking something seriously that was not supposed to be taken seriously. That was for later. I cannot remember when I was able to use the words "art" and "movies" in the same sentence without stammering. It must have been a great day for me.

So *Henry V* was different. It was a self-conscious act of creation—an attempt at a work of art in a medium that didn't do that sort of thing very often—yet also, yes, a *movie,* which, despite its elevated language and obvious ambitions, for the most part succeeded in movie terms. It was, you had to admit, kind of fun, or so it dawned on me as it "unspooled" at the Times theater on that autumn evening, as much fun to watch as most "regular" movies were.

It was also, almost certainly, the first movie I ever saw that wore its foreignness proudly, which said to me and my kind that movies could come from anywhere on the planet and entertain you—not like Abbott and Costello, but in some way that was rich and strange. Back in the day—not that I knew of it at the time—D. W. Griffith was given to prating on about the silent movies being a "universal language." That was pompous, of course. But I think this movie suggested a similar possibility to me.

I have never seen it again since that night almost seventy years ago. I think I'm afraid to. I think it might prove stiff and awkward, not what I want it to be, not what it is in my memory.

A footnote: It is possible that *Henry V* is the first foreign film I ever saw—starting at the top. But it may be that *I Know Where I'm Going!* was the film from abroad that takes that dubious prize. Either way, it had its moments. That's the lesson I learned from it.

23

Here's Looking at You, Kid

Murder, My Sweet (also known as *Farewell, My Lovely*) is one of the first film noirs of the wartime era, and it deserves mention here. At the time of its release, in 1944, it seemed most notable as the vehicle by which Dick Powell converted himself from a so-so crooner into a reliable tough guy. It has all the elements of the genre—doomy voice-overs, bad women, weariness, Powell getting the crap beaten out of him, plenty of darkness. All in all, it was a pretty good little film, and Powell—was excellent in it, as he was in most of the films that followed it in his now saved career. As footnotes go, this is a good one. Too bad that in movie history *Murder, My Sweet* has to share its year with *Casablanca*.

I suppose *Casablanca* is the most beloved Academy Award winner of all time. Okay, we must remember a basic rule of this book—try to resist the superlative unless it genuinely applies.

So let's say *one* of the most beloved Oscar winners of them all. Julius Epstein, who wrote the screenplay with his brother, Philip, and Howard Koch (and shared the screenwriting prize with them), did not think it was his best. As I recall, he liked *Light in the Piazza* better, for understandable, writerly reasons—and because *Casablanca* was a messy business. It was written more or less from day to day, with the brotherly team going off the picture to do some wartime service in Washington (which accounts for Koch's presence in the credits). This squares with Bergman's recollections. She remembered not knowing until the last minute whether she would stay with Bogart or take the plane with Victor Laszlo to carry on the fight against fascism. "Play it in the middle," she was rather unhelpfully told. But Epstein remembered precisely when he and his brother decided she had to go with Victor: They were stopped at the light at Beverly Glen and Sunset Boulevard when they were driving to the studio one morning. It was logical, and it made all the difference. A romantic sacrifice was required. If Ilsa had stayed with Rick, we would have just had a routine "happy" ending—maybe something less than that—and none of those ravishing close-ups, the cutaways to the airplane's revving engines, the weltschmerz that is the film's permanent contribution to our way of seeing the world. And don't tell me that Michael Curtiz was not a great director—every shot in the film is perfectly placed and held for just the right amount of time.

I have no way of knowing to what degree the unproduced play on which the movie was based contributed to the screenplay's wit—at a guess, not very much. But it seems to me that the miracle of the picture lies elsewhere. Umberto Eco has written that its success derives from the fact that it evokes *every* standard move or cliché of its genre. If it had skipped one—disappointed just one of our expectations—he claims it would have failed. He may have a point. But I'm not entirely certain about that—forgive me—as time goes by.

What's wonderful about *Casablanca* is that it is a war picture (or perhaps I should say a wartime picture) that has virtually no action. There is exactly one fatal shot fired in it (when the loathsome Strasser is offed by Rick). Mostly it is about Rick and Ilsa mooning about, rekindling the love they lost back in Paris some months ago. The cleverness of the movie lies in the way ideology serves as the force that keeps them apart. The damn thing has principles, which, all things considered, are worked into the narrative with a fair amount of subtlety. What it's saying is that normally love should find its way, but not when the world is in crisis. ("It doesn't take much to see that the problems of three little people don't amount to a hill of beans in this crazy world.") And it means it. Or it means it long enough for us to accept the possibility that every once in a while people can act out of their better natures. Even today the film can persuade us of this frankly dubious proposition.

In reality, I think Rick and Ilsa would have found a way to get together again. *(Go. Drop me a line when you get settled.)* But that's too cynical a note even for the ever cynical critic to strike. Besides, Bogart has by the film's end persuaded us that he loves his misery too much to surrender it easily. He'll always have Paris, won't he?

According to A. M. Sperber and Eric Lax, Bogart's best biographers, Bogie was dubious that Rick would have been able to give up Ilsa in real life; she was just too winsome to resist. That's likely true. But such leaps of faith are commonplace in the movies. They wouldn't be movies if they didn't make these demands on the audience's desire to believe in a reality that is an improvement on life's ineluctable everydayness.

Of course, all deeply successful movies, movies that worm their way permanently into our consciousness, require some luck to get there. There are a number of movies in this book that I regard as highly as *Casablanca* but that are not automatic favorites of the rest of moviegoing mankind—or even necessarily known to it except as rumors, things one means to get around to someday. Part of this film's luck was in its dialogue—

that blend of wisecracks and dark portent that would, as we'll see, shortly become the lingua franca of film noir. This movie had many more writers than have credits on it, and how they got together on this style remains a mystery, but it suited Bogart better than any of the words in the movies that had fired his recent rise. I suspect Wallis—who was very hands-on with this project—had something to do with it. He was a phlegmatic guy, but a very smart one.

Then, too, there was the casting. Sydney Greenstreet, Peter Lorre and "Cuddles" Sakall were Warner regulars doing familiar turns, and that was comforting, I suppose. Paul Henreid was noble without being too much of a pain in the ass, and, of course, Bergman simply melted in everyone's mouth. *Casablanca* was about as perfectly cast as any movie can be. There was talk at the time of other casts—Ronald Reagan gets a mention, and Ann Sheridan, too. The former would have been a disaster and, worse, turned the film into a B picture. Sheridan was a perky, winning actress—but she had nothing of the soulfulness the role required. One wonders about these rumors—were they just batted around the room for a day or two, or were they seriously considered? Again, I think Wallis was the deciding factor. He was serious about this thing, and Ronnie Reagan was not to his taste for *Casablanca*—*Kings Row* notwithstanding.

But the best luck of the film was luck in the purest form. In January 1943, President Roosevelt and Prime Minister Churchill met in North Africa to discuss war aims. It was the first time the president had left the United States in wartime, and it was at this meeting that the two leaders advanced the (controversial) idea of insisting on unconditional surrender as a prerequisite for ending the war. The meeting took place at, yes, Casablanca—within days of a certain film's release. The picture, of course, had nothing whatsoever to do with the conference, but the venue was on the front pages for days. And Warner Bros. did nothing to discourage the notion that it might just possibly have something to do with high politics instead of sex and stuff. I begged and whined to see the film, despite the fact that my parents thought it perhaps too "sophisticated" for a ten-year-old. They weakened in the end, and I loved the movie. I understood it, if not completely, then well enough.

Which is not quite the end of the *Casablanca* story. A year later, it was nominated for a bunch of Academy Awards and won some (best director, best adapted screenplay), and when it came time for the best picture award, Hal Wallis was primed and ready—it was the logical choice, and everyone knew it was, well, you know, his vision. Sure enough, its title was called out. But who should beat Wallis to the stage but Jack Warner, whose name as producer was included—a courtesy credit if there ever was one—with Wallis's in the main titles. So far as anyone could remember, he'd had virtually nothing to do with the movie, but that didn't faze Jack as he beamed his gratitude to the Academy. Wallis resigned from the studio within days, going on to a long and distinguished career as an independent producer, with no apologies from Jack as far as we know. Warner's stepdaughter, acting under the name Joy Page, was in the picture—she's the girl tearfully joining in the singing of "La Marseillaise" (and getting more than her share of close-ups from Michael Curtiz) and is, come to think of it, the fulcrum of the plot. It is she and her husband who need those letters of transit so they can get the hell out of Casablanca. Not that we much remember that plot point, what with all the romantic hoo-ha going on.

Speaking of which, we must pause over the Epstein brothers' next film, which they also produced: *Mr. Skeffington* (1944). As I said earlier, it starred Claude Rains in the title role, opposite Bette Davis as his wife. Directed by the underrated Vincent Sherman, it is an important Hollywood venture in that it is almost the only American film that takes up the subject of anti-Semitism, which as far as the studios were concerned was the great unmentionable of the war years. Mr. Skeffington is, in fact, a Jew, up out of the slums and prospering in banking. He marries Davis, who is rich and careless, a kind of playgirl, and she makes him miserable. They decide to turn their marriage of convenience into an inconvenience. He moves his operations to Europe, where in due course he is jailed and tortured by the Nazis, in the process losing his sight and his wealth. In the meantime, his wife falls ill and loses her looks. At which point the movie goes O. Henryish on us: He cannot see her decline, which, in the movie way of illnesses, doesn't actually look too bad, and, chastened, she realizes that she loves him after all.

Reduced to a plot summary, this sounds like cornpone, doesn't it? But that reckons without the passion of its playing, and without the serious—at least by local standards—moral point the movie is desperate to make. Somehow, the damn thing works. It is so earnest, despite its wild manipulations. We care about these people, who have taken two whole lifetimes to attain happiness. We can even imagine a postscript in which Skeffington gets an eye operation. And Davis, for godsake, calms down (well, no, not really). The picture reminds us of Noel Coward's remarks about the power of cheap music to move us to tears and the resolve to be better people. I cannot justify my fondness for this movie, but I cannot ignore it, either. It moves me whenever I encounter it. I suppose that's because it's one of those films that hints at those large emotions, known only to grown-ups, which we fondly, erroneously, believe we will someday fully understand, and which we forgive when we learn that they are, in fact, cornpone—but in the grand, sweeping manner.

The dialogue and lighting of *Casablanca* might seem to qualify it for consideration as a pioneer of film noir. But it's too softhearted for that. I think we have to call it sui generis, note its influences on all sorts of filmmaking and look elsewhere for the beginnings of noir—possibly to *Shadow of a Doubt* (though I have my doubts). At least it brings Alfred Hitchcock, perhaps belatedly, into this conversation. As of 1943, the year of that film's release, Hitchcock had been in the United States for four years, having established himself with creditable English thrillers touched with some nice humor. Here, he had made more ambitious suspense dramas *(Rebecca, Foreign Correspondent, Suspicion, Saboteur)* and was becoming a force to reckon with—though not yet the grand figure he was to become in the years ahead.

Still, this movie (in part written by Thornton Wilder) was an extraordinarily good one, probably the best he had yet made. Hitchcock told François Truffaut, among others, that it was his favorite film. Certainly a case can be made that it is among his best. Its setting is the small California town of Santa Rosa, where at the time Hitchcock maintained a second home. There lives a restive girl called Charlie (Teresa Wright), who dotes on her uncle, also called Charlie, and played by Joseph Cotten. He represents to her the big-city glamour she craves. What she does not know is that he is a serial killer, the so-called Merry Widow murderer, who preys on rich widows, and that he is not in Santa Rosa for a family reunion. He is hiding out from the law. He tips his hand at a family dinner when he launches into a soft-spoken tirade against "idle, useless" women feeding off their men. This is misogyny raised to flash point, and as the girl comes to the conclusion that he is a murderer, we in the audience reach the near certainty that he will kill her to protect his secret, which he almost does.

The marvel of the film is Cotten's chilling performance. He had come to Hollywood with Orson Welles and his Mercury Players, and he had been excellent as Jed Leland, the drama critic obliged to eviscerate the performance of Kane's mistress in an opera the newspaper mogul paid for. He was scarcely less good in *The Magnificent Ambersons,* as the man who observes the rise and fall of the Ambersons. By all accounts Cotten was a likable man, given to practical jokes, and a loyal supporter of Welles and his ways, but his work in *Shadow* is extraordinary as he explores and exemplifies the possibilities of the psychopathy that may underlie charm. (See Hitchcock's work with Cary Grant; he alone could bring out the danger that lies beneath charm, about which Hitchcock was always—I think rightly so—suspicious.)

Cotten went on to other good roles (in *The Third Man,* for instance), but one always has the uneasy feeling that he was a second-choice charmer, which was perhaps all right with him. In *Shadow of a Doubt,* though, he was first-class, because he could let the menace in his character out early; his obligations to charm were cursory. He could get on to being scary early and let the darkness in him take flight.

I don't know if *Shadow of a Doubt* is really a noir film. It is not particularly dark in its mise-en-scène, and it's not wise-cracking in its ways (rather the opposite). On the other hand, like many of the true noirs that shortly followed it, the film makes a point of bringing evil close to ordinary life—an intrusion that is not necessarily as rare as we are generally pleased to believe in our well-defended bourgeois culture. In any case, it is a good picture, one that Hitchcock was right to be proud of—the first but by no means the last time he adumbrated what was perhaps his greatest theme—the need for our fat, happy, predominant middle-class culture not to let its guard down, to be aware that it will sometimes brush against people who do not mean it well. We must always allow for the possibility—not necessarily murderous—that there are people out there who want, at the least, to take advantage of us. Yes, there are.

Just ask Charlie. Or for that matter Walter Neff, of *Double Indemnity* (1944), a full-fledged noir. In their excellent encyclopedia of the genre, *Film Noir,* Alain Silver and Elizabeth Ward cite movies dating back to 1927 as having aspects of noir about them, and in the 1940s they list such titles as *The Glass Key, I Wake Up Screaming* and *This Gun for Hire* as noirs. They will get no argument from me. But I want to be something of a purist on this point. It seems to me that *Double Indemnity* (adapted for the screen by Wilder and Raymond Chandler from the James M. Cain novel) has elements that must be present in this genre if they are to be called noirs. Otherwise they are crime pictures—some of them very good—borrowing style elements from noir but missing some points that are crucial to, let's call it, genre satisfaction.

In 1992 I wrote a small book about *Double Indemnity* for the British Film Institute's admirable "Film Classics" series. It was basically a love letter to the picture, which I began with a quote from Woody Allen: "It has all the characteristics of the classic forties film. It's in black and white, it has fast badinage, it's very witty, a story from the classic age . . . and the tough voice-over. It has brilliantly written dialogue, and the perfect score by Miklós Rózsa. It's Billy Wilder's best movie . . . practically anybody's best movie."

So, yes, that dialogue. You can't have first-class noir without it. But Allen omits the nexus of it: the central male-female thing. The film has got to have a man willing to be manipulated by an amoral woman, ready to bring him down—to death or, at the very least, dishonor or disgrace. That, to me, is the central mystery of noir, never played out more brilliantly than in *Double Indemnity*.

Where did these films come from? There had been nasty and scheming women in movies from their beginning, of course, but not quite of this determinedly evil nature. Why should they suddenly appear in the midst of World War II, when the most basic drive of the movies was otherwise: to show loving couples enduring all sorts of separation, including death, under the terrible impress of world war. I have never seen a persuasive explication of what we might call the Stanwyck-MacMurray phenomenon. Maybe it was very simple: Everybody was just tired of simpering, good-natured films.

But let's be a little more tough-minded. Noir is a literary conceit, not a cinematic one. Movies, since sound came in, had always had good dialogue, but of a rather genial nature. The kind of hardness noir featured came out of the tough-guy crime novels—Hammett, Chandler, Burnett—which began attaining popularity in the 1930s. Those damaged protagonists liked

tough dames with lip and a taste for fraudulence. It was probably Mary Astor who pioneered the type (deliciously) in *The
Maltese Falcon*. Her Brigid O'Shaughnessy does not, I reckon,
ever once tell the truth in that picture, but Bogart loves her,
even as he "sends her over" at the end of the film. Brisk needed
to become brusque. The type needed to gel, to harden up (à
la Stanwyck), if she was to assert her spell on guys like Walter
Neff—and us.

Noir also needed a sympathetic character, which is where
Edward G. Robinson comes in. His part was expanded from
the novel by Wilder and Chandler so that his relationship with
Neff became, as Wilder said to me (and others), "the love story
in the picture." I think it is about as good an adaptation as
has ever been made. It cleaned out a lot of arty bunkum that
marred the ending of Cain's novel, and in MacMurray it found
the leading man that it needed.

It was not easy. Wilder, logically, approached most of Paramount's tough guys for the role. George Raft, who became
something of a specialist at turning down great roles, rejected
this one for lack of a "lapel" scene—where he would turn
over the collar of his jacket and reveal the badge pinned there.
Wilder found himself eyeing MacMurray, a sometime dance
band saxophonist whom Paramount was using as a light comic
leading man. He was by no means a dope, but on the other
hand he was not the sort of man one readily thought of being
led to murder—which, as Wilder considered the matter, was
precisely the point. He was perfect in the part, an emotionally
stunted wise guy.

The picture was released in September 1944, and it did all
right—decent reviews; fair, but not spectacular, business—
and Oscar nominations the next spring. Paramount had two
horses in the race: this picture and Leo McCarey's soppy *Going
My Way*, which was popular (can't beat Bing Crosby as a singing priest and Barry Fitzgerald as an older, funnier brother
in Christ) and made a ton of money. In effect, it ordered its

employees to vote for the priests, which they largely did. Wilder was reduced to watching McCarey bustling down the aisle to collect his laudatory hardware. Forty-seven years later, sitting in his one-room Beverly Hills office ("If I'd made *Home Alone* it would be a suite"), he stuck a shoe out in my direction. He had been sitting on an aisle as McCarey came past one last time. Wilder wiggled his foot for me as he apparently had those many years ago, upon which "Mr. McCarey stumbled precipitately," he said, smiling happily at his ancient mischief.

Of course, the larger last laugh is Wilder's. McCarey is sort of a footnote in Hollywood history; Wilder, thanks to *Double Indemnity* and other wonderful films, shines far more brightly in the annals.

It seems to me that the first years of film noir are among its best. It is a genre that hit the ground running. Personal note: I was just the right age for noir—ready for it and sick to death of *A Date with Judy*. Or maybe I just had a previously unrecognized fondness for people who were kind of screwed but trying not to be. People like Mildred Pierce, for example. I don't know how I happened to see this 1945 movie, but since it did not include any on-screen murders, I guess my parents thought it was on the morally okay list.

So there I was as Mildred (Joan Crawford, of course) built her restaurant business with the wisecracking aid of Eve Arden, playing her sensibly smart-mouthed assistant and trying to keep her daughter Veda (Ann Blyth) from self-destructing (not a chance). The kid is a monster of materialism and avaricious sexuality, too. This was a comeback picture for Crawford (she'd been fired by MGM and hired by Warner Bros., where she belonged all along), and she gives a very good performance (for Michael Curtiz), fully deserving of the Oscar she won—mostly because in some ways she underplays the part. She's tense, but she's never nuts. She's the victim, not the criminal, here.

She has her own romantic tribulations, but she is mostly, against all odds, keeping it grimly together. I think the film works—not that I saw this at the time—because Mildred is a kind of everywoman. In some ways, she keeps hoping against hope that Veda's just an adolescent "going through a phase," that their relationship is not unlike thousands of real-life parent-teenager relations, one that will eventually come out all right once the hormonal firestorm of adolescence runs its course. You can't blame Mildred for not realizing that Veda really is a psycho.

A case can be made that *Mildred Pierce* is not really a film noir, that it's just "a woman's picture" (as the cliché then went) raised to flash point. But it has the style of a noir, particularly in the lighting. And—herein lies its largest claim to originality—it has a noir antiheroine. She is not who she is supposed to be. We keep expecting Crawford to turn into her. She's the right age for the part, and her Hollywood history makes her seem right for it, too. But Veda's the first-class schemer. You can't really blame Mildred—or us in the audience—for failing to notice that until it's too late. Among other things, the kid is making a play for one of Mom's lovers. I'm not entirely certain on this point, but I think she's the first teenager to be shown as irredeemably awful. Let me make one of those big statements I'm sure I'll live to regret: Some part of our American innocence is lost with *Mildred Pierce.* Ever since Veda, we've always had to consider that adolescents carry within themselves the possibility of corruption—of themselves, of everyone they encounter along their twisted paths.

Having said that, I want to retreat to a smaller generalization. So far, I've neglected the character actors who brought so much to the movies in these days. Two of them are outstanding in *Mildred.* One is Jack Carson. He could play dumb. He could play a smart aleck. He could be affable and he could be mean as a snake. (Remember him as the dreadful press agent who finally brings down Norman Maine in the second version of *A Star Is Born,* or as the father of the "no-necked monsters" in *Cat on a Hot Tin Roof?*) Here he's one of Mildred's lovers, who, had he been wise instead of merely a wise guy, might have been part of a peaceable solution for this drama—not that we would have wanted that. And then there's Eve Arden (like Blyth, nominated for a supporting Oscar) giving balance to the picture; she lent common sense and perfectly delivered zingers to lots of films in her day, but never more effectively than she did here. She saves it from the lugubriousness that is always lurking around this film; she saves it for sanity.

Figures like the ones played by Carson and Arden are vital to movies that, like *Mildred Pierce,* aspire to be something more than genre pieces. George Cukor, that shrewdest of directors, once remarked to me that almost all American films are based on convention and that it is their business to penetrate to the reality—that human truth, if you will—that sustains those conventions, gives them those quirks that draw us into engagement with them, despite their "been there, done that" clichés of plot and structure and, often enough, their star performances.

Take Arden in this film, for instance. Wisecracking women looking askance at the muddles the leading players fall into were a staple—and a delight—of talking pictures from their beginning. They were a convention of romantic comedy, spokeswomen for the audience's commonsensical view of the nonsense proceeding among the movie's leading swells. But remember, this stock character—like all the other "types" in movies—was once upon a time founded in a somewhat forced-up reality. And in their way, they remain connected with that reality. They are the relief from the hugger-mugger of the main plotline, and we bless them for this vital service, a reminder that there is a real world clamoring for admission to the closed, conventionalized, sometimes really weird world that most movies—and especially film noirs—present.

At any rate, the mid- to late forties were glory years for noir, beginning, I suppose, with *To Have and Have Not* (1944) and ending with *White Heat* (1949). These years contain, I think, more authentic masterpieces of the genre than any other era. In the former, Bogart finds real-life true love in the form of Howard Hawks's discovery Lauren Bacall, as well as a cheekiness that rounded out his screen character to perfection. A perfect example occurs in *The Big Sleep* (1946), in a little throwaway scene where he has to enter Geiger's Rare Books to pursue a lead. He did the scene, and Hawks pronounced it kind of dull. Bogart asked for a retake. He turned the brim of his hat up nerdishly and adopted a prissy lisp as he peevishly asked the salesgirl for an obscure edition of a particular volume.

The key to the success of *To Have and Have Not* lies in its insolence, especially Bacall's, and in Bogart's willingness to cede the screen to her, so smitten was he when she was purring her invitations to him. These are not, perhaps, great movies; there came a time in *The Big Sleep* when it was not just improbable, but impossible for the characters to be where the script wanted them to be. But then everyone realized that was not the energy the picture was running on. It was the casual, carelessseeming "badinage" that gave the film its appeal. So everyone relaxed and had a good time exchanging zingers. If you've been away from it for a while, these seem to be as fresh as the day they were coined.

In that same year (1946), there occurred a noir masterpiece: *Notorious.* Hitchcock, Cary Grant, Ingrid Bergman and, much publicized at the time, the longest screen kiss—up to then—in the history of the medium. But it is so much more than that. A case can be made that it is the first fully realized Hitchcock film. Bergman is the daughter of a Nazi, recruited by Grant (a federal agent) to penetrate a ring of German agents, nominally presided over by Claude Rains but actually run by his mother, Leopoldine Konstantin, operating out of Rio. Bergman is initially presented as a careless, not to say feckless, woman, whom Grant wishes to introduce into Rains's circle. They, of course, begin to fall in love (hence the big kiss). She is obliged to marry Rains, who begins to poison her. Can Grant rescue her? Can he obtain the wine bottles filled with uranium, with which the Nazis intend to build an atomic bomb and, one supposes, mount a comeback?

Hitch was rather dismissive of the uranium. It was, in his view, just a MacGuffin—it could as well have been industrial diamonds, he thought. But in the aftermath of the atomic bomb, this scary form of energy was on everyone's mind, and he went with it. He never cared much about what device set his characters into elegant motion, and the motion in this motion picture is ever elegant. Grant's dark side is always showing itself, but alternating with his smooth side. Bergman is ever in a dither, but slowly coming back to her best self. And Rains comes close to being a tragic figure—loving her almost despite himself, yet unable to free himself from his scheming mother. It's a lovely tangle, written by Ben Hecht at his best. No one ever raises his or her voice in this film, which at the plot level is nonsensical, I suppose, but at the emotional level entirely gripping. There is one scene in which Grant and Bergman discover the uranium sequestered in the wine bottles (they actually break one of the bottles) that is, I think, one of the best suspense scenes the master ever concocted—essentially out of nothing but a moment's carelessness, a rescuing handkerchief, and some narrowly avoided menace. It's glorious, like everything else in this deliciously understated, underplayed masterpiece.

I have at least two favorite noirs out of this period, starting with *Out of the Past* (1947), featuring Robert Mitchum and company and the best overripe dialogue of a period that did not lack for hard-guy poetics. There are writers like David Thomson who are dubious—in a loving sort of way—about this movie, and I take their point. It's wildly overplotted and, truth be told, Mitchum's character sometimes seems too ready with *le mot juste;* you sometimes wish he would give the metaphors a rest and state his case simply. But then, more or less helplessly, you see the film again and are seduced anew by Jacques Tourneur's cool direction of hot material, by Nicholas Musuraca's impeccable cinematography, by the plot (which makes very little sense, come right down to it), by the sense of doom hovering over Mitchum—a smart guy rendered stupid by Jane Greer's machinations—and the film's utter refusal to cut him a break, which is so often one of the glories of noir. He says in the course of the film that he doesn't want to die, but if he must he wants to be the last to do so. We keep hoping he will evade his preordained fate, but in our heart of hearts we know almost from the get-go that he won't. Raoul Walsh once remarked that you could kill off Cagney at the end of his movies and the audience would accept his demise equably. Mitchum was of his ilk.

He's so languid—almost dreamily so. Sometimes you want to reach out to the screen and shake him. Can't he see—really see—the peril around him? He's almost smug in his indifference. There is an all-American imperviousness about him that's delicious at its best. Once I was shooting an interview with him for some TV show or other. It was in the early morning, and the director, a very bright young woman, was fussing over last-minute details. Mitchum was settled in his chair, a very large drink to hand. She thought to remove it from the camera's sight. He pushed her gently away and murmured, "Stand up, Mr. Roosevelt, and we'll get a few snaps." He, of course, gave us a terrific interview, which included wicked impressions of studio bosses being both gangsterish and idiotic. At one point in the conversation he gave this opinion of the star actor's life: "You don't get to do better. You just get to do more."

There was a lot of weary truth in that statement, as there was in many of his best roles. I don't want to pretend any intimacy with the man, but I wish I might have achieved it. He was one of the great minimalists among the stars. He very arguably was a cynic, and surely a hard drinker, but he was always a disciplined actor and a shrewd judge of bullshit. On the only other occasion we talked, he had just finished work in *Ryan's Daughter*. He was only too happy to tell you why he thought David Lean's movie was dreadful—too long in Ireland and not much to show for it. He found his greatness elsewhere, in pictures people didn't pay much attention to, until he wasn't around to make them anymore, and we found ourselves missing them, and him. He was sui generis, one of the few movie stars who understood that you never wanted to be caught acting until you were on the way home.

A few years later there was *In a Lonely Place* (1950). It features Bogart as Dixon Steele, a more or less psychopathic screenwriter who may be a murderer (in the book on which the film is based, he is) but has a potentially redemptive love affair with Gloria Grahame, who can also offer him an alibi for the crime. He is, however, an extraordinarily angry man, and his potential for violence sunders their affair and any chance they might have had for "normalcy." Directed by Nicholas Ray on a knife's edge (it may be his best film), it offers us Bogart more angry than we have ever seen him. We understand that he is only accidentally (and technically) innocent of the crime; he could as well be guilty. That's what's really scary about this dark, tangled movie, which leaves this actor in a radically lonely place for all eternity.

Movies that explore only one emotion—in this case anger—are comparatively rare, but their single-mindedness compels our attention and eventually a sort of perverse sympathy. *Poor Dix,* we think. The world outside chatters blithely on, but he is trapped forever in his nuttiness. Been down so long it looks like up to him.

Also around this time was *Act of Violence* (1948), Fred Zinnemann directing. Here we have Van Heflin versus Robert Ryan—the former hiding a wartime secret, the betrayal of his men in a prison camp, the latter determined to have his vengeance for this act. Ryan was an actor who mostly did not get his due but was reliably dour and complex when, often, there was no need to be; he simply couldn't help himself. Offscreen, he was a gentlemanly fellow (I knew him slightly), very composed and watchful, and never better than he was in this film, which is, I think, one of Zinnemann's best—sort of a B picture with A aspirations that are fulfilled, not least by Ryan's limping implacability.

We also need to mention Ryan's very fine performance in *The Set-Up* (1949). He's a boxer who's supposed to throw a fight and can't bring himself to do so. The film is a comparative rarity in that its running time precisely matches the narrative time it covers (rather a neat trick). It is directed very efficiently by Robert Wise, and Ryan is, I think, brilliant in it—so glum, so used up. The film comes to a "happy" ending. (At least Ryan's character does not die, though he logically could have.) Some critics have objected to that. I don't. It sacrifices no relentlessness to the grim mood it establishes and maintains throughout. It's clear Ryan is not going to find many triumphs in this life. It is a unique boxing picture in that he is not going to find success playing the violin.

We need, as well, to circle back on Mary Astor, playing a hooker who more or less knows all the picture's secrets, as she did in most of the hundred or so movies she made. Her name keeps coming up in this conversation, doesn't it, more so than actresses of more fame? It's belatedly time to give her the credit she never quite attained in her prolific career.

She's the perfect lover in *Dodsworth,* the perfect liar in *The Maltese Falcon,* the perfect mom in *Meet Me in St. Louis* and now the perfect whore in *Act of Violence.* The range represented by these four films perhaps outlines her problem: She was a star with too much range. That is to say, she was an actress who could do pretty much everything, so she just did it, never establishing a reliable persona the audience could count on. Offscreen, some hot correspondence with George S. Kaufman made her seem a bad girl when she was, in fact, merely free-spirited. She's wonderful in *Act of Violence,* in a relatively small part that is crucial to the plot's unfolding. That was her way. She later wrote a cheerful tell-all autobiography and some novels and stayed in work forever. Zinnemann was, I thought, a rather prissy perfectionist a lot of the time—an exception or two to be made in due course—and a case can be made that this taut, modest film is perhaps his best work (though I'm sure he would not have agreed).

Mary Astor was a lovely actress, both passionate and good-natured, and she deserves to be remembered more fondly than she is. As does *Act of Violence*. It's a mean-spirited little picture, not easily likable, yet not easily forgettable, either.

In 1945, a film called *Rome, Open City* was released in Italy and, shortly thereafter, around the world. Directed by Roberto Rossellini, it is a fairly simple story of wartime resistance, in which most of the people we care about in the film eventually endure violent deaths. The most important thing about it is that it was made while the war was still being prosecuted in Italy. It used a number of nonprofessional actors (not including Anna Magnani, who became a major star as a result of this film). You got the sense that much of the film was grabbed on the fly by Rossellini and that its "realism" had an authenticity that had not previously been attained in other films that aspired to that quality. Indeed, "neorealism" became the description of choice for this kind of filmmaking, particularly after it won the Palme d'Or at the next year's Cannes Film Festival.

Oddly, neorealism as a film form did not travel very well. All of its masterpieces were Italian in origin, and its reign as an important genre was relatively short—from the year of *Rome, Open City* until roughly 1952, when *Umberto D* was released. Yet I have a great deal of affection for it. I suppose that's largely because these films made their way to the art houses of Milwaukee and Madison when I was of an age to appreciate how they were different from the other films on offer.

As I look back on neorealism, I find that, for me, two films stand out in memory—one fairly early in the cycle, one quite late in it, and I'm going to let them stand for all the pleasures that cycle gave me. The first is Vittorio De Sica's *The Bicycle Thief* (there is some confusion about the title), which actually came in at number one in the 1952 *Sight and Sound* poll. (A decade later it had slipped to seventh, and a decade later it was gone forever.) The second is *Umberto D,* also from De Sica and rarely on anyone's best films list—except mine.

The Bicycle Thief tells a very simple story: A wife pawns the family's bedsheets to get her husband's bicycle out of hock, and he uses it to get a job posting movie posters around Rome. He is accompanied on his rounds by his son, Bruno. Quite early on, the bicycle is stolen, and the rest of the film is devoted to their attempt to recover it. At the end the pair simply melt back into the crowd.

At the time, there was considerable hoo-ha in America because Bruno takes a pee in the street. You would have thought from some of the response to this innocent moment that the kid had committed a capital crime. Eventually, it was seen as merely a part of the film's easy naturalism—and as part of its charm. It was a small milestone on the road to accepting some new level of honesty in portraying the reality of ordinary lives on the screen.

That thought does not, however, quite convey the full quality of this film. It is rich in incidents, which, considered separately, don't amount to much but, taken together, create an extraordinary panorama of ordinary life in our time. At first glance, *The Bicycle Thief* has an almost thrown-together quality, which it maintains steadfastly and by no means cheerlessly. It only slowly begins to show us a relationship between father (Lamberto Maggiorani) and son (Enzo Staiola)—both nonprofessional actors, I believe—as rather casually developed in the script by Cesare Zavattini (and a boatload of collaborators), that is probably more delicately and thoroughly explored than any in the history of film. The sheer number of people who contributed creatively to this movie poses perhaps the greatest challenge to the "one man, one film" theory of how to make a great movie. Sometimes, it really takes a village.

Umberto D is more simple in structure than *Thief.* A retired professor is living on an inadequate pension, his sole companion a winsome though not particularly attractive dog named Flike. He is a burden on Umberto (played brilliantly by Carlo Battisti), who keeps trying to lose him—except that he can't be lost for long. The main suspense of the movie derives from the eventual loss of Flike (the professor fears the pound and euthanasia). The main joy of the film derives from Flike's recovery and Umberto's acceptance of the fact that the joyous little creature is his for life.

It doesn't sound like much, but it is among the most heartbreaking movies ever made. Very simply, it says, I guess, that we do not choose what or whom we love, that somehow the object of our affection chooses us—and we reject that choice at our peril. Umberto cannot, in the end, reject Flike's love. Nothing much changes in his life, which remains at best marginal. But there is redemption in his acceptance of the dog's love. The ending leaves us awash in sentiment. This deal is for life, which we understand is probably nasty, brutish and short—but better than nothing.

I lose all critical perspective when I am in the presence of this film, so desperately do I want it to be true and not a sentimental fairy tale, which it doubtless is. Sometimes you have to will belief in a movie. *Umberto D* is for me such a movie. And the great, monumental trick of it is that the stern realism of its style seems to guarantee the truth of the tale. Umberto and Flike are for me immortal signs that the better angels of our natures are real—if, naturally, extremely rare.

24

The Best Years

We come now—reluctantly in my case—to *The Best Years of Our Lives.* It is, of course, about veterans coming home at the end of World War II and their problems adjusting to the postwar world. It's about Dana Andrews, a bombardier on a bomber during the war, returning to civilian life as a soda jerk and to a marriage with Virginia Mayo, in which he's just a jerk. (Never mind—Teresa Wright is just around the corner.) It's about Fredric March being, oxymoronically, a liberal-minded banker. It's about Harold Russell having hooks instead of hands, and trying to force Cathy O'Donnell away from his damaged self.

It was written by Robert Sherwood, directed by William Wyler and produced by Samuel Goldwyn, in 1946. It was the last outcry of wartime liberalism—expressing the sense that we had fought a good war for a better world, which would now arrive on schedule, despite the hardships endured. It was a huge and beloved success. It comforted people—everything would be okay now—and ignored the issues and conflicts that actually marked the postwar world. For example, it never mentions the great issue of postwar America, our struggle with racism. Or, for that matter, McCarthyism. Or anything else that really disturbed us. Mostly the movie is about sorting out a variety of love affairs—the right man with the right woman.

We don't often care to test likable films against historical reality. But *Best Years,* as I had occasion to discover, elicits a defensive passion that is quite remarkable. Its fans cannot bear to accept that mostly things did not work out the way the film confidently insisted they would. Credit the filmmaker with good intentions. But if you return to the film now, it is in my estimation close to travesty.

There is, though, one sequence in the picture that is authentically great. Dana Andrews is in a field full of parked and disarmed bombers—war's grim detritus—that seems to stretch for miles. He climbs into one of the planes, seats himself in the bombardier's seat in the nose of the B-17 and recollects, with the help of sound effects, the days when he was a pilot—the heroic past—and forgets the reality of being a soda jerk, while imagining a better future. It is a long, lovely moment, beautifully realized by Wyler, and by Andrews. It is at the heart of the picture's optimism. It achieves the greatness the rest of the picture aspires to.

As of 1945, ninety million people went to the movies every week, the largest number since 1929. As of 1950 that number had dropped to sixty million. By 1980 it had fallen to around twenty million, give or take, where it has more or less hovered ever since. The reason, of course, was television. Once you bought a set and paid your electric bill, it was essentially free. Social commentators seriously debated whether the movies had a future. A couple of studios went out of business. All of them truncated production, and long-term contracts with talent virtually ceased. It would not be until the 1980s that the business stabilized on the much more modest scale that still pertains. Movies for me, by and large, then became less entertaining, though not at first. It required a few years for them to decline naturally.

Genres largely ruled routine production during this period. It was a great age of science fiction and westerns, very few of them immortal works, but many of them entertaining, inexpensive and well made. "Serious" filmmaking focused, to a surprising degree, on political and quasi-political topics *(Crossfire, The Killers, Criss Cross, Cry of the City)* as well as social problems—mental illness *(The Snake Pit),* alcoholism *(The Lost Weekend)* and, of course, racism in many of its aspects *(Home of the Brave, Lost Boundaries, Intruder in the Dust* and *Pinky* among others). These movies tended to be soberly reviewed and earnestly discussed, though they have not worn well over time. I would not willingly seek out any of them today.

It may be that the quintessential filmmaker of the era was Stanley Kramer, earnest and inept, making politically correct, totally leaden movies on "important" subjects and, upon his death, receiving front-page coverage and a full inside page in the *New York Times*—twice the coverage (as David Thomson has pointed out) accorded Robert Bresson on his passing. He survived many a bad review and many a box office disaster, and it is hard to think of a movie, other than perhaps *The Caine Mutiny,* that one would now encounter with anything less than dismay—and he only produced that. He, among many, was a master of demographics: He made movies for the liberal-minded, people who cherished political correctness over such aesthetic values as the movies rather carelessly—certainly unprogrammatically—promoted. Please don't guess who's coming to dinner—you already know anyway.

Whatever was happening, commercially speaking, to the American movie in the years between 1945 and 1950, a case can be made that these twilight years of Hollywood's ascendancy were good years. Within the industry there was concern, of course, about falling receipts—how could there not be?—but there was also a sense that its troubles might be temporary. Good American pictures were still being made, and, individually, many of them continued to prosper.

Elia Kazan's first movie, *A Tree Grows in Brooklyn* (1945), is possibly the best movie we have had about a child growing to maturity (and they are not a few, these films), with a lovely, clear-eyed performance by Peggy Ann Garner, an angry, bitter one by Dorothy McGuire as her mother, and James Dunn winning an Oscar as her feckless, charming, doomed father. It is not a "great" movie, but it is rich in nonsentimental values—in common decency, if you will. Kazan made better, more aspiring movies, but none, I think, more heartfelt. And none that, at some simple, uncomplicated level, affects the viewer more directly.

This was his high time. He did not much care for *Gentleman's Agreement* (1947); it was not a lasting monument to his style, his manner—nor that of his actors. I came to know and like Kazan—and to write a book and make a film about him—and I came to believe that for roughly a decade he was the greatest of American directors, a man who had an inimitable way of recording something truthful about American life.

The previously mentioned *It's a Wonderful Life* is a sort of faux Kazan. I don't need to go over its component parts again. Though, as I've said, I cannot label it even a very good movie, it is one to contend with, a triumph of sappiness over common sense. More than once I heard Frank Capra say that movies are "lies like truth," and I think we have to give him that in this case. And perhaps we should recognize that Lionel Barrymore's banker really is the meanest man in this little world, and at least Capra doesn't let him reform—that's what the film has in the way of integrity. He is not present at the Christmas tree when everyone and everything comes out all right, as of course we always knew it would. *It's a Wonderful Life* represents a peculiarly American form of corruption—the cheerful kind. It is not alone in this respect. But it has an eerie perfection in its field.

If I may, a personal footnote: Around the time of my Capra film, the National Society of Film Critics was in the habit of inviting directors to its monthly meetings for off-the-record conversations about their work. I was serving a term as the group's chairman. We invited David Lean for such an evening. Not everyone in this crowd liked his work, but I did—*Ryan's Daughter* excepted. (This was pretty much the majority opinion of the picture, incidentally.) He gamely showed up, somewhat jet-lagged, and expecting, I think, a gentlemanly exchange. Which was not to be.

The problem was that virtually everyone hated his movie. Attacks on it broadened to assaults on his entire body of work, about which he was vague and evasive. This had happened once before, with John Frankenheimer. But John was a tough guy, perfectly capable of defending himself, and it turned out to be a lively evening. Putting it as pleasantly as possible, Lean was no Frankenheimer. As chairman, I did what I could to lead the conversation to calmer waters—not at all effectively, I'm sorry to say. These supposedly civilized critics turned into a baying pack, led by Pauline Kael, who had always found Lean too genteel for her taste.

It was ugly. Lean retreated into himself, the group yapping at his heels. Pauline was like that—basically a bully, and a relentless one when she sensed weakness. Her trick was to pretend she was telling the brutal truth, which everyone else was too cowardly to do. A lot of the time she was just showing off for her coterie—the Paulettes, as Richard Corliss immortally dubbed them.

Lean did not make another film for fourteen years, and he put it about that his treatment on this occasion was the cause of his silence—which was nonsense. Worse—from my point of view—he blamed me for leading the charge against him, when the opposite was true. I tried to make amends, mostly by writing part of an overenthusiastic *Time* cover story about *A Passage to India* in 1984. But still, it was as shameful an hour or two as I ever endured as a critic. My defense? I was too young and green to command the meeting, tell everyone to just back off.

My peculiar chronology now happily brings me to *Red River* (1948), which is, in my estimation, the best cattle-drive western of them all. John Wayne was initially a little dubious about young Montgomery Clift playing opposite him. He seemed awfully willowy to the Duke—and he was fairly young at the time. But Hawks persisted. He thought that if, eventually, Clift took a poke at Wayne, the sheer surprise of the act would startle the older actor, leading to a fight that would demonstrate their love for one another—which Joanne Dru helpfully points out to them, even though at the moment she has an Indian arrow planted painfully in her shoulder. Walter Brennan is crankily along for the ride as cook and conscience to the venture, his main question to Hawks being whether to wear his teeth in or out. The latter, of course. Much funnier.

It's a joyous, quite linear movie, unfussy, the way Hawks liked them to be. And more than *Stagecoach*, it established Wayne not just as a star but as an institution, a force of nature. He is just such a powerful presence in the picture—humorous, difficult and forced by Clift to work hard to keep up with his canny, counterpunching portrayal. His surprise when Clift finally abandons his passivity and strikes back at him is a great movie moment.

Wayne had been a footballer at USC and had a summer job at Fox Studios—mostly tugging and hauling—a big, handsome guy you couldn't help noticing around the lot. He did minor bits and pieces there, and then, the story goes, Raoul Walsh observed him handling heavy props with a light touch and gave him the lead in *The Big Trail* (1930), a so-so western in which he was awkward but somehow authentic. Thereafter, he worked regularly—some small parts in biggish pictures, and vice versa, but mostly westerns, some of them of the singing variety, hard as that may be to believe. He was nominally a star—but only nominally. He was, as we all know, rescued by *Stagecoach* in 1939, given at last a star's entrance by John Ford. This might be a good moment to reflect on the question of masculine beauty. By the time he was making the cavalry westerns and the other epic works of his maturity, he was rather a heavy screen presence. He looked okay, but he was scarcely a dreamboat. He was by now a good actor, alert to the ironies of his screen persona. We just plain liked him. Anyone who could woo flinty Joan Didion to sympathy was obviously a man of parts.

But think back to 1939, and the sheer beauty of the man. Yes, beauty—no other word will do. Some of it was owed to the panchromatic film stock, which made everyone look better than life. Then, too, there was the standard of the time—no man or woman dared aspire to stardom without possessing extraordinarily good looks, which is no longer always the case. The entire Hollywood system, from directors to grips, was, in effect, a conspiracy to present everyone in his or her best light.

I have no idea if Wayne was a likable man, but some glancing contact with him made me think he probably was. He at least had a sense of humor. And there was an ease, a grace, to him that was very winning. He came to define—as much as anyone—what stardom was. He made his share of lunky pictures—too many of them, because he was a bear for work. But you also have to say that within his genre limits, he made a great many fine and memorable movies, ones that I would happily throw into the machine tonight, reveling in that flat voice, that dry humor and a certain quizzicality. He was not the greatest actor of them all—there were men of greater subtlety working in Hollywood's golden era—but he was sui generis: There was a power in him and an anger (see *The Searchers,* for example) that is beyond compare. He also faced down the cancer that carried him off at the comparatively young age of seventy-two with exemplary courage.

While we are on the subject of westerns—or perhaps I should say more-or-less westerns—I want to mention a group of three from this period.

One is virtually unknown and unsung. *No Name on the Bullet* (1959) is one of a small raft of low-budget action pictures that Audie Murphy made after he returned from World War II as America's most decorated soldier. He had a baby face and was from Nowheresville, Texas, but he was authentically tough. An example: A bunch of TV cowboys were amusing themselves by having a quick-draw contest and, so the story goes, asked Murphy if he'd like to join in. "Sure," he said, "if you use real bullets."

John Huston liked his affectless quality and starred him effectively in some A pictures, but he settled into Bs for the most part in the fifties. I found him there in the aforementioned movie. He plays a guy mostly sitting on his western porch, not doing much. But just the same, he's scaring the daylights out of the town. Obviously, he has deadly business hereabouts, but he's in no hurry to conduct it or, in fact, to identify who his eventual target is. This means virtually everyone in town is in a dither, as they are all possible victims.

The film is seventy-seven minutes long and is directed by the action master, Jack Arnold, and it has a twist ending that is very satisfying. I'm not arguing that it is a forgotten masterpiece or that Murphy is a great actor neglected (though he did come to a premature end). But there is an unpretentiousness to him that is very satisfying—more so than you will find in pictures that huff and puff far more grandly than his did.

Movies of this sort—never many, but on the other hand not a few, either—were one of the pleasures of moviegoing up to the 1960s. When the studios were grinding out B pictures (often in series like *Dr. Kildare*), they clung to a certain standard. They were testing grounds for directors and stars, and these people worked hard and took them seriously. They offered a way up, and also a place for the audience to stay in touch with treasured retainers. There were few undiscovered masterpieces at this level of American filmmaking, but there were few major disappointments, either. This was the place where many solid talents waited to make the transition to television and the belated stardom it afforded them.

The second film is *Gun Crazy* (1949). It's a Bonnie and Clyde sort of story, starring John Dall and Peggy Cummins— not exactly big-time stars. It was written by the odd couple of MacKinlay Kantor and Dalton Trumbo and directed by Joseph H. Lewis, a reasonably reliable B picture operative who somehow attained auteur status in France (go figure). The lead characters are precisely what the title says they are—quite coldly so. They work for a while on the right side of the law, in carnivals and the like, and then slide over to the dark side, eventually staging a series of robberies that lead to their demise. It is a very chilling little movie. They share a passion for shooting, of course, but not, it seems to me, for one another. Yet the movie has attained cult status—deservedly so. There are very few films in which the protagonists' mad passions are not for each other but for . . . I guess you could call it a hobby of sorts. They are, in tandem, a whirlwind of destruction.

In any case, the movie eventually attains a sort of cool frenzy that is quite rare, especially in this era. It's possible that everyone connected with it just simply forgot that Dall and Cummins should have shown some passion for something other than those shiny firearms, which are the sexiest things in the picture. That, however, works well for the film, which was made in low-budget haste. Sometimes what you leave out of a film is what gives it some special (possibly lunatic) quality. It was one of what are said to be eighteen movies—there are doubtless more—that Trumbo worked on during his blacklist years, at cut rates and in something of a manic way. There are pictures of him writing in his bathtub, cigarette in a jaunty holder. (He died of lung cancer.) There was no time for nuance; there was only time for one central, pretty big idea, to be explored at breakneck pace.

As a result, *Gun Crazy* becomes one of the few movies to say something worthwhile about, well, America's gun craziness. I love its bleakness, its blankness, its meanness.

We come now to *The Treasure of the Sierra Madre* (1948), which you will recall is about Humphrey Bogart going bonkers digging for gold in Mexico while Walter Huston, indulged by his son, the director John, steals the picture with what is probably the greatest goatish performance in the history of the movies. The problem, of course, is that they find their treasure. This drives Bogart's Fred C. Dobbs into paroxysms of paranoia. That is a state of mind not rare in the movies, but I'd venture to say that Bogart forever defines it. He snivels, he snarls, he is from the outset of *Treasure* "unsound," if we may put it mildly. We also feel sorry for Tim Holt—deft, calm and doomed as the only sane member of this party. If the fortune hunters had not found gold, it's just barely possible that Fred C. Dobbs could have clung to his sanity. But they do—and round the bend he goes. His attempts to protect his "goods" (his share of the treasure) are mad as well as manic. In effect, he cedes the picture to the elder Huston, without quite surrendering it to him.

Huston was a great character man. He could be kindly, dignified and, yes, a very respectable Abraham Lincoln for D. W. Griffith. But he didn't let slip the bear within until this movie. He danced, he capered and yet he was keeping this ill-assorted bunch on as even a keel as possible. The subtext of this performance is, I think, its lack of expectation. He has been hunting for gold all his life, with no great success. Now, at last, it is in his hands. But if experience has taught him anything, it is that something can always go wrong. He is prepared for that, even good-humored about it. He is the locus of the film's irony—huge, of course—and no one has more richly deserved his Oscar than Huston.

The Treasure of the Sierra Madre, though based on a very sober novel by B. Traven, is, in its screen incarnation, a great shaggy dog story. Huston won Oscars for writing and directing it. It was not an instant hit, but enough of us loved it from the start to keep it alive. I was just fifteen years old when I first glimpsed it. Yet its ironies were not all that difficult to comprehend. It had its surface madnesses to amuse us, but beneath them there was something deeply, elusively squirrelly about the picture. Few movies are so perfectly pitched on the borderline between farce and tragedy.

25

Fasten Your Seat Belts

In 1950, the nature of screenwriting changed—a little. I continue to contend that the great age of that art or craft was the 1930s. Risking a generalization (with obvious exceptions), I'd say that the writers of the earlier era were at some pains to write a spoken rather than a written language, unless they were adapting some high-toned novel or play. Especially in comedies and romances, their words tended to be casual, off-the-cuff, a pretty good imitation of the way people spoke in real life—but, of course, edgier, a little more pointed. *Bringing Up Baby* is a good example, but there are dozens of others. Unless we're talking about the Marx Brothers or some other highly stylized— that is to say, surreal—sort of film, there was a kind of bemused murmur to the dialogue of the typical light American film. The writers weren't going for zappers most of the time. That's what made such minor—but delightful—movies as *Easy Living* and

Hands Across the Table (and dozens more) so engaging. Maybe *easy to take* is the right phrase for them. Bob Hope's frantic gag comedies, endlessly going for the boffo, are examples of what we are not talking about. They are a sort of illustrated radio—lots of good jokes, lots of not-so-good ones.

As we've seen, during the war—Sturges excepted—the movies lost much of their sense of humor, and they didn't regain it with the ending of hostilities. The lightsome actors of the 1930s were still around, but they wanted to make *The Lost Weekend* now. Humor simply stalled or went soft and sentimental. Maybe it was because the performers and the writers and the directors were older now.

Into this breach there eventually stepped some wits of a different kind—notably Joseph L. Mankiewicz and Billy Wilder. They were up out of the writers' buildings, where before the war they had written some notably funny movies. During the war they wrote some notably sober movies. Now they wished for something more mordant.

Take *All About Eve,* for example, or *Sunset Blvd.,* both from 1950. These movies are, I think, written more than spoken—very polished. Gemlike, you might say. "Fasten your seat belts, it's going to be a bumpy night." "Why do they all look like nappy rabbits?" That sort of thing. People did not speak like that in real life, but we could be persuaded they might. (The lines above are from *Eve.*) Upon repeated exposure, such lines at times seemed arch, even perhaps oddly sentimental, or sententious. But Bette Davis was a marvel in the film, clinging hard to her slightly fading stardom while fighting conniving Anne Baxter to a draw (I guess) in the title role. Mankiewicz wanted to be witty in the film, which he often was, but he also wanted to say some important things about life in showbiz's faster lanes, which worked out less well on the whole. But it was something new, and people liked it at the time, though I think it has not worn well with the passing years. It didn't sweat a lot, though—give it that—and like its predecessor, *A Letter to Three Wives,* it won for Mankiewicz the best writing and best directing Academy Awards simultaneously, an unprecedented and unduplicated feat. He hung around quite a while, an endlessly witty man who eventually became essentially blocked as a writer-director, but still a gallant figure. One always wished him well.

Sunset Blvd. is to me quite a different case—if only because it is that rare instance of a movie narrated by a dead man; offhand, I can't think of another. Down on his luck and chased by the cops, Joe Gillis (William Holden) ducks into a driveway on the title avenue and enters the weird world of Norma Desmond—"I *am* big; it's the pictures that got small"—played by Gloria Swanson, possibly filling in, it is said, for Mary Pickford. She is a onetime silent picture star rattling around in a mansion and encouraged by Gillis (who has a perfectly nice romantic foil in Betty Schaffer, played by Nancy Olson). He is a weak man, seduced by the older woman, and they get to canoodling. Every once in a while, silent picture stars of her era come over to play cards, and pretty soon she is buying him clothes, riding him around in an ancient car and thinking of a comeback, which he encourages.

What sends her around the bend is a call from Cecil B. DeMille. She thinks he wants to cast her. In fact, it's not DeMille but a studio functionary who wants to rent her car for a scene DeMille is shooting. DeMille keeps calling her "young fella," which doesn't help much. Then the lighting guy, Hog-Eye, turns the light on her and gives her her moment. And her ruination.

It is from time to time a funny movie, in a weird sort of way. Norma is forever poised perilously on the edge of madness, and Holden is using her (though he's under the impression that he's a nice guy and at the same time a sort of genial cynic). He does not love her, but on the other hand he doesn't have much to do, either. He is—well—feckless, an idler. At worst, he thinks she's probably something of a neurotic, not so different, perhaps, from other women he may have toyed with in the past. Madness is simply beyond his ken. Until, of course, it's too late. And he is dead and she is entirely crazy and, you will recall, "ready for my close-up."

A lot of people—inside and out of Hollywood—hated the picture. It was never a great commercial success. There was, putting it simply, no one to like—except perhaps Ms. Olson, and there was not enough of her. There was a pre-release screening of the film at Paramount, and the word was awful. Louis B. Mayer was present and held that the film was unreleasable. Wilder is said to have told him to go fuck himself. Mayer suggested a fund to buy the thing up and bury it. The film just sort of fizzled, except among the cognoscenti, like James Agee, who among other observations noted that movies about Hollywood seemed to be better than novels about them, which is likely true.

But there it is—*Sunset Blvd.* Mordant, by God. Always ready for its close-up.

It is still 1950, and along comes *All the King's Men,* written and directed by Robert Rossen. It wins the best picture Oscar, as well as the prizes for best actor and best supporting actress. It does not, however, win the best director or writing Oscars—they are denied Rossen because of his politics.

He was forced to wander wide, largely abroad, in search of work in largely inferior films that did not cohere into the very good career that might have been his. Rossen had been a playwright and a very successful screenwriter before turning to directing with *Body and Soul,* in 1947. He had been a Communist, but had come to a bitter break with the party around the time of *All the King's Men.* Some of its members, it is said, visited when he was preparing the movie, urging him to abandon it. Whatever for? he wondered. It seemed to him impeccably anti-fascist. Well, er, that was the problem: In a certain light, Willie Stark could be seen as a Stalinist figure. Rossen sent the party members packing, but their association cost him the personal honors that were almost automatic in these instances.

Rossen also suffered from ill health for some years and died at fifty-eight. But he kept working, in good times and bad, and seemed to me rather gallant. Rossen was the first movie director I ever met, and I probably should say that I liked him. I liked this film, too, though most people do not. It is something of a lost film. In fact, I think it's better than the novel it is based on.

I did not always think that. Robert Penn Warren's book seemed to me, when I first read it in the late 1940s, a major American novel, a work of high ambition and considerable achievement. (The last time I encountered the book, it seemed to me wildly overwritten.) What Rossen did in adapting it was quite radical. He stripped it down to its plot, in effect clearing it of the underbrush of fancy writing and stressing its highly melodramatic story. He simply tells the tale of a man rising from humble beginnings to command a backwater southern state, and Rossen made a rollicking movie out of it. Its author graciously endorsed the movie, for good and sufficient reason, I think.

The film was shot with Northern California standing in for the South, and it featured some bold casting, notably of Broderick Crawford as Willie Stark, the fast-rising, hard-falling southern governor. He was a crude actor, though the son of performers, up out of undistinguished westerns, comedies and suchlike. But he had a noisy power, and he was perfectly type-cast in the role, as were Mercedes McCambridge as his secretary and John Ireland as a cynical journalist. Crawford did a rather good—if again loud—impersonation of studio head Harry Cohn in *Born Yesterday* but then declined to inconsequence in genre pictures and television (*Highway Patrol* most prominently). He was a hard-drinking man, and young actors, working the show as they were breaking in, observed him pasting his lines around the set—open a drawer, read a few lines, shut the drawer, glance in another direction and read a few more until the scene was finished. All along, he kept nipping at his bottle. By afternoon, such acting as he was capable of was finished.

We come now to Marlon Brando, about whom it seems I've been writing all my life—including, yes, a book. He once called me on the phone to protest the use of some clips in an Academy Award tribute to Elia Kazan that I was producing (it turned out okay). He had it in him to be a great actor, and occasionally he was. He was also a lazy and self-indulgent slob, whining often and tiresomely about the actor's fate in general and his own in particular. He made weird and unpredictable choices as an actor. He could be both dainty and crude, often within virtually the same moment on film. He had an almost surreal way with words in his interviews. But to get to the essence of it all, he simply changed the face of acting in America, indelibly.

One imagines that his family despaired of him as a kid—military school and all that restlessness—so they shipped him off to New York, where his sister, Jocelyn, was studying acting. He took a surprising interest in the subject. He quite soon came under the influence of Stella Adler, who was for some, Brando notably, a passionate teacher. She was something of a Stanislavskian apostate, but she gave Brando a discipline he had previously lacked. It is perhaps not too much to say that what he learned of acting technique he learned from her. When he began to get roles in the commercial theater, he did well. People could see that he had something they couldn't quite describe, but he was arresting. They could imagine a career for him on Broadway. And so could he. From 1944 to 1947, he was pretty steadily working there, culminating with *Streetcar*. People thought he was going to be a star in something like the usual way. And so did he.

He was an eccentric, of course—the pet raccoon and all—and a man whose moods affected his performances, night in and night out. He was a challenge to act with, no question about that. But he was good in ways that people had not seen before. And the run of films leading up to *On the Waterfront*, in 1954, was near to unprecedented. There were complaints, of course—mumbling, self-indulgence—increasingly from Brando himself. Acting was such a childish activity, especially for him, since it was relatively simple for him to do. He seemed to think, for a time, that politics was a more serious activity than acting. He made a number of unworthy movies, in most of which he managed at least moments that only he could create. He made some films that were better than his critics would admit *(Mutiny on the Bounty, One-Eyed Jacks),* but he basically put it about that doing anything worthwhile was but "a chilly hope." Then of course there were his masterly returns to form in *The Godfather* and *Last Tango in Paris.*

We are left with a mystery. My generation had such hopes tied up in him, and I guess we are obliged to say he failed them. But consider *Streetcar,* which some have suggested is the best movie adaptation of a play ever made. They will get no argument from me. The brutality and tenderness of Stanley Kowalski is an ever-renewing miracle, with his co-stars not far behind. And what about *On the Waterfront?* And to think that he affected not to give a shit. This least professional of players (and his colleagues) made of acting a profession, of all things.

There were good movies being made then—though it was scarcely a golden age—but so much of the talk was about the actors. Brando, Clift, even James Dean preoccupied us more than their vehicles. Stars were fewer now than they had been, but they had about them a mystery that was larger, I think, than it had been earlier.

There was another way of looking at this—Laurence Olivier's. If Brando acted too little, Lord Olivier probably acted too much. He liked to say he did it in order to leave behind a decent estate for his family, but there was more to it than that. Acting fascinated and defined him. Try to imagine Brando in such a role. Possibly in the dark night of his soul, an unadmitted idealism may have fitfully stirred, to be tamped down with a contemptuous comment. He could unquestionably have done more, but he could have done less.

The quintessential movie of the 1950s was, I think, *From Here to Eternity* (1953). It is, as I said earlier, probably the best movie ever made by Fred Zinnemann, that cautious, whiny, occasionally mean-spirited craftsman. The film is a quite accurate adaptation of the James Jones novel, mainly by Daniel Taradash. It's very well acted by Deborah Kerr and Burt Lancaster, among others, and features the comeback performance by Frank Sinatra that established him as a star forever and a day. The roll in the surf by Kerr and Lancaster is without a doubt an iconic moment in the modern history of the movies.

Eternity is typical of the films that received the most sober critical attention at the time—mainly adaptations of middlebrow novels, made with sometimes fussy care and now held at somewhat of a discount by critics and the knowing public. I still like it, though. There is a craftsmanship, a professionalism—call it a sheen—to it that is admirable. And an under-the-surface passion in its players that grips the viewer harder than he may expect.

The genres, though, were not entirely neglected in these days. In sci-fi, there was *The Day the Earth Stood Still* (1952) and *Invasion of the Body Snatchers* (1956). In the former, Michael Rennie, not a particularly well-known actor at the time, plays an alien who pilots a spacecraft to Earth in order to issue a warning: *Give up your warlike ways or face obliteration.* His ship is crewed by a giant robot named Gort (actually the doorman at a Los Angeles hotel), sewn into a seemingly seamless metallic costume, who can be deterred from defending his ship violently if one utters the phrase *"Klaatu barada nikto,"* which it falls to Patricia Neal to utter. Rennie proposes a demonstration of his powers; he will—why yes!—make the Earth stand still. He does so while incidentally solving an equation that has been puzzling an Einstein-like scientist (Sam Jaffe). There is a nice ease to Rennie's performance—indeed, to Robert Wise's entire picture. It is graceful. It does not breathe hard. The film is charming, likable. It makes its unexceptionable point without undo preachment, ere it draws out of sight with the usual "We'll be watching" warning. Too bad Neal and Rennie can't act on their obvious liking for one another, but you can't have everything.

Don Siegel's *Invasion of the Body Snatchers* is a more intense film. Starring two minor but agreeable actors, Kevin McCarthy and Dana Wynter, it tells the story of the citizens of a small town who are being replaced by "pods," look-alike creatures that are essentially blander versions of the real folks. They take over when the citizens fall asleep, so what we have here is basically a townful of insomniacs—and an allegory that, depending on your taste, is either anti-Communist or anti-McCarthyite. It is, like many of Siegel's films, trim, efficient and smoothly scary.

Somewhat later, I kept company with Dana Wynter for a couple of delightful years, and she had a tendency to pooh-pooh the thing. She was a very beautiful woman (also a charming one). She was loaned out for this B picture and was a good sport about it. She was a completely professional actress, but not one who took the work all that seriously. She was a devoted mother and had a wonderful, throaty chuckle that continues to resound happily in my ears. It seemed to me her attitude toward *Body Snatchers* was rather larkish. She had made at her home studio (Twentieth Century Fox) more "important" movies, which had been more ponderous than popular. This was the only picture that people paid attention to, and its eventual cult status amused her, as it should have. She was, like a lot of performers of those years, trapped in the conventions of the times—so many heavy-handed adaptations of "literary" works. I never heard her name one of those that she thought was any better, so she settled for *Body Snatchers*. It was what she had in the way of immortality, which is, after all, more than most people have.

26

Don't Unfasten Those Seat Belts Yet

If you were serious about the movies in this period—and God knows I was—your attention often shifted abroad. Foreign films were, well, just different—in their styles, their themes, maybe simply in their appeal to those of us in the younger audience who wished to transcend genres. We were taken with a new thought: that the movies were an art form just as valid as any other, which we wanted to help define. There had always been adults who believed that, but for us it was a generational thing. It was one of the things that helped set us apart from an older crowd, for whom, on the whole, movies were nothing more than an evening's entertainment.

Case in point: *The Earrings of Madame de . . .* (1953). My resistance to superlatives remains steadfast, and yet I cannot help but think—sometimes—that this Max Ophüls film is one of the greatest films.

It is always mentioned in those books that list and discuss the masterpieces of world cinema, though an entirely coherent account of its plot is rarely given. The decor, the costumes, the breathtaking camera movements are described with proper awe, but the story line is not always clearly defined. It is in some sense quite simple: Madame de . . . (Danielle Darrieux) is in debt and must sell something to lift that burden. She settles upon some earrings, a gift from her husband, the surpassingly suave Charles Boyer. In due course, they reappear in her life when she takes as a lover the elegant Vittorio De Sica. They fall into real love, which becomes something like a tragedy.

In a very rough outline like this, *Madame de* sounds, I suppose, like a fairly routine romance. But that reckons without the elegance of Ophüls's realization. The swirl and sweep of his camera—often in tight spaces, at that—has few comparisons. And the playing of his principals—restrained, yes, but with passion throbbing just beneath the surface—is similarly intense. When Darrieux and De Sica in effect dance out the entire story of their passion, as the musicians one by one withdraw from the ballroom and the lights are gradually extinguished, it is, to my way of thinking, one of the grandest romantic moments in all of cinema.

Ophüls made other romances equally as potent—*Letter from an Unknown Woman* is an excellent instance—but *Madame de* is the one I like best. I love the air of sadness that haunts it without overpowering it, the curious calmness with which it confronts the storms of the heart. You wonder how Darrieux can go about her days—eat her lunch, choose her frock, get her hair done—gripped as she is by relentless passion. Possibly this is the great, almost unnoticed miracle of this film: It does not entirely surrender to its grand passion; it leaves a little room for the quotidian, for the flow of ordinary life, which goes on despite our breaking hearts.

There's no particular rhyme or reason to the films of the 1950s. There was a nice little line of women's pictures (mostly

Jane Wyman, weeping her eyes out). I'm leaving out *High Noon* and *Shane* because I don't think they were as good as people thought they were at the time. In retrospect, they seem too stiffened with the desire to rise above their station. There was, though, the musical, which, in this decade, is the history of the collaboration between Stanley Donen and Gene Kelly. This sublime pair rescued this genre from its reliance on backstage stories. The history of Hollywood would be poorer by far without the exuberance of *On the Town, Singin' in the Rain* and *Seven Brides for Seven Brothers,* among others. Their unique blend of effervescence and joyous romanticism is without parallel in film history.

In particular, Kelly brought to these enterprises something that was quite new to the movie musical. Vincente Minnelli defined it as a kind of earthiness that had been missing from male dancers before his arrival. (Astaire was great, but he was more ethereal.) In a sense, Kelly's athleticism made it all right for little boys to like dancing. He had, to be sure, ambitions (some might call them pretensions) for musicals—those ballets that became his staple—and though one stirred restlessly as they rolled on and on, who could deny the sheer joy of something like the staging of *Singin'*'s title song (among other immortal moments)? For the most part, Donen's best work was based on original material or on minor sources that could easily be "adapted" for the screen with no one "knowing" that was happening. Decline, to a degree, set in when members of the "Arthur Freed Unit" began making versions of hit Broadway musicals at MGM, though even then there were lovely moments (for instance, the great "Steam Heat" number from *The Pajama Game*).

If I had to choose a musical for my peculiar pantheon, it would have to be *Singin'*, for the perfection of its development at a fairly early stage in the musical revival of the fifties. But I'm going to pick another one, too, also written by Betty Comden and Adolph Green, though directed by Vincente Minnelli:

The Band Wagon (1953). It has a shimmering score by Arthur Schwartz and Howard Dietz, some gorgeous dancing by Astaire and Cyd Charisse, and a superb comic performance by Jack Buchanan, as a producer-director-star who must be cured of his own pretentiousness. This is what sets the movie apart. It sends up the musical's new desire to, you know, "make a statement." It is a rare thing for a movie musical—a movie anything—to satirize its own premises. But *The Band Wagon* does it with high spirits and good cheer. It deserves a higher place in memory than it has—it's a lovely, merry movie.

It's a surprise that this era of the musical was so brief: We can identify its beginning in 1952, with *Singin' in the Rain,* and declare it over with *Damn Yankees,* in 1958. Musicals, of course, continued to be made in later years, but rarely, and they were largely versions of Broadway hits. They seemed to me more dutiful than inspired. There were no replacements for directors like Donen (who mostly made comedies in his later years) or stars like Kelly, Astaire and Charisse, who did straight roles with mixed results. I wish that were not the case. Movies occasionally need to sing and dance and be sort of giddy. I miss those qualities and I want them to make a comeback. I doubt they ever will. The skills they require are lost to Hollywood now.

27

Mixed Baggage

In 1955—or maybe it was 1956; sources differ—a man named Jean-Pierre Grumbach, operating under the pseudonym Jean-Pierre Melville (the name, of course, borrowed from American literature), made a movie called *Bob le Flambeur (Bob, the Gambler)*. I did not see it at the time (few Americans did), but it was re-released some years later, and it was welcomed warmly in the United States—a trim crime story about an assault on a casino in Deauville. It was the kind of thing we liked to think the American cinema held a patent on, though it had more or less lost the knack for the genre by this time.

Melville's crime dramas, efficient and engaging, are valuable ornaments, none more so than *Bob le Flambeur*. It is that it is so unfussy, which is true of all Melville's movies. There are, it seems to me, no more clean-cut narratives in our recent movie history. As important, they are brisk and hypnotic. He was heard to murmur that he did not really know what his movies meant until he saw the finished print—by which time it was, naturally, too late to make changes. It sounds slapdash, but the films don't play that way. There is nothing careless about them.

Take *Bob*. It moves right along, but it is actually a very patient movie, laying out its plot carefully, making sure we always know its ins and outs. Melville's films always make perfect sense. They are also fatalistic and romantic in an offhand sort of way. And very tough-minded. I have never seen a bad one, or, to be honest, a truly lovable one, either—unless what you love is impeccable craftsmanship in aid of criminal enterprises beautifully laid out.

The Searchers also appeared in 1956. There is little need to describe this very straightforward movie by John Ford—hasn't everyone seen it by now? A girl who will grow up to be Natalie Wood is abducted in an Indian raid on her home, and John Wayne, as Ethan Edwards, abetted by Jeffrey Hunter as Martin Pawley, go looking for her. Many miles and many years later, they find her. She is, of course, "spoiled" by her relationship with Scar, the savage who perpetrated this deed, and there is little doubt that she has come to love him. So when Ethan and Martin at last find her, will the former kill her or forgive her? There is a subplot in which Hunter's wedding to Vera Miles is endlessly delayed by the obsessive search.

There are things wrong with the movie: sentimental songs, for example, and a rather feckless story about an Indian woman who is in love with Martin and is also—curiously—crucial to the development of the plot. It didn't win any prizes and did no more than respectable business. I was mildly dubious about it; it seemed to me not quite routine, but also not all it might have been. I had not, however, reckoned with the enormous power of John Wayne's performance. In its rage, in its implacability, in its sheer command of the screen, its complexity, it is towering. He comes home belatedly from the Civil War, still in love with Olive Carey but not daring to speak of it, since she is married to another. He is scarcely settled before Debbie is abducted and the near-endless search begins. Eventually Wayne is required to hold two contradictory thoughts in mind simultaneously: that his niece must die for loving Scar, and that she must be forgiven for a fate that she can do nothing to evade, save committing suicide. It is possibly the central glory of this performance that we never know which way he is leaning. We know only from the odd outburst that he is in agony. Mostly, he is enraged by the cruelty of the position in which he finds himself. When at last he corners Debbie, we expect him to kill her—in some sense the higher logic of the story demands it. But he cannot. The logic of movie heroism—this is, after all, a John Wayne picture—argues otherwise. He lifts the terrified girl skyward and quietly says, "Let's go home, Debbie." And we would not have it any other way.

In reality, this was not a foregone conclusion. There were many abduction narratives on the frontier, and though I don't think any ended in murder, they often ended in misery. The abductees often made lives among those who held them captive, and did not settle back gracefully or gratefully into their former lives. Something like that happens in *The Searchers,* but (as far as we are allowed to see) the victim is Ethan Edwards. He restores Debbie to her home, though we are not permitted to know her state of mind at this turn of events. We see Wayne outside the door of her ranch—in Monument Valley country, which could not support any sort of agriculture. He is not invited in. Instead, he grasps an arm in a gesture borrowed from the deceased Harry Carey, the door closes on him and the film ends. Ethan is fated to wander the West without the comforts of home and family.

It is a harsh fate—a hero's fate, bleak and lonely, to be suffered in silence. And possibly in pain unimaginable to us ordinary folk. It has been said that this ending is the most sublime moment Ford ever staged or Wayne ever played, and I will not argue the point. The film rises above its flaws.

Is it the best western ever? I don't know. It transcends its

genre, really. It tugs at us, haunts us in ways that few of its ilk
do. It keeps some of its secrets close, rewarding our renewed
attention from time to time in the mysterious ways that good
movies do. Ford got his Oscars elsewhere. Wayne got his later,
for the good humor of *True Grit*.

From the Wild West to the less-than-wild Alfred Hitchcock,
in *The Wrong Man* (1956). Manny Balestrero plays the bass at
the Stork Club—an anonymous sort of man of no importance.
He finishes his gig one night and heads home, where he soon
finds himself accused of a crime he did not commit. It will take
him—Henry Fonda (he does keep coming up, doesn't he?)—a
very long time to prove his innocence. In the meantime, his
wife (Vera Miles) goes insane. She simply cannot bear the pressure put upon them both by his being the wrong man. It is only
by accident that the right man, as it were, is discovered.

The film seems to me entirely without precedent or follow-up
in Hitchcock's canon. There is no wit, no cheekiness, to be
found in it; it is unrelentingly grim. Yet I think it as great as
anything he ever did. It is undervalued by his following—sort
of a "yes, but" in his large body of work. One thinks of the
line in *The Iceman Cometh*: "What did you do to the booze,
Hickey? There's no damned life left in it."

What the film has, though, is real tension. It simply has none
of Hitchcock's waywardness. We have no certainty that Mrs.
Balestrero will ever be completely restored to herself. Sources
are not definitive about what drew Hitch to the project, except
that it's a fine, creepy story with far more at stake in its unfolding than banter and wit and "suspense." Death is not at stake
here (is it ever, really, in a Hitchcock movie?), but life is. What's
that phrase in leases? The right to the "quiet enjoyment" of your
rental. That is what's disrupted by this film. And, curiously, it
turns out that the real criminal bears only a vague resemblance
to Henry Fonda—Hitchcock's sly little joke on how hysteria or
something like it can disrupt perception, cause us to not quite
believe our eyes.

I wish Hitch had made more films of this sort. In its realism, it is as elegant as his better-dressed work. In my conversations with him, I learned that he was not a funny guy. If you wanted to discuss film with him seriously, and set that sort of tone with him, he was your man. He would go on endlessly about the techniques of film—the creation of style, or styles—appropriate to his subject matter. When he set aside the jokey manner he reserved for his television show and other public appearances, he was as serious and sober about movies as anybody I've ever encountered. He was truly a master. I don't know if he ever thought of anything but film—not really. *The Wrong Man* is a masterpiece that is essentially without compare in the body of his work. In time, it will rise in everyone's estimation.

Forgive me if I take on his films a little out of order here. *North by Northwest* came along just three years later, and it is, I think, the most elegant of Hitchcock's five collaborations with Cary Grant. He had, I think, a need to somewhat degrade the actor in this film, a need to bring him low (before letting him off the hook). He had a great sardonic villain here (James Mason) and the divine Eva Marie Saint purring ambiguous invitations to Grant as he is chased from pillar to post mostly in an unwelcoming Midwest. The crop-dusting scene is a small masterpiece of efficient degradation. We love seeing Grant get his suit mussed. Better still, we love seeing his character, glib Roger Thornhill, discover such humanity as he possesses—more than you might think—under the impress of mass villainy. It turns out that he has the right stuff after all. It's just that he previously had not been called upon to access it in his silly and superficial life.

I suspect that in the history of movies, many heroes are stillborn. Circumstances do not conspire to test their ordinary virtues. It is a large part of Hitchcock's art: to get these fellows into trouble and show them to be made of sterner stuff than we ever would have imagined. It is here that we forge our identifications with them—sure, we could do whatever they're asked to do in the realms of bravery and cleverness, if only we were asked. Therein lies the art—all right, the artifice—of *North by Northwest.*

One time Hitch let slip his discomfort with Grant to me. He was so smooth—too smooth by half, I think he was implying—and that made the director uncomfortable at times. (The heavyset director, the impeccable star—it's understandable.) They were not bosom buddies. But they could collaborate brilliantly—one of the best director-star partnerships in movie history—and this is, to my way of thinking, their best and wittiest work. The plunge of the train into the tunnel that brings the film to its conclusion is simply a masterstroke—bold, funny and absolutely right.

"Come back, Sidney," cries Emile Meyer's corrupt cop. "I want to chastise you." Sidney Falco (Tony Curtis) is not buying that invitation. He's not expected to. That's the way things are in *Sweet Smell of Success* (1957), which is one of the most genially corrupt movies in our history, and a huge, delightful surprise. It was written by Ernest Lehman, based on his thoroughly nasty little book, with the gleeful help of Clifford Odets. It was directed by Alexander Mackendrick, who had developed a nice little line of chucklesome English comedies but had never done anything remotely like this. Burt Lancaster is an evil gossip columnist, determined to break up the love affair of his sister and, incidentally, bring down any nice person who wanders innocently into his path, which he accomplishes with flea-flicking ease. It is among the meanest movies ever made in America—and therefore a flop when it was released. I love it very much.

Maybe this is where Marxism went to die. By that I mean that Odets, who had been in the distant past a Communist, and remained a man of the left for a lifetime, and Lehman, whose politics were certainly liberalish, understood that by this time formal allegiance to ideology was not viable—unless you count anarchy as a possibility. That's the case here. There are hints of decency in the film, but they are limply stated, benchmarks to remind us that somewhere there are values of a better sort. But the nice people in the film are there to be squashed.

There are anecdotes of Odets madly writing dialogue on the set, quick, wise-guyish, baleful stuff, perhaps the better for being written in haste. Its rhythms are marvelous; they set the pace of a film beautifully shot by James Wong Howe. Its relentlessness is exemplary. It is a movie that revels in its own perversity. The world of Broadway press agents and their tribe is sufficiently distant from us that we can, if we like, regard it as a fantasyland—except that this is one of those rare movies that is simultaneously distant and achingly real. How Sandy Mackendrick came to be mixed up with these characters is a mystery. It's a cruel masterpiece, and it is among the best films Lancaster, Curtis and everyone else connected with it ever did. It never lets up, and it never lets you down.

Vertigo came a year later. Nice Jimmy Stewart becomes afflicted with the illness in the course of a rooftop chase. After he quits the police force, a friend asks him to follow his wife (Kim Novak), who has become obsessed with an ancestor named Carlotta Valdes, who killed herself a hundred years ago. Novak seems almost a sleepwalker. She falls into the water of San Francisco Bay, and Stewart rescues her. They fall in love. She escapes him, climbs a tower at a mission nearby and falls to her death, his vertigo preventing him from saving her. A little later, he sees a woman who is a dead ringer for her (Novak again), except that she is cheap and tarty. He wonders, though, if she might be dressed and coiffed and made into the simulacrum of his lost love. Thus the divine circularity of this movie.

It was a failure, critically and commercially, when it was released in 1958. Today, as mentioned previously, it has supplanted *Citizen Kane* atop the *Sight and Sound* poll of the world's best movies. I'm not sure I'd go that far, but it is a very fine movie. It also has its implausibilities. Discussing it, David Thomson says that if you want perfect logic, you should perhaps be reading novels—you are not, as he writes, "a creature of the cinema." He has a point. The movie has a certain chill that's not fatal to our pleasure in it—we love being manipulated in certain circumstances.

We are fond of saying that we "love" movies, by which we mean, most basically, forgiving them their implausibilities— yes, their stupidities—because they are just so damn much fun. *Vertigo* is not a movie of this sort. It is not cuddlesome; it is deadly serious. If you are not prepared to deal with it in that way, I think you will possibly emerge from it puzzled, put off, needing to see it more than once, as most of us do. It is not a movie to love. It is a movie to "respect." This is a movie that cries out for an asterisk of some sort. But also for an attention more unwavering than most.

28

To Live

The 400 Blows appeared in 1959. Seeing it for the first time was one of my most memorable moviegoing experiences. So it seems curious to me that both the director, François Truffaut, and the film that launched his fame (*The 400 Blows* won the best picture prize at Cannes the year it was released) seem to be somewhat discounted now. Partly that's because he died before his time. Partly it's because some of his later films *(Day for Night, The Last Métro),* though pleasant and popular, did not seem quite the major events the audience expected—not quite the thumping statements that a director of his supposed stature was to bring forth on a regular basis. Partly it is because he made five films featuring the protagonist of *The 400 Blows* (Jean-Pierre Leaud always played Antoine Doinel), all of them nice enough, none of them as potent as the first film.

I think *The 400 Blows* remains an extraordinary film that is diminished in retrospect because it seems to be a rather simple tale, though in fact it is more complex than it at first seems. On one level it is the story of a boy with a powerful oedipal attraction to his mother, who is also a wanderer, getting into and out of trouble, sometimes comically, sometimes not so comically, on a pretty much ad hoc basis. Basically he is on the run in this movie, which ends with him at the seashore, unable at last to run any further. We never dislike him; he retains our sympathy, and he retains our exasperation, too.

If that were all there was to *The 400 Blows*, it would be a minor film, maybe even a cult film (which it may be in danger of becoming). There are, though, other layers to it. In particular, it is a movie—not really a "film," with all that implies—that has a quite inspiring open-endedness. This boy is so improvisational, constantly inventing and reinventing himself, never settled, always on the move. There are very few movies in which we are less certain about the outcome than we are in this one—how a scene will play out, let alone how the whole picture will "come out."

Truffaut was, by all accounts, a shy, not to say skittish, man. When he was shooting *Fahrenheit 451* in London, he took all his meals in his hotel room, leaving it only to go to the set. Afterwards he said he had no impression of actually having been in the city. I don't think he was exaggerating. Later, he loosened up somewhat (wives and children have a way of doing that to a man), but his diffidence was large, if not particularly forbidding.

I don't mean to suggest that Truffaut made anything less than a number of fine films, or that many of his failures were anything but interesting, and often stimulating. But I do believe that in some sense his career was disappointing. Recent writing about him has about it a "yes, but" quality—Jean-Luc Godard's reputation going up while Truffaut's goes down. Reputations are such strange things, aren't they? Truffaut gave us in the beginning such pleasure, such promise. Now there is something grudging in the talk about him. You cannot gainsay his accomplishments, which are of first importance in the history of cinema. But they seem now less than they were. You wonder if his repute can recover, or if he is drifting down the page toward the footnotes. I hope not. There is much loveliness in his work.

A female friend of mine will strike me upside the head if I ignore *The Seven Samurai* herein. This is not a problem; I'm deeply fond of this 1954 movie, so relentless in its action. (Forgive me for jumping around in the fifties.) But Akira Kurosawa is, I think, something more than a mere action guy (though he is, God knows, masterful with it, especially with the mass movement of crowds and the staging of heroic action). What I most like about the film is its air of derision; Toshiro Mifune seems always to be asnort with that quality.

It is in one sense a simple film—just the samurai defending a village that is annually set upon by raiders intent upon rape, murder and general destruction. Yet you can watch it as often as you like and never tire of it.

It is a measure of Kurosawa's range that the film that came before *Samurai* was so different from it: *Ikiru,* which translates as "To Live." He was a director who made every sort of film, which is why, I think, he is somewhat discounted by the critics. No one doubted his mastery of many film forms or his energy. But I think a certain dubiety clung to him. His curse was to be prolific, especially when he was contrasted with such competing Japanese masters as Ozu and Mizoguchi.

Energy is, I believe, the most mysterious force in filmmaking. Some people have it and some people don't, and observers tend to fret over it unduly. Shouldn't he slow down? To which I reply, Why should he? We cannot escape our internal rhythms. Why not surrender to them—an epic one year, a chamber piece the next? Especially when the overall quality remains high.

Ikiru (1952) is quite a simple film: An elderly man, sublimely played by Takashi Shamura, learns that he has cancer and has only a few months to live. He has done little in life, but now he devotes his last months to building a small park. This he accomplishes, a small affirmation achieved. He will die content. And we are moved more than we think we possibly can be.

Is it a "great" movie? I suppose not. It does not bowl you over; rather, it tugs at you—quietly, insistently, persistently. Yes, we will surely die, but somehow we will sit on a swing in the rain as it approaches, doing better than we ever imagined we would.

We are not quite done with minimalism yet, with *Tokyo Story* (1953) unconsidered. According to one source I consulted, Yasujirō Ozu's masterpiece consists of just twenty-four shots, only one of which moves—very slowly. I pretty much have to take it on faith that it is his masterpiece, for his films are difficult to see in the United States. Mostly, his camera stays close to the ground, quietly observing people in conversation. Nothing, in the usual sense, "happens" in the movie. Some elderly people visit Tokyo for the first time to see their children (which is undoubtedly also the last time they will visit them). They are shunted about. The mother becomes ill on their trip home and dies. Their widowed daughter-in-law—altogether the kindest person in the film—makes funeral arrangements and is urged by her father to remarry. She doubts she will. The end.

Yes, it is a masterpiece, though I'm not altogether sure why. People mention Chekhov when discussing it, but that somehow seems inadequate. "Humanity" is evoked to not entirely satisfactory effect, either. I have never seen a piece about it that adequately explains its mystery, the way it grips you so tightly. Maybe it has something to do with the way it forces you to lean in, to try to discern what it means. I am tempted to see it as a sort of mystery story about the often banal ways we try—and fail—to communicate with one another, though we wish it were otherwise. There is so much silence in this movie, so much loneliness, too. I remain in thrall to *Tokyo Story*, but it is ineffably sad. Everyone somehow means so well and fails so miserably to connect in any but the most routine and frustrating ways. I think it is one of the most poignant films I know. And also one of the most haunting. I wish I could come more firmly to grips with it.

Setting aside the prodigious outpouring of work from Japan, the New Wave—or the *Nouvelle Vague*—was the most important body of work in the cinema of the moment. To oversimplify, it was the product of a generational revolt of sorts. That is to say that during the war, Europe was cut off from the rest of the world's films, and its own films seemed somewhat sclerotic, particularly to its young cineastes. Then, with the end of hostilities, a pent-up flood of film—particularly from America—was unleashed. No longer were these writers and scholars obliged to write wistfully about movies dimly glimpsed from afar. The possibility of actually making movies of a new and different kind arose. Subject matter expanded, and so did stylistic options. Films became looser, freer. The tradition of the well and carefully made traditional film—which had its glories, naturally—was discounted, not to say held in contempt.

This split was largely along generational lines. Theories abounded, arguments were expounded, books were written—and new kinds of films began to be made. "What is cinema?" Bazin repeatedly asked. And the answer came back, "Anything you want." It was, putting it mildly, a heady time. It was also significantly different from other eras of large ventures in the movies, in that the impetus for the New Wave did not come, at first, from commercial impulses but rather from people who had about them a certain, well, purity—at least at first. Hollywood was faltering, but an alternative cinema was flourishing. The streets were alive with the stir of the new.

So . . . *Breathless,* or, *À Bout de Souffle,* to be utterly correct about its French title, in 1960, by Jean-Luc Godard. Jean Seberg finally makes her belated mark. And Jean Paul Belmondo setting some kind of record for talkative sullenness. It is really a Frenchified version of a goodish American noir movie—never more so than when Belmondo confronts a poster of Humphrey

Bogart and sighs, "Bogie." How desperately he wants to be him. But he can't. French, you know.

It ends in nastiness—murder. But yet it seems to me rather a cheerful movie, smart-mouthed, sort of cheeky—and technically venturesome in that its sound was created entirely via post-synchronization: There were no annoying microphones cluttering the set. All of this helps to move the movie along at something like a breakneck pace. It's really a cool little movie, with an underdeveloped undercurrent of angst that's not too heavily laid on. I think, honestly, it is Godard's best vein, and one he chose not to explore as often as he could and should have. He was soon deep into heavy-duty filmmaking. He lost and rarely regained his lightness of being—though some American critics stood by him. Personally, I lost patience with him. *La Chinoise, Weekend*—they seem to me joyless films.

There is one film of Godard's, however, that I dearly, maybe even perversely, love. That's *Bande à Part (A Band of Outsiders)*, from 1964. Yes, I know, it's sort of a cheesy crime picture (though some critics huff and puff over it). Basically, a couple of students (Anna Karina and Sami Frey) and a friend (Claude Brasseur) learn of a cache of cash and plan to rob the mysterious lodger at her aunt's. In this they do not succeed, and something like tragedy strikes. So far, so routine—the film is based on a not exactly upscale American crime novel. But it is a comedy of the highest order—giddy, insanely logical, occasionally murderous and, above all, relentless. It is, of course, a farce, played with great sobriety, with at least some of its people getting off without the cash, but at least with their lives.

One wonders why this director succumbed to sobriety—for that matter, why so many do. There is no real answer—perhaps it's just people telling them they have serious themes to explore. Then again, you know the saying: "Dying is easy. Comedy is hard."

29

Bergman—At Last

I had been seeing films by Ingmar Bergman well before I knew I was seeing films by Ingmar Bergman. He had made his first feature, *Crisis,* in 1946, and it was pretty good as I recall—sort of sexy in an earnest kind of way. But of course, I didn't know who the auteur was—no one did. He was then one of a number of Scandinavian directors doing interesting work, offering glimpses of bums and boobs and a few sober reflections on sexuality that justified the nudity. In recent years, a few critics have suggested that maybe some of these pictures deserve a second look, though I'm not among them.

It was not until *Smiles of a Summer Night,* in 1955, that audiences in Britain and the United States began to reckon seriously with Bergman. It was, I thought, a somewhat dim, but intricate, comedy that to me, at least, did not reach its full potential until it was remade as a musical (*A Little Night Music,* by Sondheim) in the seventies. Certainly it did not prepare us for *The Seventh Seal,* two years later.

I absolutely hated it then, and I still don't like it very much. Playing chess with death and a troupe of merry players consoling the populace, and lots of other pretentious twaddle, crammed into its relatively short running time made my teeth ache.

I must concede I am not the ideal audience for this movie. I don't give a hoot about debating the existence or nonexistence of God. But, of course, millions of people think otherwise. And I have to acknowledge that this is a subject that has never been taken up in such a—what can I say?—"showmanlike" way in the movies.

It was a sensation, no question of that. It was a handsomely made film—some of its images are immortal, though there was a certain slickness about it. A consensus has grown that it is not a masterpiece. But at the time, I should have recognized the mighty ambition in it. Bergman was daring so greatly with it, you knew it risked ridicule with people like me. Woody Allen, his greatest admirer, has said that it doesn't make any difference how you rank his films, and he is right. With a few exceptions, it is a body of work second to none. This was something I would have to begin acknowledging when in 1957 Bergman created what I am convinced is his first masterpiece, *Wild Strawberries,* a work entirely different in tone—except, of course, for its seriousness and its demonstration of range.

Victor Sjostrom, Sweden's greatest director prior to Bergman (and a protean actor as well), played Isak Borg, an elderly professor being driven by his daughter-in-law (Ingrid Thulin) to a ceremony where he is to receive an honorary degree. Along the way he encounters, in dreams and reality, significant memories of his not entirely happy past. They pick up some hitchhikers, including a vivacious Bibi Andersson, who reminds the old man of the great lost love of his past. Other relatives are also recollected. No great redemption ensues, though a greater understanding of this life, now obviously drawing to a close, does occur. Indeed, I think it is in Bergman's refusal to suffuse the final passages with blinding light that much of its greatness lies. When we grow old, it is not possible to fully reform, to be what we might have been when we were younger. A little bit—some smallish grace notes—are what we can manage, and Bergman permits these to Sjostrom/Borg. They are enough to satisfy us.

It was not, apparently, the easiest of shoots. The old actor insisted on quitting promptly at 4:30 in the afternoon, and he wanted his shot of whiskey just then, too. Bergman indulged him. Thus fortified, the old boy would occasionally return to work for a few shots. The result was one of the great naturalistic performances—and films—in movie history, or so I believe. Bergman would, of course, create more complex films, but none—dare I say it without sounding like a sentimental fool?— more heartfelt. It is so perfectly judged in that respect—so dry, so warm.

In this period, culminating with *Persona,* in 1966, Bergman achieved an extremely potent mastery. He drew together a "stock company" of actors who were uniquely responsive to his will, led by Liv Ullmann, who was his lover and fellow resident of the island of Faro, off the Swedish coast. They made great films in this period—in addition to which she made two fine pastorals with Jan Troell in the United States. She also made a good deal of piffle, which for a time damaged her international career. She retreated to Sweden, and the pair eventually ceased to be lovers, but they remained friends for life. Better still, they were collaborators, notably on *Faithless,* a fine and complex film that she directed. It is not *Persona*—but what is?

Persona may well be a great work, though it is also relatively short, frustrating and mysterious, too. In essence, a famous actress (Ullmann) loses the basic tool of her trade (speech) and is put in the care of a nurse (Bibi Andersson). By the end, the illness has been transferred from patient to nurse, and we have learned a terrible lesson: The artist must discharge her neuroses somehow; if she cannot do so in imaginative works, she will do so more destructively, by imposing them on other people. The high point of the film is a long monologue wherein the nurse recalls a day and night of sex on a beach that Pauline Kael has called, quite rightly, one of the great erotic passages in movie history, even though not so much as a button is unbuttoned.

I have never read a fully persuasive critical account of this film. People seem to fall back in confusion before it—as I do, no matter how often I encounter it. This usually argues some flaw in the filmmaking, and I suppose that's possible. For such an elegantly made film, it is one that has engendered a surprisingly outraged critical commentary. But it is, nonetheless, a hypnotic film. If there is a lack of clarity in it, a lack of coherent conclusiveness to it, so be it. That's why we are constantly drawn back to it—seeking the key to its elusive meaning. It is one of the movies' great enigmas, and it is one that I have gone back to three or four times at least to arrive at the tentative conclusions I have advanced here.

It seems to me that over the long haul of the next decades, Bergman for the most part embarked on a slow process of simplification. The development of his stories was certainly simpler and more direct on the whole, though they were not less terrible in many of their outcomes. They were also much less concerned with metaphysics, which was a great relief to me, at least. He did Mozart (delightfully, I thought) and marriage (not always a snarling tangle), and there is an intimacy of scale in these films that very rarely tightens to the claustrophobic. It actually expands most wonderfully in *Fanny and Alexander* to a potent mix of terror and charm.

We will come to that in its time. In the meanwhile, there is the matter of Pauline Kael's argument to consider. She was not entirely pleased with *Persona*, which was her privilege. She concedes it its "ingenuity" but finds audiences being encouraged to let the movie "happen" to them rather than to engage with the film critically. She has some kind of a point here (hence the wide variety of interpretations offered for the film). But still, this was a remarkably fecund period for Bergman. It's possible that no director has ever made so many films of such high quality in so short a period (from 1973 to 1983). Kael was always more of a ditherer in her reviews than she liked to let on, and in this instance—even more than usual—she did not come firmly to grips with her material. It eluded her, and we can sense her frustration, which reflects our own. This movie tests us as few others do critically. In some sense it is the film that we have to conquer, and never fully do. That's the best thing about it: its insolubility. There are a very few movies that we will never "solve."

30

The Criminal Life

David Thomson calls *Anatomy of a Murder* (1959) "perfect." He is not a man easily given over to such superlatives. I don't think he means that this is a perfectly elegant film or that Otto Preminger was his favorite auteur. What he means, I think, is that it was a well-executed, intricate adaptation of a well-plotted, very popular, rather witty best seller with a lot of good actors—young, old, in between and led by canny James Stewart—easing gracefully along in their traces. Repeated mention was made of "panties" (they were a significant plot point), there was stunt casting that actually worked (Joseph N. Welch, the flinty lawyer who as much as anyone brought down Joe McCarthy, played the judge in the film with expert wasp-ishness) and George C. Scott was Claude Dancer, from far-off East Lansing, wonderfully snarky, a man we were going to have to contend with in the near movie future. Did I mention

Eve Arden? She was sharp as a tack, as usual. Duke Ellington was beyond cool. It was fun, smart and tricky, and everybody we like in the movie basically gets screwed, which is okay—it's plotted so that no lasting harm comes to anyone. Wendell Mayes's script is sharp, and it is realized gorgeously by the extraordinary cast. (There was often a lot of good acting in Preminger's films.)

Anatomy is Preminger's masterpiece, though peace on the shade of Andrew Sarris, there were not as many of those by Preminger as the late, great critic thought. Preminger made *Laura,* of course, a rather elegant and cloudy romance, and a group of crime stories—including *Fallen Angel, Whirlpool* and *Where the Sidewalk Ends*—that were modest, expert and glum, before succumbing to less-than-divine adaptations of fatheaded best sellers *(Exodus, The Cardinal, In Harm's Way)* that were of dubious merit, though I guess he thought they were important films. He was a supreme cynic, but also a man who carried himself as an artist no matter what anyone else thought.

Preminger wanted to be a middlebrow (though he thought he was being some kind of intellectual). So he huffed and he puffed and made it to that state, leaving behind his best self except, instinctively, this once. You can watch the film as many times as you like with some kind of pleasure. Do not, however, go near *The Cardinal* or anything else with a Saul Bass title design. These designs were handsome; the problem is that they were almost always the best thing about the movie.

In this period, a change of sorts came over film noir. Charlton Heston, always intellectually ambitious, conceived a film to star Orson Welles, who was also signed on as director. The year of release was 1958, and it was called *Touch of Evil.* Welles bulked up (more than usual, if that's possible) to play a corrupt cop who contrives to get Heston's wife (Janet Leigh) into a peck of trouble; basically she is tied to a bed and subjected to some really scary humiliations by a gang of goons led by Mercedes McCambridge, herein one of the most sadistic females in the history of the movies. Leigh is plucky, but you're never in doubt that her danger from this cackling harridan is real. Universal didn't know quite what to do with the finished product, so they released it on the bottom half of the bill, where it was discovered by a privileged few.

The film has felicities above and beyond its B picture budget, beginning with an opening sequence—some three minutes in length—that is one long, dazzling tracking shot that proceeds through a lot of elegant moments that are almost thrown away. The movie may have been based on a fairly trashy mystery novel, which Welles rewrote, but he still had plenty of directorial chops at that point. The movie's final edit was a studio job, dissatisfying to Welles, and forty years later (!) a restoration was made from his notes that, most significantly, removed the credits from the opening sequence and tightened the film up in many minor but significant ways. It is no longer a blighted film. It is a tight, tough, tricky movie, which is what it started out to be before everyone started futzing with it—a first-rate second-rate piece of work, perversely sexy and enjoyable. It was a harbinger of some things to come.

It was almost a decade later that *Bonnie and Clyde* came along. It was five years later that the first of the *Godfather* pictures arrived, and two years after that *Chinatown* appeared. There are never many game changers, but there don't have to be. Influence is not a matter of quantity; it is a question of impact.

In the sixties and seventies, film noirs continued to be made. They did not have their former impact and became a predictable part of the Hollywood mix—which was not so bad. Warren Beatty to the rescue. It was two young writers, Robert Benton and David Newman, who had the idea for *Bonnie and Clyde,* and they enlisted Beatty in it. Arthur Penn was reluctant, but Beatty is nothing if not persistent, and eventually Penn signed on.

In the making, the picture became both more brutal and

funnier than it had been in the beginning, but in its first release it was dimly, even fecklessly, received. Bosley Crowther thrice attacked it (ensuring his long-delayed demise as the *New York Times'* film critic). Pauline Kael rose to its defense, and many critics (me among them) re-reviewed it more enthusiastically than we had at first. It became a cause célèbre. Robert Towne did rewrites and Beatty fought for and won a re-release, which ensured Oscar nominations and eventual prosperity.

Penn recalled being utterly confident that he knew exactly how to direct the picture, how to mix the comedy and the bleakness of it and to create one of the great ensemble casts in film history. The hail-of-bullets ending is without parallel. It simply tears your heart out. There is an exchange of looks between Bonnie and Clyde as they acknowledge their demise that is sublime.

The book on which the *Godfather* movies are based was a mighty best seller, deservedly so. I remember gulping it down in one long sitting, with brief breaks to gobble down sandwiches. I remember thinking it was sort of trashy, yet I was helplessly in its thrall. The first film derived from it was made in 1972. There is Brando, suddenly paying attention in one of the most gripping character parts in movie history. In the second part (1974), Robert De Niro builds on what Brando laid out. (The third film is negligible.) Al Pacino is masterful as the son meant to escape the crime family—to be perhaps a senator—yet hopelessly, helplessly caught in its toils. The casting is ever perfect in these films. Here, Francis Coppola is a great director.

Most gangster films, of which formerly there were so many, are rather small in scale; Cagney, for example, was mostly seen running a fairly modest operation. An example: There is a still in which sharpshooters are aiming machine guns at him while he rather casually awaits their fire. This is not a guy, we think, running a major crime syndicate. It suited Hollywood in the 1930s to play organized crime as an anomaly—"shame of a nation" and all that, but not a genuine threat to our comity.

If not that, the gangsters were seen as "nut jobs" (in Cagney's phrase), people not just beyond the law, but beyond sanity as well.

The *Godfather* films changed the scale of organized crime in the movies. They presented crime as a business like any other. Its leaders spoke on equal terms with the leaders of other major enterprises. They dared to contemplate marriage with women of completely respectable families. They might think of the Ivy League for their children. They might, in a generation or two, think of leaving the life of crime entirely for the law or even politics. Yes, of course, "wet work" was sometimes still a regrettable necessity and handled with due dispatch.

I don't suppose any of us thought the pictures told the literal truth about how organized crime was actually organized. One imagined that Robert Duvall's calculating lawyer was more the norm than James Caan's hothead was—though that scarcely mattered. What still matters is the yearning to go straight on the part of Michael Corleone and the hopes his pop harbors for him in that regard. If there is tragedy in these films—and I think there is—it lies in the failure to shake off that yearning. One has to believe that the grandchildren have their summas from Harvard and their Wall Street partnerships and that the stories they hear of the criminal past sound like tall tales, something the dotty old codgers make up to verbally enliven an otherwise uneventful past.

Which brings us to *Chinatown* (1974), and something close to perfection in my estimation. You know the story. It is ostensibly about water—about bringing it in plenitude to California. But it is most significantly about incest—not the first movie on that topic. There was *Scarface,* in 1932, which everybody said right up front was about the forbidden topic. *Chinatown* has John Huston—so evil, so funny—in a crucial role; Jack Nicholson, so slippery, yet in his way so curiously honorable; and Faye Dunaway, utterly tragic when she finally cracks ("My daughter! My sister!").

The film is a writer's film—Robert Towne's, to be specific—
though the script contributions of the director, Roman Polan-
ski, are significant and absolutely first-rate; it was he who
insisted on the shattering ending, for example. But it was
Towne's story—not exactly an autobiography, but something
that captured the fragrance of the Southern California in which
he grew up. You can almost smell the sweetness of the land—or
is it corruption?—within the film's frames.

It was always an ambitious project—dreamed of as part of
a trilogy, tracing, besides water, land and air as avatars of the
unique ambience of Los Angeles. It wound up being carried out
in two movies—though the less said about the second one, the
better. Sequels, we know, are usually not very good. It is reasonably safe to say that never has a movie as good as *Chinatown*
been so ill served by its successor.

People chip away at *Chinatown*. They say its pace is draggy,
that the orange filters suggesting nostalgia are ludicrous. This
and that gnaws at both critics and ordinary viewers. I didn't
much like it on its initial release. Then one night I watched it in
a motel room and I fell for it: the intricacy of it, its odd blend
of wit and tragedy and, yes, Nicholson's nose job. (A hinge was
used, though sometimes the filmmakers lied about it and said
they did it for real.) Anyway, it dawned on me that it was a great
movie of a kind, mostly because of its attitude, which holds, as
Huston puts it, that we are capable—sometime, somewhere—
of doing anything, no matter how vile.

I like it that we live in a world that has at least one movie
that holds this truth as self-evident. Whenever I watch it, I am
hypnotized by its cruel ambivalences. "He was some kind of
man," Marlene Dietrich murmurs of Orson Welles in *Touch of
Evil*. We may say something similar of *Chinatown*. It is some
kind of movie.

31

Clint

I have written books and innumerable articles about Clint Eastwood and made several films about him, too. I have no similar relationship with anyone else in the movie industry. We have been friends more or less since we met in 1976. We have dined together, laughed together. And I cannot recall the exchange of any cross words. I have no objectivity about his work. I think he is a major American film artist.

I will say, however, that I was not immediately smitten by his work. I drifted into a screening of one of the *Fistful of Dollars* pictures in the mid-sixties and drifted more or less immediately out of it. I like the Leone pictures very much nowadays. Back then they were too harsh for me, too anti-traditional, and maybe too sardonic. It was the same way with *Dirty Harry,* in 1971. I wanted more gallantry from Clint. I missed entirely any sadness or loneliness. Jay Cocks, my reviewing colleague at

Time, did not. His wife, the actress Verna Bloom, had worked with Clint; they became friends, and one night the three of us had dinner together. I was astonished to find Clint easy and quiet, a listener rather than a talker. I liked the man before I began to appreciate the actor. We took to calling one another when he was in New York or I was in Los Angeles, and that went nicely. Though he was more politically conservative than I was, he was on social issues as liberal as any of my other friends.

He made some okay movies in the early seventies—nothing astonishing, but solid and interesting. I thought *The Outlaw Josey Wales* (1976) was a wonderfully spacious movie, recounting Josey's return from bitterness to a new appreciation of community. Clint took over direction of the movie after a few unhappy weeks—he said it was the hardest professional decision he ever made—and the picture had grace and ease (without sacrificing a certain harshness). It marked a turning point for him. Some years later, he casually remarked to me that he thought *Josey* was every bit as good as *Unforgiven,* the picture that, of course, marked his annunciation to a more knowing audience. It was just, he said, that people like his bête noire, Pauline Kael, were not expecting it—indeed, didn't think he had so thoughtful a film in him.

He had a point. He also had the habit of inconsistency in those days. He followed *Josey* with *The Gauntlet,* for heaven's sake. He thereafter did some movies that were decently ambitious—promising—but not quite, I think, what he hoped for them to be. He was a self-taught director, learning by instinct. An indicator of that: His worst picture, *The Rookie,* preceded his best (to date), *Unforgiven,* then a lot of so-so work before he began the very good run of films that started with *Mystic River,* in 2003.

Since then, not all of his films—we'll come to some of them later—have been hits, but all of them have been aspiring. Mortality dogs his heels, as it does all of us who are in our eighties. It pretty much takes a year to make a movie, and how many years are there—even if you are the fittest man on the planet? He made *Jersey Boys* simply because he wanted to have a musical in his résumé. The challenge, you know.

Clint is a dedicated worker. There have been years in which he made two movies. He does not "develop" films. He secures them in the open market, and there are times, he says, when there is not much around and he takes what he can find there, for better or worse—though in recent years he has been more careful in his choices. He has a somewhat belated sense of his own importance as a filmmaker—not that that veers toward self-importance. Sometimes you wonder what he sees in this or that project, but they tend to come out pretty well. There is an ease about him, a lack of pretense, that is one of his most attractive characteristics.

32

Belle de Jour

Catherine Deneuve is naked to the waist, her perfect breasts threatened with flogging while she awaits her punishment without affect—or so it seems. She shows no fear. No writhing. It has been argued that she may be a virgin. I rather doubt it; I think it more likely that she is at this early moment in *Belle de Jour* (1967) merely frigid. In any case, she was instructed by the director, Luis Buñuel, not to act in any way in the movie, and she did not—brilliantly. Later she is recruited to be the title character of the film, working only in the afternoons and returning at night to her safe, sane and, one suspects, not very interesting home and husband.

Belle de Jour is one of the most beautiful and mysterious movies ever made—elegant, handsome, enigmatic, in some sense inexplicable. As the film moves along (in great beauty, let it be said), it does not unravel itself (not fully, at least). It is ostensibly clear and ultimately opaque. It is—yes—surreal.

The film makes clear that Buñuel is one of the great direc-tors. His filmography, which includes *The Discreet Charm of the Bourgeoisie* and *That Obscure Object of Desire* among so many other great films, is a major one. And no one else has had the wit to make a movie in which the guests at a dinner party refuse to leave.

33

The Apu Trilogy

These films were made in the 1950s by the Indian filmmaker
Satyajit Ray. They have about them great simplicity and a
greater power than we first noticed, as they trace the rise of the
boy Apu from childhood to (fairly) young manhood. There are
deaths in them and a degree of other misery, though in the end
things come out all right, relatively speaking.

They also contain the danger that "humanistic" cinema is
always freighted with. There is a certain predictability: birth,
death, big topics oversimplified and sometimes rather tiresome.
In the early 1990s, a friend of mine named Gilbert Cates was
producing the Academy Awards telecasts, and for several years
I produced the little tributes to the winners of the honorary
Oscars, including one in 1991 for Ray. There were no air-worthy
prints of his work in India or the United States; they were
located in Great Britain, where—one should have known—

they had the year before had a Ray season complete with gorgeous prints, in prime time, incidentally. There is something to be said for having a movie culture—that is, a capacity to pay heed to minority tastes.

Coming upon the Apu Trilogy anew, I was struck by the lasting power of its strong, simple imagery and by the cumulative power of the three films (*Panther Panchali,* in 1955; *Aparajito,* 1956; and *Apur Sansar,* 1959). You really have to see them back-to-back-to-back, which is difficult to do. They truly constitute an epic, ranging as they do over two decades and through both city and village life in modern India. They reflect as well the most basic and tender emotions in a patient way. Most important, all three films speak indirectly to a single theme: the ineffectuality of the male in a colonial and postcolonial society.

The trilogy begins with a portrait of Apu, an adorably curious and eager boy in an agricultural village, undaunted by the tragedies that surround him, which include the death of his young sister and the passing of his father when they move to the city. Apu acquires a teacher-mentor and eventually goes to college, though a certain languidness overtakes him—there are so few opportunities for young men, and the possibilities for corruption abound. He finds happiness in an arranged marriage (of all things), but his wife dies and he surrenders to bitterness, in the process abandoning his son (and the novel on which he is working). He eventually recovers, though the conclusion of this work is ambiguous. One thinks Apu, chastened by the bitter experiences he has undergone, is now settling for a rather bland domesticity, for making a living like the rest of us, instead of the life that was occasionally promised by the trilogy.

It is not a tragedy. Neither is it a study in more than a muted and occasional bliss. It is, well, just "life," I guess. And I can't think why the trilogy haunts me as it does. I suppose it's because there are so few movies like it—the flow of life in its ordinariness (and occasional alarms). It is everything as we experience it, not melodramatized.

I have to say that it is an odd work for me to care so greatly about. I am, I suppose, Eurocentric in my taste for movies from abroad (as this book probably proves). There are simply more cultural congruities between Americans and Europeans than there are between us and, for instance, the Indians. You have to work harder, on the whole, to appreciate their nuances. That said, there is a great clarity to the Apu Trilogy, a simplifying force, if you will, that grants it an uncommon grace. Ray could sometimes dither (he made some thirty films, not all of them masterpieces), but his is a great body of work.

34

Fellini

Pirandello is evoked. Existentialism is mentioned. And, naturally, "the silence of God." Check, check and check again, when it comes to Fellini.

But what about show business, of all humble things? Or perhaps we should call it "low business"—the realm of clowns and magicians, chorus girls and lecherous impresarios, working the provinces, the less salubrious big-city music halls, on rare occasions, from childhood on lured, tempted and occasionally dismayed the great director. They were the subject of his first film (*Variety Lights,* co-directed with Alberto Lattuada), and they are a crucial element in the last of his films to be released in the United States, *Intervista.* Whether he touches upon it only briefly or muses upon it at length, low business has never been absent for very long from the thoughts of Federico Fellini. It is the topic of his masterpiece, *8½* (1963).

It is an oddity of Fellini's filmography that he so often makes pictures about this or that aspect of show business and that the critical commentary about it so infrequently alludes directly to it. The critics are always chasing various forms of big think in his work. But consider: His first great success, *La Dolce Vita* (1960), was about the Roman demimonde and its relationship to, among other things, low-level journalism. (It also contributed an immortal word to the language—*paparazzo*—the name of a character engaged in scuzzy journalism, the plural of which is *paparazzi*.) There are others, of course, beginning with his very first film and including the delightful *I Vitelloni* (1953), which is about the *fumetti,* photographic comic strips, not to mention *La Strada* (1954). And let us not forget *And the Ship Sails On* and the late-in-life *Ginger and Fred,* which has Mastroianni and Giulietta Masina as a retired dance team brought back for one of those god-awful nostalgia TV shows (she wants to do it, he doesn't), which is, I think (I'm in the minority here), sad and funny and curiously moving in its minor way.

There are those who are not susceptible to Fellini's charms. They think he's the avatar of cheesy sentiment. They are being too stern with him. *8½,* for example, is a film in which fantasy and reality get into an interesting muddle. Mastroianni is Guido, a blocked director, committed to a film's start date and flat out of ideas for it. The set is built, the cast is ready, but the problem, he thinks, is that the medium cannot contain his vast vision and Guido will not again compromise that vision, put on just another "show," crowd-pleasing though it will probably be. He cancels the shoot.

And then, out of the shadows of the set, a magician appears, ready to work, and the clowns parade out. Guido tentatively starts sorting them all out. Others whom we have met during Guido's dreams and reveries amble into view as well, to be shaped into some semblance of art. Among the voice-over lines we hear: "Life is a holiday; let us live it together."

In other words, forget the mighty personal statement. Settle for putting on a show, albeit one that looks as though it will have a big finish after all—brassy, sentimental, full of good feelings. I can see why this looks like a compromise to some people. Sure. Possibly. Then again, an awful lot of more aspiring movies have come to a lot less. I like the message of *8½*. A lot of the time, less is more; and a lot of the time, more is just terrible. There is a lot of posturing in this film, a lot of silliness too, but it keeps delighting. I want masterpieces as much as the next guy, but they are rare—as rare as first-rate entertainments.

35

Strange Loves

A ny movie that is set in large measure at Burpelson Air Force Base, where Sterling Hayden is defending his vital bodily fluids, cannot be ignored. Indeed, *Dr. Strangelove* is the 1964 comic masterpiece from Stanley Kubrick, in which the world comes to a screeching halt as Peter Sellers, playing three roles, patiently explains to his Russian commander-in-chief counterpart that one of the nut jobs under his command "went and did a silly thing," consisting of setting off a nuclear strike that cannot be called back. Strangelove himself (another Sellers role), his wartime activities grand now that he has switched sides, cannot prevent his arm from flying up in the Nazi salute. This is one of the rare American comedies that is about something more than moon, June and romance.

George C. Scott as General Buck Turgidson explains that we will get our hair mussed in an atomic exchange, but with casualties in the acceptable twenty-million range. If you think that's funny, then this is the movie for you. I do. Its last image is of a lone airplane flying into oblivion while a song plays "Somewhere we'll meet again, don't know where, don't know when."

What I like best about *Dr. Strangelove* is the way it stays relevant. As I write, it is precisely fifty years old, and more than most movies—especially movies with a "topical" bent—it has not aged. The events depicted could still happen pretty much as they do on the screen. It is still wildly funny and wildly terrifying. It's as Howard Hawks once said, "The great trouble is people trying to be funny. If they don't try to be funny, then they are funny." To which, "Amen." These people are completely sober. There is not a moment when they signal they are just kidding. This is probably because Kubrick, though one of the most intelligent men I've ever met, never in my hearing cracked a joke. He was all intensity—ferociously so. No one on a Kubrick movie was ever allowed to fool around. People around the movie game were sometimes dubious about him. Those who actually made movies were awed by him; those who reviewed them or otherwise theorized about them often had their doubts. He seemed not to have any idea how funny he was.

The Monty Python troupe was definitely trying to be funny as it set forth in pursuit of *Monty Python and the Holy Grail* in 1975. And they were. The film was produced on an absurdly low budget, which is why they clopped along with coconut shells imitating the sound of horses' hooves. There was no budget for actual horses, and no time for, shall we say, the nuances of plotting. (At the press screening in New York, they gave out the shells as souvenirs, which my children and I proudly bore away with us at the end of the show.) They were an extremely merry group and totally without pretense, which was the best thing about them. They just sort of banged along their loose plot line, advising us to "look on the bright side of life" (as they did in the very good sequel *Life of Brian*, which ends with the boys crucified, but game as ever. That was the thing about the lads: They just didn't give a damn. I got into modest trouble with William F. Buckley on that one. I saw no reason why religion was not fair game for satire. He begged to differ. Snarled to differ, actually. A nice little dustup).

But maybe we need to make a serious point here. This is actually one of the bravest films I write about in this book. If you cannot make a movie sending up religion, you don't really have a free screen. Everything has to be fair game in the movies—as it is in all the other arts. This film—which is not as flat-out funny as *Grail*—claims that right (pomposity coming here) for the screen. It is, to my knowledge, the only movie to do so. We obviously live in a secularizing age, which proceeds apace. I haven't seen *Grail* since it was released. I don't know if I'd still think it was funny or challenging or whatever. But that's not the point. The point is that it got made, a small miracle.

Let's make a couple of great leaps forward to two movies in the spirit of these pictures. In 1984: *This Is Spinal Tap*. You have got to love a movie in which the guitar amps go to 11, which is, of course, one more than normal. Rob Reiner's "mockumentary" maintains that standard consistently. It's all wretched excess, perfectly sustained. There's even a representation of Stonehenge in miniature, which is sublimely stupid. I suppose it's sketch comedy (though there is a plot of sorts, something about the band breaking up), but the point of the exercise is simply to be giddy, at which it succeeds brilliantly. It just keeps rolling deliriously along, its parodies of the music and the attitudes of the band remarkably deft amid the hubbub. There are so few laggardly moments, so few miscues.

Four years later, along came *A Fish Called Wanda*. It's a caper comedy that turns on the communication skills of a man with a really bad stutter. Need I say more? The film was directed by Charles Crichton, a routine operative, who rose to something like greatness on this occasion. The movie has pace and sass, good jokes and nice situations—in short, a laff riot. But in its way it's rather an intricate piece, which includes a psycho thriller, erotic folderol and plenty of bad luck all around, before everyone flies off to paradise. The performances by Jamie Lee Curtis (up out of horror films), Kevin Kline (up out of nowhere) and John Cleese (a onetime Python) are superb, though I think the acting prize must go to Michael Palin, stammering his way to glory. The whole thing is a beautiful piece of work—one of those comedies that does not make any important miscues, and which is very rare and treasurable.

36

___

Getting Started, or,
I Thought You'd Never Ask

I began reviewing movies in 1965, as I believe I said earlier, more or less by accident. I was hanging around the little section devoted to reviews—books, plays, etc.—at *Life* when its editor, Dave Scherman, always semi-short of copy, said he needed a movie review pretty quick. I said sure, why not. The movie I chose was called *Sammy Going South,* about a little boy trekking from one end of Africa to the other. It was a minor, agreeable little film. I wrote my review, I was rewarded at the going rate ($300) and the next week Davey asked me to do another. That was in the spring. By the end of summer I was the lead movie critic (I was even given a contract), and I hung on there until the magazine folded, in 1972. They had just paid me rather generously (they had just signed me for a new year) and I figured I would find something to do by the time I ran through that money. A few days later, Henry Grunwald, *Time*'s managing editor, called and asked me to move over there, which I happily did. I was making my first TV series, and I had to work pretty hard for a few months, but I had a lot of energy in those days, and it worked out. Jay Cocks had the *Time* job, but he was welcoming and thinking of doing some other things anyway. We shared the space for a while. Then Jay moved on to screenwriting, while I stayed and stayed, enjoying the work.

I pretty much learned on the job, which I did respectably. I'm still doing it, though for another place nowadays, as I said. If nothing else, it's a habit of which I've never tired. Truth to tell, it's easy work. Counting portal to portal, it takes only maybe three hours to see a movie (a little longer if you stop for lunch) and a similar amount of time to write the review. It's a lot easier than slogging through a book and not necessarily less stimulating. Additionally, there's plenty of time left over to write books and make television programs.

When I began reviewing in 1965, the heat was with films from abroad. There were large bodies of work building there (we've mentioned quite a few of them already) and they were quite stirring. Even *Life* wanted to pay attention to Bergman and other foreign directors. We paid due heed to American films, naturally, but for me it was marvelous to write about the films from foreign climes. Looking back, I am somewhat surprised by the amount of space we devoted to the likes of *Blow-Up, My Night at Maud's* and *The Red and the White.* I am even more surprised that no one around *Life* objected to this bias. After all, it was not exactly *Partisan Review.* But it was desperately trying to reinvent itself just prior to its demise, and management wasn't paying all that much attention to the review section. We sort of stood out by being so la-di-da. People noticed, and that redounded to our credit—lucky us. The grumbles from the bosses were few and far between. Lucky me.

I want here to speak of the modern-day auteurs: Woody Allen, Scorsese, Spielberg, Eastwood (again). They have dominated our screens for a very long time. They remain productive, and they remain expert. They range in age from their sixties into their eighties, and they are still among our finest filmmakers. I can see no great falling off in their skills. I will start with Woody arbitrarily and move on to the others in subsequent chapters.

By 1977 Woody Allen had made five movies, most of them genial and witty and all of them increasingly sophisticated structurally and technically. The world appeared to be his oyster—except, of course, to him. He let it be known that he was unhappy at not being Ingmar Bergman. People suspected him of a false modesty that was not entirely unattractive, yet not entirely attractive, either. I met him on a short-lived television program where he did occasional comic monologues and I reviewed books.

I went a few times to a comedy club in Greenwich Village where I enjoyed his work. At some point we started having dinners and lunches on an occasional basis. It was clear to me, and by no means to me alone, that Woody had a kind of genius— for jokes. Good jokes. Before he was out of high school, he was taking the subway to Manhattan, writing jokes as he went— dozens, hundreds of them. Still in his teens, he was selling them and then venturing into stand-up on TV and so on, beginning the career that is now familiar to us.

This business about his genius for jokes is, I think, worth pausing over. It is so easy for him. He has told me that he can work up a monologue while he's standing in the shower. Therefore, he doesn't value this gift. Art—and there is an art to comedy—should be effortful, painful. Ease betokens the casual. Did Bergman take his work lightly? Doubtful. Allen is trapped by his gift. I devoutly wish he could enjoy it more than he appears to. Maybe he does, in the recesses of his soul, but he's never going to admit it in public.

Over the years, I made a television show about him and wrote a book based on the interview I did for that program. I even appeared in court on his behalf, in some action I cannot entirely recall. We had mutual friends, and the meals continued to be agreeable. After I moved to Los Angeles, we continued to stay in touch, as we still do. He is an intelligent, sober companion, and I do not believe—have never believed—any of the preposterous things that have been said about him by Mia Farrow and others.

Which takes me well beyond 1977 and *Annie Hall*, which was a huge hit—at least by Allen's standards. It won four Academy Awards, including best picture, best director, best screenplay and best actress for Diane Keaton. The fact that its original title, "Anhedonia," was changed to the one under which it was released certainly helped its cause. It was a charming movie, though scarcely an overpowering one. It holds up nicely. It represents a considerable step forward in his filmmaking skills.

It is not, however, one of my favorite Woody Allen films, and I suspect it is not one of his, either. It seems to me too casual, less aspiring, than his best work. What I don't think it predicted was his fecundity—virtually a movie per year every year since—or the ambition of many of those pictures. I don't believe any American director has made as many films as he has (excepting, perhaps, the dimmest Hollywood hacks of the studio days), or so many that have their merits. He's had his failures—inevitable, working at his pace—but it seems to me that his is one of the great careers in modern American film. It has a scale that is not epic. His films, to be sure, are modest, not overwhelming. But still, I am told by one of his associates that they never fail commercially, which is in itself remarkable, given the range and ambition of the topics he has taken up—a subject not much discussed by the critics.

At the time *Zelig* was released, in 1983, all the talk was of the very demanding work Allen and his crew did on the film to assure that it achieved an authentic antique cast as it records the history of a nonentity who yet contrives to be present at many of the twentieth century's most significant moments. In this it succeeded brilliantly, but all the attention came at the expense of the picture's larger meaning, at least at the time. The truth is that Zelig was (unknowingly) a fascist, rescued at the last minute from very dire circumstances. It is a movie at once scary and hilarious and one that Allen, for once, thinks well of, as he should. To most people it's all about its superb trick, not about its very powerful message, which is, among other things, about how close we can come to being both innocent and ugly at the same time, how, indeed, they are aspects of the same all too human impulse.

The Purple Rose of Cairo (1985) is, I think, a wonderfully mixed bag. It is, at least nominally, a comedy—a good one—but it is also a rather serious film in its way. Cecilia (Mia Farrow) lives in a fantastic cinematic world—all white telephones and such—and Gil (Jeff Daniels) is a movie star, making a super-silly film that bears the same title as this movie. They form a connection, and for a time her bleak life is saved by film fantasies in which she lives virtually daily. Except that at some point she realizes that she must choose between delight and reality. She opts for the latter. As Woody puts it, "Some instinct in her tells her that she's got to exist in the real world, because to exist in the fantasy world is psychosis." He adds: "By choosing the real world, which we all must do, she is inevitably crushed by it, as we all inevitably are."

Doesn't sound exactly hilarious, does it? But this is a movie in which Woody hides his hand expertly. It is funny—until it's not. He is very firm on this point: You simply cannot live sanely within fantasy. *Purple Rose* is among the most exquisitely judged of Woody's films. It veers neither too far toward satire nor toward the tragic. Its tone is perhaps best stated as wryly compassionate—the proportion of magic to realism in haunting balance.

Radio Days (1987) at first glance looks to be a slight little movie. It is about—well—radio days, that comparatively brief period when radio was a glamorous enterprise in New York, and its curiously anonymous "stars" were the subjects of breathless profiles, which had them whisked here and there by care-fully timed taxis as they fulfilled their many assignments on the airwaves. They led seemingly giddy lives, and the film has a gently busy, yet minor, air. We need not be taken in by that. It is, I believe, one of Woody's most accomplished films. There is, to begin with, the disparity between the way these people look—unprepossessing—and the way they sound when they are acting before the microphones, with only a ricky-ticky orchestra and a sound effects man supporting their often gran-diose work. It's just inherently funny. But it's more than that. *Radio Days* is a marvelous conceit, unlike any other movie. At the end of the film, the radio people head to the roof to see in the new year and see out the old. The electric signs of Broadway stretch out before them; optimism is in the air. The moment passes, and Wallace Shawn, one of the radio stars, reflects on the ephemeral nature not just of radio but—this being a Woody Allen film—of existence. It's a brief, lightly managed moment, but the film's heart and meaning are contained in it. This is the way worlds end, with a whisper. Not a word is said about televi-sion being just around the corner, or about the wreckers' balls transforming Times Square into something unrecognizable, or about changes in fashion, rendering Woody's more gracious New York an historical artifact. "I just wanted to illustrate, in an entertaining way, that there's no God," Woody said to me one time. It is probably my favorite sentence of his. He set himself a difficult—no, impossible—task. Yet it is here accomplished.

Deconstructing Harry (1997) is possibly Woody's most shock-ing movie. In its language alone, it's utterly different from any-thing he's ever done—a mad barrage of obscenities reflecting, I think, the impotent rage Woody felt at a time when he was engaged in a brutal custody fight with Mia Farrow—complete with charges that he had sexually abused their daughter (a nasty business that recurred in 2014). The film is about a trip Woody's Harry Block (the name has a certain resonance) undertakes with a friend to drive to a college he once attended to receive some academic honor. The friend dies along the way. It is the most charmless movie Woody has ever made—deliberately so, of course. It simply refuses to insinuate itself with the audience, which was happy to oblige with its indifference. There was some bleak wit in the film—some things never change—and Woody felt that it represented a moment when his audience had to make a choice about him: They could indulge his dark whims or they could take their leave of him. They were nice about it, he thinks (no animus, no anger on the part of either party to their unspoken agreement), and they could in the future reconstitute their arrangement. But he had to go his own way when the spirit moved him.

The obvious thing to be said about these movies is that they are extremely disparate—a charming fantasy, a larkish memory piece, a flat-out comedy, a very sober and aspiring film. It seems to me that critically, Woody does not get enough credit for the extraordinary range of topics he takes up—perhaps because he does not himself allude to it. He simply gets on with the ideas that occur to him. He speaks of finding scripts and ideas for them in drawers in half-finished form and returning to them as ideas for finishing them come to him. It is one source of his fecundity, which does not seem remarkable to him—only to us.

Work rhythms are a mystery and carry no moral or aesthetic weight. It's all right with me if the reader chooses one or the other of these films as his best. But I can't quite leave him like that. In 1994, he made *Bullets Over Broadway,* which seems to me remarkable because it is a kind of reversion. It just means to be funny, which it gloriously is—the story of people putting on a show, with Chazz Palminteri brilliantly playing a gangster named Cheech, who has a gift for writing plays, and John Cusack as a playwright who has all the desire and none of the talent for his craft. It's gorgeously funny, beautifully gagged and, come to think of it, has a point, one that's ever on Woody's mind: that our lives are always ruled, more than we care to admit, by chance. Cheech is an artist who has no self-consciousness. He is simply born with talent, which starts to leak out as a play begins to take shape in rehearsal. He also has the savagery to defend to the death what is increasingly his creation. This film is proof that Woody can just be funny when he wants to be.

He is obviously a protean figure. He is one who is generally underestimated by a public that first met him as a star and director of comic productions and is, I think, reluctant to abandon that comfortable identification. There is a dubiety about him as a serious filmmaker, which needs to be abandoned. He has long since earned the right to succeed (and fail) on a higher plane when the spirit so moves him. It has been an amazing career, by no means finished, and his glum sense that he has mostly failed to make the great films he set out to make needs to be taken with a grain of salt. So he is not Bergman—who is?

37

The Wrath of God— Or Is It His Silence?

In 1972 there came along a movie called *Aguirre, the Wrath of God,* directed by Werner Herzog. It is set in the wilds of South America, and it stars Klaus Kinski, who was, so they say, kept on the location under threat of murder by the director. It is one of the most astonishing movies ever made. Essentially, it is about being up the Amazon without a paddle—and, eventually, without sanity.

It's an important film because there were not many before it that were essays in pure insanity. Even after it, there are only a few. Significantly, this one made it all right even to take up the topic in the movies. Aguirre and his little band are simply lusting after gold, which is supposed to be located in El Dorado. On their raft they float toward it, beset by marauding Indians, disease, hunger and, finally, murder, madness and a troop of monkeys. It ends, inevitably, in chaos (as we always knew it must). It is, quite frankly, a horror show, though occasionally it is also a very, very dark comedy. It is an allegory—or is it a metaphor? For me, it's a certifiable great work.

But, putting it mildly, it is not everyone's dish of tea. As the years wear on, it comes to seem more important than we perhaps realized. It opens doors to the possible—though only for the brave of heart. It suggests that there are now no topics that are necessarily beyond the reach of the movies.

I don't imagine that it is much seen today, or "liked." But oh, those monkeys! and the sheer irrationality they represent—the sheer damn chaos that lies at the heart of all human enterprise. No mere movie so unblinkingly makes this point. You must see it, at your peril.

38

Marty

I did not care for *Mean Streets* when it first appeared in 1973. It seemed to me clumsy, awkward—somehow unpersuasive. In this opinion I was virtually alone. I must confess: I still don't like the film. Over the years I have made my peace with it—especially with Robert De Niro's marvelously wacky performance. And, of course, Marty Scorsese has fulfilled in the four decades since all the promise others saw in him.

I wrote a book about him and made a film about him and have enjoyed the pleasure of his company on many occasions. One time we discussed this issue. We came to the conclusion that I was too much the Midwesterner, he the New Yorker, for us ever to have a meeting of the minds about *Mean Streets*. Which raises the question of why I admire so many other pictures in his filmography.

Official acknowledgment of his gifts was a long time coming. There seemed a possibility that he might, like Hawks and Hitchcock and Raoul Walsh, never receive an Academy Award. That was an absurdity after he had made *Taxi Driver, Raging Bull, Goodfellas* and *The King of Comedy.* I suppose it had something to do with the violence of these films. They were so painful. (And not necessarily hugely profitable.) They were not, on the whole, date movies—putting it mildly. But everyone noticed their expertise. How could you not?

Of this group of movies, I think *Raging Bull* (1980) and *Taxi Driver* (1976) are the masterpieces. The first asks no quarter, and gives none, as it recounts the career of Jake LaMotta, played brilliantly by De Niro. It opens with yelling between him and his mother and ends with the boxer quietly reciting the "I coulda been a contender" speech from *On the Waterfront* in his nightclub act. At the very least, it is the most brutal boxing picture ever made. The audience flinches and winces as it is taken through Jake's career in the ring. I love the sprays of sweat and blood in the boxing arena. No fight film has ever been so intimately detailed, and none has asked more of its star.

But in a way, boxing is only the context of this picture. In my conversations about it with Scorsese, he has suggested that it is really about a man seeking grace without fully realizing that is his quest. He is, at best, stumbling, half-blindly, toward that goal. Scorsese thinks that if LaMotta attains some recognition of his humanity (which he does in time), that will be victory enough for him, all he can hope for—not that he ever fully articulates that aim. That is for us, watching, to impute to him—which we do painfully. I do not know of any movie that pulls us down this path in such dread. I think it is a great work.

So is *Taxi Driver,* powered by Travis Bickle's terrible anger and incomprehension. He's played by De Niro, who, to begin with, doesn't know that Cybill Shepherd is toying with him. He thinks perhaps he may aspire to her, which is, of course, a mad idea, plausible only to a man who is probably as innocent as he is crazy. And then there is Jodie Foster, in a performance that seems almost unconscious (or uncalculated) in that she says things and does things that seem so unplanned, so shocking, really. There is no sentiment in her work. This child-woman has no pity. The story in some sense comes out all right—that is to say that some kind of "happy" ending is arrived at (in the sense that not everyone ends up dead or maimed) and Travis ends up a "hero" in the world's eyes.

But the film does not really end. Here is Travis in his cab, still on his rounds, but uncured. He is a time bomb still ticking, ready to explode. Here is the city, still essentially rain-washed and malevolent, ready to extract its price from him—from anyone—who dares let down his guard in its presence. The center of the film, the half-improvised scene in which Travis challenges himself in a mirror, is a masterpiece of paranoia and of split personality—not uncommon movie topics—but, in effect, shot in a broom closet, which intensifies its terror (and its weird humor) to unbearable levels. This movie addresses things movies do not ordinarily speak about, and it achieves levels of nuttiness few achieve. I don't need to see it again, because it is indelibly etched on my brain—broad strokes and dreadful details both. It is perhaps the most terrifying great movie ever.

There are other movies in the Scorsese canon that are nearly as good—*Goodfellas* (1990), for example, which takes its protagonist on the long path to the Witness Protection Program in an odd and witty way. In *The King of Comedy* (1982), De Niro is Rupert Pupkin, a man desperate for fame and, by God, achieving it—he kidnaps a talk show host, Jerry Lewis, the ransom being an appearance on Lewis's show. The farcical elements in the film are spun brilliantly (who says Scorsese can't be funny when he feels like it?), and the eerie confidence of De Niro's playing is masterly. Written by movie critic Paul D. Zimmerman, the film has a mad self-confidence that never falters. It also has an element of terror that is held in check but is more than palpable. It's a haunting film, the best part of which is that Rupert—God help us all—succeeds in becoming a star. It's one of the more original comedies of recent times. One wonders what a sequel would bring.

Scorsese falters, of course—every director does. As I was writing this, he brought forth *The Wolf of Wall Street,* which I thought was both lame and frenzied. But we are always talking here about bodies of work, and I think we need to speak of his range, which is far larger than we think. His topic is largely the criminal class—but he has given us *The Age of Innocence* and *The Aviator,* too. One of the things I most respect about him (and the other directors we are discussing) is the expanse of his ambition, his willingness to come a cropper. Sure, there is room for comedy specialists and all the other genre operatives, too. But a willingness to fall flat on your face from time to time is vital. Not too often, of course. But some movies have to grow—sometimes for years—before they attain their true stature. And Marty is a director capable of making movies of that kind. Woody Allen famously said that mostly a career is about showing up ready to work on cockamamie projects. If you don't, you just go stale. Ambition is everything—well, almost everything. I mean, surely we don't judge Spielberg by *1941,* do we?

39

Earning It, or, Spielberg's Way

Steven Spielberg is, or was, a prodigy. The story of how he left the Universal Studios tour and wandered the lot for a summer, making people think he was an employee, is part of his legend. So is the astonishing fact that he began directing features when he was only twenty-four years old. There are far fewer prodigies in the movie business than we think there are, and fewer still who succeed so spectacularly at such a tender age.

He was making TV movies when he was only twenty-three, and he made his first feature, the admirable *Duel*, in 1971—a television movie that was transformed into a feature release in 1973, when he was twenty-six. A year later he made *The Sugarland Express*, which was his first official feature release. By that time he had made nine TV episodes and was zeroing in on *Jaws*. I do not think there is any filmography to match this one for productivity in its early years.

Steven is an agreeable man who keeps what must be a powerful energy in check. He drives (or drove) his kids to school, often left work early in order to spend time with his family and, in my many conversations with him, never has made me feel rushed or hurried.

It was *Jaws,* in 1975, that made him rich and famous, though it was a close call. As we all know, the shark kept sinking, and lots of other things went wrong. There was talk of canceling the whole enterprise. But, obviously, they did not. Years later, when the American Film Institute named its hundred best movies, *Jaws* was one of six Spielberg films on the list.

Taking nothing away from *Close Encounters of the Third Kind* (1977), the most significant subtext of which was the need to communicate (if we could do it with aliens, why couldn't we do it with each other?), it seems to me that Spielberg's first unquestionable masterpiece is *E.T. the Extra-Terrestrial* (1982). It is the ultimate of Spielberg's several "lost boy" films—except, of course, the lost boy is a cute alien desperate to return from Earth to his faraway planet, abetted in that aim by the good-natured youngsters from Earth but hindered in that desire by clumsy (grown-up) scientists who want to "study" him. I honestly think the moment when the kids on their bicycles achieve liftoff in their quest to return E.T. to the place where he belongs is one of the truly wonderful moments of cinema. (John Williams's magnificent scoring of the sequence is an incalculable aid to it.)

I want to pause here to make explicit what has probably been implicit throughout this book: I believe in popular cinema, probably more so than I do in "art" cinema. Obviously, there is room for both kinds of expression in film, and I think I've given a fair shake to them both herein. But it seems to me that sequences like the liftoff in *E.T.* are every bit as rare as, say, the conversations (or their lack) in *Persona.* They come from the same inexplicable place in the artistic spirit and run similar risks of failure. The flight sequence could have been only so-

so. Happily, it works beautifully. But the point is this: It has an infectiousness, a joyousness, that more aspiring efforts do not attain. We appreciate the latter, and we can analyze them forever, but something like *E.T.* just takes us over. I never see it without misting up over it. I don't know what's operating there, but I'm pretty sure it's mostly instinct rather than close calculation. For all his other achievements, Spielberg himself never again soared to this height, in my view.

He was looking for something else. Movies like this one, he has said, carried a slight air of popcorn about them. He is perhaps being overly modest, but I'm persuaded by his argument that he was liberated for his other major works by relative failures. "I don't think I could have made *Schindler's List* or *Empire of the Sun* without *The Color Purple*," Spielberg has said. "I didn't have the maturity, the craft, and the emotional information to acquit the Holocaust in an honorable way without bringing shame to the memory of the survivors."

Purple (1985), which tells the life story of a poor African American woman, does not soar in any of the typical Spielbergian ways. It is quite grim and more than occasionally plodding. But one takes his meaning. It never sells out to his instinctive impulses for adventure or comedy—for relief of some sort. It is, I think, a movie that in some sense we owed him. Call it, perhaps, a rite of passage that he more or less forced us to take with him. It paid immediate dividends in the form of a very good but slightly neglected movie, *Empire of the Sun* (1987). Based on a book by J. G. Ballard, with a script by Tom Stoppard, no less, it is another lost-boy story, part factual, part fictional, in which a boy, the excellent Christian Bale as Jim, becomes separated from his family as World War II breaks out in Asia and stumbles his way to maturity, with the significant help of John Malkovich. It is a handsomely realized film, and it essentially ends with one of Spielberg's finest sequences, when Jim wanders into a stadium filled with the detritus of his past life: Biedermeier and Josef Hoffmann furniture, cheval glass, Rolls-

Royce cars, all the vestiges of a lost empire—the refuse, now useless, of a society that did not see the war coming. You get the impression that Jim is prematurely aged (Spielberg stressed that his eyes are those of an old man) and that he will not stay long in this place, that he will become what Ballard became—a permanently rootless wanderer on this earth. The film presses as close to real darkness as Spielberg allowed himself to come in those days. It was not a commercial success, but he would say, correctly, that it was the first film he had made solely to satisfy himself, which means it was of the highest importance in his career.

Let's talk about the little girl in the red coat, the most controversial shot (or short sequence) that Steven Spielberg ever made. It appears in *Schindler's List* (1993). Aside from a short opening sequence of a flickering candle, it is the only touch of color in this black-and-white film. It was criticized as a shameless touch of show business in an otherwise austere, not to say bleak, masterpiece. Spielberg's critics correctly admired the film, which is one of the two or three best he ever made, but this scene seemed to be a blot on Spielberg's record.

It didn't bother me. What do a few seconds of screen time matter in a film as powerful as this one? Virtually every movie contains some mistakes, although you try to keep them to a minimum. Spielberg kept his own counsel about the shot, defending it by saying it was fully calculated, fully meant. He explained that he simply wanted to say that the Holocaust was as obvious as a little girl in a colored coat, that people in vast numbers knew about it and could not blink it away. She was there, indelibly. By extension (I am imputing this to him), far from being a mistake, this little sequence was symbolically close to being the heart of his film's meaning. I suppose the point is arguable.

Directors do such things. It is what their art is about. You can say it is showbizzy, but I do not believe that was his intent. To think otherwise is to call into question his integrity, and in my years of knowing him I have never had any reason to question his integrity. The fact that he has made so many lark-ish movies counts against him, I suppose, for some critics, but even those movies are made with great seriousness of purpose. We have to concede him this shot, its plainness of purpose, its strength.

It was five years later that Spielberg fulfilled a long-standing promise to his father and made a movie about Americans in World War II. In the interim, he had, I think, flagged a bit, making only two movies of his own. The notion of doing a war film still nagged at him, and one day a script was deliv-ered simultaneously to him and to Tom Hanks; by the end of that day they had both committed to *Saving Private Ryan*. His father would grumble about it a little—it was not a story about *his* war, flying the hump in the China-Burma-Indian Theater. Spielberg thought that was irrelevant. The picture was to be a tribute to all the men who had fought in the war. It didn't mat-ter to him whether the film made a profit. He guessed it prob-ably would not—too violent. He thought maybe Hanks would give him a profitable week or two.

War movies come in two basic modes. Those made when a country is at war endorse what we might call the heroic fallacy—the war is thought to be a good one, and no sacri-fice, no brutality, is too much for its winning. Those made in peacetime take the opposite view: War is a madness, not to be endorsed. The military necessity is seen to be a tragic one. These films can be full of rip-roaring blood and guts, but their message must finally be a pious one: Never again!

Saving Private Ryan is actually pretty silent on that subject. The war simply is, no big questions asked. Private Ryan has gone missing and needs to be found. Hanks's Captain Miller commands the nine-man unit charged with finding him amid the chaos of war. He is a schoolteacher and a low-key, dutiful, not particularly heroic fellow who in the American way will get the job done. The film begins with the D-Day landings at Normandy, with what I am convinced is the greatest combat sequence in the history of American film. Ironically, it's atypical of Spielberg's usual practice.

Normally he's a director who likes to storyboard. In this case, he did not. D-Day was chaos, and basically he let the filming capture that. For close to a month, it was improvisation on a vast scale, probably as close as fiction ever comes to the confusion and horror of war's reality. He found that, though the work was exhausting, it was also exhilarating, and that set the tone for the whole film. That spirit returned in the battle that concluded the film, when Captain Miller finally meets his end.

This being a Spielberg film, there was some controversy attached to it. That had to do with the sequences that bookended it, in which a soldier, many years after the fact, visits the Normandy cemetery, which stands on the onetime battlefield, to commune with his fallen comrades. The words "corny" and "sentimental" flew around. Spielberg said that those bookends seemed to mean more to the veterans he talked with than any other aspect of the film. They are old men doing what they do as their time shortens, and they seek to recall the heroic days of their youth. Their sentiment to me seems honest.

There is honest sentiment and dishonest sentiment. This seems to me to be of the former kind, and I think we ought to let it rest there. *Saving Private Ryan* deserved its success. At the end, the dying Captain Miller says, "Earn this," by which he means that those who are spared must not waste the rest of their lives, must spend the years left to them decently, bearing in mind the unique experience they shared—not brooding, but not forgetting, either. This is an honorable, even an extraordinary movie about war, and it goes about its work—I am choosing this word carefully—in a manly fashion. Its heroics are not false. Nor is there anything in it of G.I. comedy or of romance sundered by wartime exigencies. It is neither pro-war nor anti-war. It is that rarest of war films, in that it simply accepts combat as an ugly thing that happens and must be borne with what grace we can muster.

40

Clint Again

In spring 1992, when Clint Eastwood was about to turn sixty-three, the *Los Angeles Times* published its customary preview of the movies forthcoming that summer. It mentioned that he was about to release a western that was entitled, temporarily, "The William Munny Killings." It was scarcely exciting news; he was no stranger to the genre. The piece identified him, however, as Warner Bros.' "fading house star," which probably hurt, if Clint happened to notice it—as I suspect he did.

It was not entirely an unfair characterization. His last movie had been his worst *(The Rookie)*, and he was in a generally fallow period—a number of movies had not worked out too well for him in the preceding years, though two of them, *Bird* and *White Hunter Black Heart,* had been decent and ambitious, if not critical successes or box office winners. There was, however, this "William Munny" project. It had come to him as a sample of David Webb Peoples's work something like a decade earlier, when the writer was being considered for another project. Clint judged the screenplay extraordinary and decided to purchase it. Among other things, it had a sound structure and a very good ear for vernacular dialogue.

He wasn't eager to put it into production, though. He thought he needed to age some more to play the part. I suspect, without ever having talked to Clint on this point, that it was his ace in the hole, something to turn to when he needed a strong project in a genre he virtually owned. Colleagues around Malpaso, his production company, talked of it impatiently. They wanted very much for him to make it.

So he inched his way toward production. He tried some modest rewrites on his own but then told Peoples he was improving it to death and went back to the original script. The studio, aware that Clint had generally been the sole star of his films, argued that there were three strong supporting roles in this film and encouraged him to cast major actors in them. Clint did so, in the persons of Gene Hackman, Morgan Freeman and Richard Harris. A location in Saskatchewan was found, and the expert production designer Henry Bumstead outdid himself, building a picturesquely muddy western street down a Canadian hillside—very realistic it was.

A couple of weeks before the company decamped for Canada, I asked Clint if I could read the script. He sent over a copy, which I read before having dinner with him one Sunday. I thought it was masterful. I said to him, "If you don't screw this up, it can be your masterpiece."

Clint chose to fly reasonably close to the ground on this one. He didn't title it—*Unforgiven,* of course—until a few weeks before its release, and it turned out to be (borrowing a phrase from the script) "lucky in the order." There had not been a serious western in some time, and the world was ready for one when it went into release in August 1992. The critics generally liked it. It stayed long in the theaters, eventually grossing more than $100 million and generating serious Oscar buzz and, eventually, a number of Academy wins, including a director award for Clint, which I felt he deserved.

Unforgiven is a well-plotted film. Clint's Will Munny hears that a group of hookers are offering a reward for doing a potentially murderous job in a remote town. He is aging and no longer what he once was—one of the faster guns in the West— but he's broke, a widower, and he reluctantly decides to take a chance at winning the reward. Along his way he picks up two companions—Morgan Freeman and Jaimz Woolvett—and proceeds to get a severe beating when he reaches his destination. He ultimately triumphs over Hackman's sadistic (and gorgeously played) sheriff. It's a brutal yet at times humorous film. "I was lucky in the order," he comments mildly after the great shootout that brings it to its climax, when, single-handedly, he kills all his enemies in one fell swoop.

At a stroke, the film restored Clint to the top level of his profession, from which he has not retreated in the years since. He has made some fine works during that time, and endured a few disappointments. On the whole, however, his run has been spectacular: the wonderfully complex *Mystic River;* another Oscar winner with the powerful *Million Dollar Baby;* two potent war pictures, *Flags of Our Fathers* and *Letters from Iwo Jima,* which uniquely tell a World War II story from the enemy's perspective; the underrated *J. Edgar.* In this period, I think his track record is pretty much beyond compare—particularly for a man who was being written off such a short time ago.

Remarkably, he seems to me the same fellow I met in 1976— dryly humorous, attending to a vast array of interests, perhaps reading a little more than was formerly the case, but always projecting an easygoing manner. He is interested in everything. I admire him enormously, and there is no one I'd rather have dinner with. There's no one whose movies I anticipate with more pleasure. He is the only movie person I have known across so many years with so much good nature. Make of that statement what you will. Has it affected my critical judgment? You be the judge.

41

Tarnished Gold

A vein of slightly tarnished gold runs through the sixties and seventies. I'm thinking of *Blow-Up,* and other films of Michelangelo Antonioni. *L'Avventura. La Notte. L'Eclisse.* They might get booed at Cannes (as the first named notoriously was), but they also had something that tugged at some people. I know a completely intelligent fellow who for a period of some weeks went obsessively to *L'Avventura,* so smitten was he by its mysteries. (A woman disappears and is not found.) I think it is firmly of its time and place; I'm not sure I'd like it now.

Films so moored don't seem to me to travel very well from the moment when they are all the rage. But yet they have a conviction that cannot be denied, which complements their sometimes maddening languidness. These are the movies that Pauline Kael characterized as coming "dressed as the sick soul of Europe," and she had a good point. You had to admit, though, that you felt awfully smart in a world-weary sort of way, running around New York appreciating the hell out of these films at the time.

There is something about *Blow-Up* (1966) that allows it to rise above its frivolities. You know the plot: A photographer (David Hemmings) goes to a park, sees a woman (Vanessa Redgrave) in conversation with a man and takes some casual snaps of them. Afterwards, she follows him home, insisting he surrender his pictures. She takes off her shirt, smokes a joint and still does not get the pictures. Now he's more interested than he thought he would be—and the film takes off cinematically. Maybe the pictures hold evidence that a murder has been committed. The photographer begins madly blowing them up to see what he has not seen. Teenyboppers intrude on the scene. And pubic hair. And what seemed a rather staid film becomes jazzy.

Against all odds it becomes, well, fun—inexplicable fun, with a certain sobriety snapping at its heels. The mystery never gets fully unraveled, but life is full of enigmas that eventually we have no choice but to shrug off. I don't suppose that *Blow-Up* is all we cracked it up to be at the time. (There's a review of it in my files that makes my ears burn now.) But I think it taught us a lesson. You start out to make a sober movie full of existential meaning that will furrow brows, then something in the process takes over and the thing becomes giddy. You fight to get it back on track, and it just won't go there—not fully, anyway. You end up with something you never planned on—an entertainment, of all things.

Possibly I tend to overvalue those; Antonioni undervalued them. He tried to rescue this film with metaphorical seriousness, with a concluding sequence in which people played tennis without a net or balls. He damn near ruined the whole thing.

42

Kubrick Again

We left Stanley Kubrick in a good place—with a comic masterpiece and much promise. Also, *Lolita* (1962) had had some nice acting in it. Though it was not Nabokov, one could surely live happily with the demented fussiness of Peter Sellers—wrong for the role, but fascinating—and the curious reserve of James Mason's grand passion. *2001: A Space Odyssey* (1968) was, frankly, labored. It was good musically, and I quite liked that cute little computer, but there was a great deal of pretense in it, too. It was not a movie that one warmed to. One was beginning to worry about Kubrick by the time he undertook *A Clockwork Orange,* in 1971—so brutal a film, such a wicked enterprise.

By now, however, Kubrick had indulgent studio backing—his movies made money, and they were events. I came to know him when I wrote a *Time* cover story welcoming *Barry Lyndon*

(1975). I liked the movie—impeccable filmmaking and existential hugger-mugger. I'm a sucker for both.

What drew Kubrick to Thackeray, I'll never know. What possessed him to cast Ryan O'Neal in the title role is also an enigma to me, though somehow his basic fecklessness suited the part. As the years wind on, the film seems somehow to gain in stature. It is such a beautiful film—the low light levels in important sequences is riveting, worth talking about, as they were endlessly when *Lyndon* went into release. But the important thing about it was its sadness. I know of few films so relentless in their sorrow, their exploration of existential pointlessness. I think the funeral of Barry's child is one of the great sequences in cinema, and the film's conclusion, in which the narrator simply says that all the people it has concerned itself with are now dead and forgotten, is devastating. There are very few fictions—possibly none—in which someone goes to the trouble of creating a complex narrative, only to conclude that the exercise is essentially pointless. I mean, everybody simply dies, which is the inevitable conclusion to all stories if you follow them to their logical end. I have no idea how Kubrick talked a studio into doing such a film—especially after diddling them for years with an unmade Napoleon project. It is, at the least, a brave and subversive film, and it moves me mightily, despite its sorrow.

Kubrick never repeated himself. Every film was entirely new when it came to subject matter. Only the attitudes he struck remained constant. His next film was *The Shining* (1980)—technically, I suppose, a horror film—about a novelist isolated with his family in a hotel closed for the winter, intending to write a novel and going bonkers because he has everything he needs except the talent to write same. "All work and no play makes Jack a dull boy," he types endlessly. There are those who think it's Kubrick's masterpiece—it is fundamentally a genre piece, though most of his pictures are, come right down to it—but I think that's just patronizing him. I like the film, but I don't think it's his best. But, hell: "Here's Johnny." And *thwack* goes the ax into the door, accompanied by a demonic cackle. It's a lot of fun. Except, of course, when it isn't.

You don't think about acting very much when you talk about Kubrick, though his films contain a lot of good performances (like Jack Nicholson's in *The Shining*). But I think his emphasis was elsewhere. He was imbued with the not uncommon belief that he was working in a visual medium. Duh! His first success—the film that made people take notice of him—was a routine but well-made heist movie, *The Killing* (1956), which starred Sterling Hayden. Typical of its type, it did not have a lot of dialogue. Shot in black and white, it consisted essentially of a lot of fast-paced and well-staged action, with a nice, ironic ending. (The loot blows away in an airplane's prop wash, just when you think the crooks are going to get away with their crime.) It's pure Kubrick, basically inarticulate, and I think it set the pattern for everything that was to follow, in more and more sophisticated form. The man really could not abide conversation. Almost all his sequences that we remember most fondly are silent. We don't notice that particularly, because they are rich in sound and knockout visual material.

He didn't really care about anything else, which is why he drives a lot of critics nuts. Let's face it: Most of the people who review and theorize about movies are literary types. They are there for the talk. That's why they remain suspicious of Kubrick. And that's why the people who revere him most highly (Steven Spielberg is a good example) are people who actually make movies. Do I think he might have thrown a few more bones to the talking-picture fans? Sure. But this way was his way. It's not the only way, of course, and I would not like it to be the movies' only way, but he achieved some sort of an apotheosis with it.

As Kubrick's career wound on, I think there is a falling off in energy in his work—not an unusual occurrence. I don't care greatly for *Full Metal Jacket* or for his final film, the posthumously released *Eyes Wide Shut*. I will say, however, that they were ambitious and contained sequences of great force. I think he gave up more than he acknowledged by his confinement in Great Britain and by the pace at which he worked.

There is one thing more to be said about this odd, halting career: It is unduplicable. He carried himself always as an artist; he was never merely a movie bozo. He found himself a studio, Warner Bros., that indulged him and was, yes, amused by him. They were impatient with him—how could you not be?—but he always, in the end, seduced you with his intelligence, his earnestness and the richness of his interests. You never had a bad time with Stanley. You never came away from time spent with him unenlightened—he told you of a book or a movie you had to see, an idea you had to pursue.

When Stanley died suddenly, people at the studio, guessing that I would probably write his obituary for *Time,* called to stress the affection they felt for him. There was no need. I felt it, too. I don't to this day know why—he was scarcely a hail-fellow-well-met. But the memorial service at the Directors Guild was rich in warm feelings for a man nobody really knew. Later, a picture by his wife arrived at many of our homes. It was of Stanley sitting calmly by a pond near his house—keeping his secrets.

43

The Force Is with Us

It is 1977, the year of *Star Wars*. It is, to say the least, an extremely entertaining movie that turned out to be a phenomenon. I came upon it quite casually. A friend and I wanted to see a movie. This one happened to be on offer—a Twentieth Century Fox film, for some reason screening at MGM.

We had vaguely heard of it. It was directed by George Lucas, who had enjoyed deserved success with *American Graffiti*. Its stars were, at the time, largely unknown, though that didn't make much difference. I later learned that Lucas's expectations for this film were not much higher than ours. It was not until it was scored, a few weeks before its release, that he began to harbor some hopes for it. The music seemed to give it an unexpected lift.

John Williams's music kicks in brilliantly right from the get-go. The dialogue is first-class in the wise-guy vein. The villain is first-rate. The action is relentless and full of nice surprises, and the actors are fresh and cheeky. Which says nothing about the pell-mell (but not careless) fun of it—I slid over from show-me mode to sheer pleasure in about five minutes. Even my somewhat more dour pal seemed to be going with it. Your first sight of a Wookie is not easily forgotten.

I'm not a very good prognosticator about a movie's potential for making money. I let aesthetics into the mix. But *Star Wars* was going to be a hit—there was no question about that in my mind. All the same, I don't think anyone could have predicted what grew out of it.

I had recently met George Lucas. We were thinking about doing a little documentary for television. A couple of weeks earlier, I had flown westward to discuss it with him and with his wife, Marcia. We had a very pleasant dinner at a Mexican restaurant. I had another gig in Los Angeles that summer, so the timing was agreeable. I was looking forward to the gig inordinately.

But we hadn't reckoned with the phenomenal success of *Star Wars*—for a time the top-grossing film in history. A short time after that became clear, I received a call from one of George's associates, asking me if I'd like to do a documentary about it. I was easily persuaded. I made the film over the summer. The largest pleasure of the job was getting to know George.

He had not expected success of the magnitude that this picture attained, and he was determined to play it cool. He kept on living in his modest house, wearing his boyish shirts and driving his usual car. He went on writing the sequels to his mighty hit, coming into the office perhaps once a week to attend to his other business. He was not going to let this unprecedented success change his ways. He would occasionally putter about in the kitchen making simple dinners, which I sometimes shared with him, as did others.

I continued to make documentaries for him. Every time a *Star Wars* sequel appeared, I put together a "making of" film about it. They were relatively easy to do, they paid nicely and George was a far from exigent boss. It was about as pleasant a job as the movies have on offer. He had thought a lot about movies, and his wit and wisdom were casually and unpretentiously on display. He, of course, made tons of money out of his work. But he was a generous man; everyone associated with him was well rewarded for his or her labors.

44

Losing It

Starting around 1985, there were quite a few good movies made (in addition to those already discussed herein): *Prizzi's Honor, Salvador, The Untouchables, Women on the Verge of a Nervous Breakdown, The Silence of the Lambs, Groundhog Day, Talk to Her, The Pianist*—there could be more, of course. These titles simply sprang to mind when I tipped back in my chair, shut my eyes and let some recalled pleasures float in.

You take my point, I'm sure. Not to be a cockeyed optimist, but pretty good, and occasionally great, movies are made on a fairly regular basis—not a lot of them, but not a few of them, either. You know how it goes: You go out looking for no more than a good time and stumble across something like a masterpiece (vice versa applies, too). Much of the fun of moviegoing derives from the way that paradox keeps working itself out. If it didn't, the movies might as well shut up shop; we could all stay home and watch the endless parade of commercials for patent medicines on television. (I had no idea we were so sickly a nation until I recently took to watching TV after a long absence.)

I'm working my way up to one final theory here. I've come to think that movies now—the best of them, the ones that concern the most thoughtful section of the public, at least—very largely concern psychopathic behavior. This is not entirely a new phenomenon. Cagney referred to his character in *White Heat* as a "nut job," beyond sanity's redemption. But full-on criminal psychopathy was not, shall we say, a favorite movie topic—until, suddenly, it was.

Why this happened when it did is something of a puzzlement. It has to do with the new kids in town, I suppose, and the continuing loosening of strictures on what was acceptable screen content. Before I develop my thesis, let me mention two of my favorite movies of the era.

Let's begin with *The Leopard,* which is based on one of my favorite novels of the late twentieth century and was made into quite a faithful film by Luchino Visconti (released in 1963). It was subsequently re-released in multiple shorter versions, none of which—putting it mildly—were superior to the 205-minute original. At its right length and in the glorious color Giuseppe Rotunno achieved in the original—a tall order, as things turned out—it is a plain masterpiece.

It stars Burt Lancaster, always an ambitious (and powerful) actor, playing an Italian aristocrat at the time of Italy's reunification, in the 1860s. He knows that he—everyone—must change if, paradoxically, the most potent values of the country are to remain intact. I think it is among the most glorious of Lancaster's performances, though the most daring thing about *The Leopard* is that something like one-third of the movie is devoted to a wedding that I never tire of. There is romance in it (between Claudia Cardinale and Alain Delon), but not much of the action we expect of epics. It has something better—or at least rarer: "crowd splendor." It's a phrase coined by one of film's first critics, Vachel Lindsay, the pop poet, and what it means is that there is a stirring and almost ceaseless bustle about the film. I'd say that's the biggest change in emphasis in the adaptation to the screen, and it works strongly in the film's favor. It gives it an energy that is sometimes missing in the novel, which is, of course, pursuing other values. In any event, it seems to me that this is among the finest adaptations of a novel to the screen, which is a way of saying that you must have a very good fiction to start with or the effort is going to be foredoomed.

The Leopard aspires to, and largely achieves, the status of high—possibly epic—art. By contrast, Jirí Menzel's *Closely Watched Trains* aspires to little more than a kind of wistful humanism. It is about a train station guard in an ignored part of the Czech hinterlands during World War II. He yearns for a woman he cannot attain and is played with an aching simplicity by Václav Neckár. The film is also about how something like tragedy sneaks up on him in the course of a film in which everyone, even the oppressive Germans, is given a fair, humanistic shake. It is entirely possible that this is the nicest movie I've discussed—though it ends in tragedy for its antihero. Neckár's character stumbles into heroism without ever quite knowing that's where he's going. His innocence is perfect, and his fate is inescapable.

It is a film that revels in its smallness. It is, I suppose, an anecdote, an incident, rather than a fully worked-out drama. It is nominally a tragedy, but a good-natured one. It could as well end with Neckár's character slipping back into peacetime and his own littleness, no questions asked. That it does not is a great credit to the film. One comes away from it thinking that tragedy—lots of heavy breathing and the imposition of large "meanings" on our activities in life—may very possibly be something of a fraud. The film proposes, rather sweetly (and subversively), that fate is more likely a matter of accident than of doom gathering inexorably around a protagonist. I'm not at all certain that I agree with that viewpoint. The conventions of tragedy are powerful and necessary to dramatic form and expectations. But let's make an exception in one or two cases. We do stumble, often enough, into existential messes and sometimes lack the luck to stumble out of them. That's the case with *Closely Watched Trains.* Can there be such a thing as an accidental tragedy—a fiction that leaves us sad but not devastated? Yes, of course, though I don't think we want this as a regular occurrence. Once in a while it's refreshing, though, especially when it comes in such a charming and impeccably presented form. There you have it in two films—vaulting ambition on the one hand, and on the other, sort of a tossed-off tragedy.

I'm going to let those two movies stand for the range of movies within the realm of "normality" and start working my thesis—with Quentin Tarantino and *Reservoir Dogs* (1992), which features an act of brutality almost unprecedented in modern movie history. Oversimplifying, it traces the bloody aftermath of a robbery gone wrong, and there are times when you want to avert your eyes from the screen and cannot. It is a masterly debut—soon enough followed by the full-on masterpiece *Pulp Fiction.*

Pulp Fiction (1994) is about the absence of Quarter Pounders in Europe (it has to do with the metric system). It's about bringing people back from death. It's about John Travolta dancing up a storm. It's about blueberry pie for breakfast. It is seemingly about anything that happens to pop into Tarantino's head, but intricately plotted so it seems to make sense—for at least as long as you are in its thrall, which exactly coincides with its running time. Above all, it is about sustaining high energy, without deteriorating into hysteria.

No, that's slightly wrong. It is about a young, movie-mad director laying it all on the line and pulling it off, producing one of the most joyous movies I've ever seen. It is serious in its way, and controlled. Tarantino has never quite matched its freedom of movement (or imagination), except perhaps in his glorious script for *True Romance.* He has never flamed out, which is always a possibility for a high-wire act of his kind. I've come away from some of his movies vaguely disappointed, but I've never felt cheated by him, never felt him coasting. He's the real damn deal. And he has set the tone for an era as much as anyone I can think of.

That era rightfully begins with *Henry: Portrait of a Serial Killer,* in 1990. John McNaughton's film is a flat, almost affectless, and seriously under-attended work, starring Michael Rooker as its title character. It is about killing people and going out for a hamburger immediately thereafter. Or about the interpenetration of the quotidian and the horrific in modern life. It is, of course, utterly charmless, and utterly fascinating, as it stresses the randomness of life in our time. We can, it says, brush against murderous death at any moment. It is very unblinking in its consideration of that possibility, and in the fact that there is no moral reckoning in sight.

Henry is by no means a film to be undertaken lightly. Yet I think it must be seen, for the perfection of its sullen statement of something ugly that has always been present in our lives but is only rarely seen in such close proximity to the ordinariness of our days. Formerly, this was seen as strange and exotic. Now, in this film and the few others like it that followed in its wake, it was brought home to us, ferociously yet calmly. It is a chilling cinematic statement of this undeniable fact of modern life.

So is *Blue Velvet* (1986), by David Lynch. In it, Isabella Rossellini, tormented almost beyond endurance by Dennis Hopper, gives one of the movies' great insane performances. The two of them live in Lumberton, one of those idyllic small towns where the firemen wave gently from their passing truck and Kyle MacLachlan and Laura Dern experiment with puppy love at the local diner.

Oops, what's this? Kyle discovers an ear severed from someone's head in a field. That's how casually evil announces itself here. That leads us to Ms. Rossellini, a lounge singer who is just possibly the most put-upon woman in movie history. Before this movie ends she will be stripped, raped and humiliated to the tune of banal pop ballads. As far as we can see, she deserves none of this punishment; she is merely its convenient target. By the time Hope Lange slips a robe around Rossellini's quivering nakedness—the movie's single act of human kindness that I can recall—we have been thoroughly harrowed by it. This is as close as the movies ever come to the merciless, if you will—and as close as Lynch ever came to greatness. It is not—let's put this as mildly as we can—to everyone's taste. But I don't see how the skillfulness can be denied. It is simply unblinking in its contemplation of evil, or maybe the simple carelessness with which people use one another when they set their minds to it. It is, in its way, a masterpiece—at once insane and curiously, utterly rational.

45

"No Animals Were Harmed . . ."

Amores Perros appeared in 2000. The title translates as "Love's a Bitch." It is the first film by Alejandro González Iñárritu. It is about dogs, dogs who bear no resemblance to chipper Benji or faithful Lassie. Three stories interlock in the film: In one, a boy cheats with his brother's wife while entering his dog in grim fights; in another a model's animal is trapped and suffering in a crawl space as she listens frantically to the sounds of his suffering; in the last of them, a hit man seeks redemption for the life he has lived. It is, to say the least, a brutally realistic film, yet one that is never less than intelligent, stylish and compelling. And unique. I don't know of any other "animal picture" that is quite like it in its lack of sentiment.

It is a very hard movie—charmless. Yet unlike any other "dog" movie I know of, it gives the animals their due. It is true to their natures. There is no anthropomorphism here, except that which we in the audience rather desperately impute to these creatures—always, I think, wrongly. It achieves something like greatness through this refusal. A title at the beginning of the film solemnly notes that no animals were harmed in the making of the film. That doesn't make the film any easier to take.

Then we have *There Will Be Blood* (2007). Of course there will. When characters aren't singin' and dancin' and cracking wise, movies shed blood in copious quantities. And why not? They are a melodramatic medium lately, when we have seen virtually everything of man's inhumanity to man in vivid and lengthy close-ups.

Daniel Day-Lewis is all ferocity in this film. Playing Daniel Plainview—wonderful name, that—he is merciless in his single-mindedness—a prospector hunting silver and then oil who achieves great wealth and no happiness with his relentless drive. What saves him for humanity is the good humor with which he slyly edges what I suppose we can call paranoia and something else: Americanism. Americanism run wild, I guess. He will stop at nothing to gain power, which he never defines. What he wants is simply more.

He is, in some sense, one of the most terrifying figures in the history of the movies. But we can understand him, if not sympathize with him entirely. Shortly after the release of *There Will Be Blood,* a few critics compared it to *Citizen Kane.* These comparisons were not completely misplaced. It definitely had ambitions of that sort. I thought, though, that it had a grimness about it that *Kane* lacked. (I think we sometimes forget what a cheeky movie *Kane* is.)

Still, *There Will Be Blood* is an awfully good try—by Day-Lewis; by the director, Paul Thomas Anderson; by everyone who worked on the film—as good, I believe, as anything we've had hereabouts in recent years. I met Day-Lewis not long after the film came out, and he turned out to be a mild-mannered, humorous fellow, as far from the character he played in the movie as it is possible to be. And why not? He's an actor, for godsake. He had, at that moment, taken time off from acting to learn shoemaking. He seemed to me as amused by that choice as I was.

46

We've Got to End Somewhere

For no particular reason, this brings me to *Fargo* (1996). I can make a case for its being my favorite movie. No, I'm not claiming it is the best movie ever, or even the best American movie. It is simply very much to my taste. As I've mentioned, I am a son of the Midwest, transported first to New York City in the 1960s, then to Los Angeles in the 1980s, rarely looking back but never entirely forgetting my roots, either. There were not a few films about life in the heartland, but I never cared greatly for most of them. They were variously patronizing or sort of sappy, in my estimation. They seemed to me created, on the whole, by people who wished to sentimentalize their pasts or to prove their superiority to them—that is, until 1996, when the Coen brothers, out of Minneapolis, gave us Marge Gunderson (Frances McDormand) and this marvelous comedy.

She's a cop. She's pregnant. She has a voice as flat as the

plains that shaped her. And she's nobody's fool. Her foil is Jerry Lundegaard (William H. Macy), who has come to a bar in the eponymous city to hire some guys to kidnap his wife and hold her for ransom. He means her no great harm; he just has a debt he needs to cover. Soon enough, people are getting killed more or less all over the place.

The Coens are, I think, the most important American film authors to come along in the eighties and nineties. They are mostly funny, sort of cheeky, but they have a serious side as well. They were good from the get-go *(Blood Simple)*, and on the whole they stayed that way, though occasionally descending to the merely cute. I don't think you can argue with the likes of *No Country for Old Men*, for example, or *Miller's Crossing*. Their films are unpretentious (on the whole) and, it seems to me, good-natured, likable.

McDormand won a richly deserved Oscar for her work in *Fargo*, and the movie also won the screenplay Academy Award. It's a deadpan comedy and all the better for its lack of affect. McDormand is married to Joel Coen and works more or less exclusively for the brothers. I wish she did more. I am grateful for what I receive. She is so eerily calm—unflappable—and endearing. She is a woman who can calmly throw up her break- fast and keep on trucking until all the crime in the neighbor- hood is settled and still remember that there is "more to life than a little money, you know." And also remember to buy her husband—of all things, a wildlife painter—some night crawl- ers for his next fishing expedition. In some sense, it is a perfect comedy, or at least a rare one, for its calmness. It is, I think, the least frenzied successful such work in American movie history. Even when a leg is discovered in the wood chipper, no voices are raised. Marge wouldn't hear of such a thing. Decorum is all.

I'm focusing on *Fargo* for another reason, too. We are some- what less reliant on genres in our movies than was formerly the case. Or perhaps more intent upon working variants on them. I think that is the most important difference between films now and films of earlier eras. It is said that Darryl Zanuck could work out a year's schedule for Twentieth Century Fox in an afternoon or two—so many comedies, so many musicals, so many melodramas, maybe one or two "important" films to compete for the Academy Awards. We were content with that—until, of course, the business of satisfying routine genre expectations passed over to television, and movies ceased to be an easily satisfied habit. Movies had to aspire to thoughtfulness for that increasingly significant portion of the audience that took reviews seriously and discussed movies with great earnestness, believed they were an "art form" to match any other. (It is interesting that this shift in attitude is so recent, a matter of just a few decades.)

I am going to resist naming a "best" movie in this book. You can't go wrong with any of the movies discussed favorably herein; all of them, in my opinion, will give you pleasure and reward a second or third viewing. I'm going to end instead by proposing sound films of indisputable quality, beginning with Ingmar Bergman's *Fanny and Alexander* (1982). It needs to be acknowledged that his long, hugely productive career is really without parallel in the history of film. *Fanny and Alexander* is a very long movie and an essentially benign one. Dickens can be evoked, and appropriately so. This is a family saga—informed, undoubtedly, by autobiography, but not dominated by it—and it is very leisurely in its telling. It achieves greatness for both its patience and its ease. Basically, it tells the story of a year in the life of a family in which a father dies and his widow embarks on a marriage to a truly awful bishop of the church. It imperils the family and tests it to the breaking point, though in the end it emerges stronger, intact.

Films of this kind are not generally my dish of tea. But there is a power to it that is, in its quiet way, astonishing. *Fanny and Alexander* is a story of survival, a sort of hymn to the tensile strength that sometimes can be found in rather ordinary people when they are put to surprising tests. It is, significantly, a film that glows with a beautiful light (the cinematography is by the masterly Sven Nyqvist), and with a sense of foreboding as well. That glow is at the heart of the film's welcome ambiguity. On the one hand, it is full of promise, offering us the hope of this family's restoration to happiness. On the other, it represents a near-to-bitter irony; the film comes close to mocking all their hopes.

Yet we welcome the hard-won, close-run, somewhat muted quality of its conclusion. For an aging master, it is a quiet masterpiece—a triumph of the will, against all odds—that appeals to our best human impulses. The film has been accused of being a shade too cozy, a little too "benevolent." That is perhaps true. But it is also a forgivable flaw. There are times in the movies when we want their characters simply to succeed in their emotional endeavors, especially when they are fairly tested by circumstances. That is emphatically the case here.

I've liked *Fanny* for the surprises it has brought me, if nothing else. And the reminder for me, as a critic, that the movies are a more joyous enterprise than we think they are as we go about our often dour critical rounds. Yes, Ingrid, they are "only" movies—that is to say, nothing—but sometimes they are everything.

Let me end with Jan Troell, who is, I believe, a major director, but one who has not achieved the reputation he deserves. He made a two-part epic, *The Emigrants* (1971) and *The New Land* (1972), both well received and nominated for Oscars. As their titles imply, they are studies of Swedish migrants finding new lives in America, and they are harsh and beautiful films. After these films, Troell faltered somewhat, with respectable but unexciting movies.

Then came a great film: *Hamsun* (1996). It is about the Nobel Prize winner of 1920, a great writer (his masterpiece undoubtedly being *Hunger,* an extraordinarily powerful work) who also happened to be a fascist, a more-than-active apologist for Hitler and a man who finally closes his eyes at the end of the film and unremorsefully pronounces himself "at peace with himself," despite the fact that his life has been, by our standards, a horror.

You cannot gainsay the power of this work, or the enigma of it. When Hamsun finally confronts Hitler, the dictator wants only to speak of art, while the artist wants only to defend himself. The film leaves him in limbo (and his wife as well), unexplained. Peter Rainer, in his very fine piece about it, speculates that Hamsun—Max von Sydow, in a towering performance—may require hostility to function as an artist, and I suspect that he's right.

He ends his life in disarray—an "imperial crank," in Rainer's fine phrase, a creature of hospitals and asylums, also a person of "dreadful waywardness" and a frantic "dabbler."

He lived into his nineties, and was ever unrepentant. Hamsun, for reasons unknown, as far as the film is concerned, somehow conceived an abiding hatred of the English. They are the opposite, for him, of the Germans. He never abandoned this principle. He died clinging to it. At the film's end, the horror of what he has done at last comes home to him. But it is, of course, too late. He can only weep. He must live out what Rainer calls "a dark fairy tale."

I do not know how Troell came to such an unpromising subject, or how he brought it off with such hypnotic power. It will never be a popular or beloved work—only, I believe, a great one.

47

That Wonderful Year—1987

While I was writing this book, I kept on my desk a marvelous book, *1001 Movies You Must See Before You Die*. It is essentially an enormous cheat sheet about film, carefully written and obviously capacious. I have virtually no arguments with its choices of movies or its solid critical observations about them. It has saved me from innumerable errors of fact, and it is altogether a pleasurable book to browse around in.

One day a few weeks ago, for no special reason, I found myself glancing at the pages devoted to 1987. It was a more or less ordinary year, as, frankly, all movie years are. Like everything else, the movies require a span of time before we can come to any firm conclusions about them.

But then I noticed within a couple of pages two films that I thought it would be a shame to omit from these reflections. One was *Babette's Feast,* and the other was *Wings of Desire.*

They could not be more contrasting. The former is basically a chamber piece in which the lovely actress Stephane Audran, under the direction of Gabriel Axel, comes to Jutland, on the Danish coast, settles in and begins preparing for the eponymous meal, which contrasts the harsh lives of the locals with the sumptuous banquet she has in mind. Never in the history of film has the simple act of eating been so resonantly—forgive me, so deliciously—portrayed. It's difficult for a movie of this kind, aiming at a kind of gentle warmth, not to descend to the sappy, but it never does. Maybe it's a minor pleasure, but it seems to me close to perfection, especially in its avoidance of sentiment, easy or otherwise. There is a briskness about it that keeps it on track.

Wings of Desire could not stand in sharper contrast. Directed by Wim Wenders and starring Peter Falk, it is a bold, bustling fantasy and, I think, the best of the many movies about angels. It is about a trapeze artist who fears falling. It is also, from time to time, about the need people have to touch and to feel, and to be hopeful. There are some reflections on the Holocaust and other big topics as well, though they are handled with deftness and a sort of slow-rolling charm. This is a film that wins you over patiently but, finally, definitively. It obviously has something serious on its mind, but it is, as well, an easeful movie, good-natured as can be.

I am playing catch-up ball with these two movies. Nearing the end of this book, I'm very conscious of its many sins of commission and omission—so many movies left out. It could easily be twice its length. I mean these two movies to symbolize all those near misses, the movies that, in years to come, I know I'll wish I had the time, patience and critical energy to contend with.

There's another point to be made about these movies. It has to do with the change in the ways movies are marketed nowadays. In the fairly recent past, they came out in a predictable way. A picture like *Babette's Feast,* in particular, simply arrived in a few theaters, got some good reviews and made its way around the country in a fairly halting fashion. No big deal— and, generally, no big profits, either. Films of this kind were strictly a small-time business.

In recent decades, that changed. Such films became events. Critical commitments—audience interest, as well—to some of them became more excited, more dedicated. For a fortunate few, it is not too much to say that they became touchstones. You could not count yourself a true cineaste if you had not seen and had a fairly complex opinion about films of the kind I have singled out here. They did not, of course, compete with the big commercial releases, but they won the awards and dominated serious conversations about film—and, in time, film history as well.

I don't know if the movies, as a whole, are the better for this development. It seems to me the ratio of good films to bad remains pretty constant, though they are fewer in number than was formerly the case. And we can say their range is wider than it was in the not-too-distant past. Neither of the films I've cited here—and there are many more like them—would have been made at all a few decades ago. This is, I think, a good thing (though much broader cultural trends play a large part in this, naturally). We get the movies the culture, in its mysterious ways, decides we deserve.

I am grudgingly content with this situation. Come right down to it, what choice do I (or does anyone) have in the matter? Movies simply are. You live with what they give you, or you lose interest in them, as most people finally do.

Let me end with a curiosity. I've always been a rather pedestrian dreamer—at least in comparison with those friends who have opted to share their nighttime reveries with me. Some of their unconscious activities have been prodigious. I have noticed, however, while working on this book, that my dreams have become somewhat more interesting. They have become more movie-oriented. They have film plots and they feature movie stars. They do not ape real movies; they are more generic than that. They are not scary; on the whole, they are rather lightsome. This is the first book I've written that has obliged me to think broadly about a wide range of films, rather than about the works of a single movie figure—a director or a star—and it has turned out to be on the whole rather a playful business. I hope I have singled out a sufficiency of sobersided movies to keep this enterprise respectable. The estimable Kenneth Turan recently managed a task similar to mine with a svelte listing of thirty-five movies. I admire his discipline. And most of his choices.

My interest in current movies has diminished. History preoccupies me more than was formerly the case. Which may mean that I'm about to put myself out of business. Which would be a shame, I guess—it's been such a pleasant way to spend my time (or waste it). Not that I worry much about it. Mortality will take care of that issue soon enough. Meantime, I hope Gary Cooper and Barbara Stanwyck and Mitchum and a whole lot of others will keep turning up in my dream theater. I'm always glad to see them.

Where movies are concerned, I'm obviously a lifer. They haunt my reveries. I never had a choice in this matter. Movies dominate more of our dream space than we care to admit. There is no phenomenon that does so in quite the way they do. There are people who are impervious to them, of course. I am clearly not one of them. I do not expect to become one of them. I expect, in fact, to be going to a movie the day before I die. Why not? They are a harmless addiction. Except when they are not; then they are instructive in ways that can be wondrous. I am grateful to them—let's leave it at that.

Acknowledgments

Thanks to Jonathan Segal, Victoria Pearson, Meghan Houser, David Thomson, Kent Jones, and Erika Schickel.

Index

A Note About the Author

Richard Schickel is a film critic, documentary filmmaker, and movie historian. His books include *Conversations with Scorsese; Clint Eastwood: A Biography; Intimate Strangers: The Culture of Celebrity in America;* and *D. W. Griffith: An American Life.* His documentaries include *Charlie: The Life and Art of Charles Chaplin; Woody Allen: A Life in Film;* and *Shooting War,* about combat cameramen in World War II. He has held a Guggenheim Fellowship and was awarded the British Film Institute Book Prize, the Maurice Bessy Prize for film criticism, and the William K. Everson Award for his work in film history.

A Note on the Type

This book was set in Adobe Garamond. Designed for the Adobe Corporation by Robert Slimbach, the fonts are based on types first cut by Claude Garamond (c. 1480–1561). Garamond was a pupil of Geoffroy Tory and is believed to have followed the Venetian models, although he introduced a number of important differences, and it is to him that we owe the letter we now know as "old style." He gave to his letters a certain elegance and feeling of movement that won their creator an immediate reputation and the patronage of Francis I of France.

Typeset by Scribe, Philadelphia, Pennsylvania

Printed and bound by Berryville Graphics, Berryville, Virginia

Designed by Maggie Hinders